THE SAMUEL & ALTHEA STROUM

LECTURES IN JEWISH STUDIES

THE SAMUEL & ALTHEA STROUM

LECTURES IN JEWISH STUDIES

Autobiographical Jews

ESSAYS IN JEWISH SELF-FASHIONING

Michael Stanislawski

UNIVERSITY OF WASHINGTON PRESS

Seattle and London

University of Washington Press

PO Box 50096, Seattle, WA 98145, U.S.A.

www.washington.edu/uwpress

LIBRARY OF CONGRESS CATALOGING-IN-PUBLICATION DATA

Stanislawski, Michael, 1952–

  Autobiographical Jews : essays in Jewish self-fashioning / Michael Stanislawski.

    p. cm — (Samuel and Althea Stroum lectures in Jewish studies)

  Includes bibliographical references (p.) and index.

  ISBN 0-295-98415-5 (cloth : alk. paper)

  ISBN 0-295-98416-3 (pbk. : alk. paper)

  1. Jewish prose literature—History and criticism.   2. Autobiography—Jewish authors.   3. Jewish authors—Biography—History and criticism.   4. Jews—Historiography.   5. Autobiographical memory.   6. Self-perception. I. Title. II. Series

  PN842.S73 2004   809'.93592000924—DC22   2004043004

THE SAMUEL & ALTHEA STROUM
LECTURES IN JEWISH STUDIES

Samuel Stroum, businessman, community leader, and philanthropist, by a major gift to the Jewish Federation of Greater Seattle, established the Samuel and Althea Stroum Philanthropic Fund.

In recognition of Mr. and Mrs. Stroum's deep interest in Jewish history and culture, the Board of Directors of the Jewish Federation of Greater Seattle, in cooperation with the Jewish Studies Program of the Henry M. Jackson School of International Studies at the University of Washington, established an annual lectureship at the University of Washington known as the Samuel and Althea Stroum Lectureship in Jewish Studies. This lectureship makes it possible to bring to the area outstanding scholars and interpreters of Jewish thought, thus promoting a deeper understanding of Jewish history, religion, and culture. Such understanding can lead to an enhanced appreciation of the Jewish contributions to the historical and cultural traditions that have shaped the American nation.

The terms of the gift also provide for the publication from time to time of the lectures or other appropriate materials resulting from or related to the lectures.

TO MARGIE, ETHAN, AARON, AND EMMA

AGAIN

CONTENTS

ACKNOWLEDGMENTS

My first and primary gratitude is to Althea Stroum, who, along with her late husband, Samuel Stroum, created the Samuel and Althea Stroum Lectures in Jewish Studies at the University of Washington. Mrs. Stroum graciously attended all of the lectures I delivered at the University of Washington in May 2002, and I was honored and delighted to spend some additional private time with her. Naomi B. Sokoloff of the Jewish Studies Program at the University of Washington invited me to deliver the Stroum lectures several years ago; I am grateful to her, to the current chair of the program, Kathie Friedman, and to the other faculty of the program—Jere Bachrach, Hillel Gamoran, Martin Jaffee, Joel Migdal, Scott Noegel, Sarah Abrevaya Stein, and Kalman Weiser—for their hospitality to me during my stay in Seattle; and to Loryn Paxton for her exemplary organization of my visit and lectures.

My study of Jewish autobiography was aided by the students in a graduate seminar I taught on this subject at Columbia several years ago, and by the members of the University Seminar on Israel and Jewish Studies at Columbia who heard an early draft of one of the lectures and provided helpful comments. I am indebted to Alice Nakhimovsky, who read the chapter on Lilienblum and Mandelstam and contributed important suggestions and corrections; to Gil Anidjar for his insights into the work and life of Sarah Kofman; to Michael Silber for help in Israeli archives; and most especially to my friends and colleagues Elisheva Carlebach and Olga Litvak, who took time from their own extraordinarily busy schedules to go over my entire manuscript with great care, and saved me from many infelicities and errors.

I wish to thank Naomi Pascal at the University of Washington Press for her graciousness as editor of this book and the Stroum Lectures Series as a whole, and the Harriman Institute at Columbia University for a faculty publications grant. I would like to thank my friend Bruce Goldberger for proofreading this manuscript just for fun; my student Dan Schwartz for producing an excellent index; and Kerrie Maynes for her superb editing and support. Finally, my greatest debt is once more to my family—my wife, Marjorie Kaplan, and our children, Ethan, Aaron, and Emma—who have tolerated my obsession with the problem of autobiographical writing for the last several years, and who make my own life-story so rich and fulfilling.

Autobiographical Jews

Introduction

AUTOBIOGRAPHY, THE JEWS,

AND EPISODIC MEMORY

The problem I discuss in these essays is the nature of autobiographical writing by Jews over the centuries, and specifically the ways in which such writings can legitimately be used as sources for Jewish history. My interest in this problem emerged while I was working on my last book, on Zionism and the fin de siècle, and discovered that one of my most important sources, Vladimir Jabotinsky's wonderful and indeed stirring autobiography, entitled in its original Hebrew *Sipur yamai* (The story of my life), was all but invented out of whole cloth—i.e., it contradicted the massive data, in black and white, in Russian, Hebrew, German, Yiddish, and Italian, that I had gathered on three continents by and about Jabotinsky, on matters both small and grand. At first, I must confess, it was great fun identifying and correcting Jabotinsky's many errors of fact and interpretation, but very soon I began to ponder the meaning and logic of these so-called "errors." In due course I realized that far more interesting than debunking Jabotinsky's own retelling of events in his life was deciphering the ways in which he had retroactively created his own mythologized, and to a large extent, mythological, life-story, constructing a supremely controlled and controlling narrative in which truth-telling necessarily gave way to the overarching purposes and goals of the work: a brilliant, but highly fictionalized, self-fashioning. To sort out this matter, I began to read literary theory on autobiography, and discovered that I had but hit upon something entirely well known: that in the last fifty years an immense body of academic analysis of autobiography has appeared, written largely by literary scholars and critics, questioning the very nature of autobiographical writing, its definition, boundaries, and relationship to what we normally designate as the truth. These studies have queried not only how an autobiography is to be distinguished from allied genres—memoirs, autobiographical fiction, and the like—but to what extent *every* autobiographer plays fast and loose with the truth: not simply that all autobiographies contain errors of fact; these one important critic felicitously called "mere friendly difficulties compared with those that belong to the very nature of autobiography,"[1] i.e., both the conscious and the far more elusive unconscious distortions of memory and narrative selection that in many ways define the very act of choosing to write one's own life story. Thus, already in 1960, that most important early theorist of autobiography, Roy Pascal, had conceded, on the basis of his contemplation of the genre of autobiography, that "the distortion of truth imposed by the act of contemplation is so over-riding a qualification of autobiography that it is indeed a necessary condition of it. . . . In the abstract, the argument remains undecided, autobiography may be a means of revealing the truth, [or] it may be a means of hiding it."[2]

In the forty years since these words were written, I proceeded to learn, autobiographical theory has become an enormous growth industry, to the extent that it is virtually impossible these days to keep up with the books, articles, conferences, symposia, scholarly associations, and entire journals devoted to the subject. Countless positions have been taken on the first of Pascal's ambitions, a definition of autobiography as a genre, and its relation to other forms of narrative, the latter itself having become an increasingly vexed and complex subject of theoretical musing. James Olney, perhaps the most engaging and productive American theorist of autobiography, confessed in his most recent tome on the subject, *Memory and Narrative: The Weave of Life-Writing*, that he has "never met a definition of autobiography that [he] could really like," and that as a result, he tends to use many terms to describe the type of writing he studies— "confessions, autobiography, memoirs, periautography (writing about or around the self), or life-writing"—without worrying about their precise generic boundaries.[3] More central to his concerns than a tight definition of autobiography has been the relationship between narrative and memory, or what he calls the narrative "imperative." Other scholars have focused more on the memory side of the equation, i.e., the mechanisms, both psychic and physiological, by which we remember things and forget them, both individually and collectively. Indeed, although literary theory and hard scientific research are often at war with each other, epistemologically speaking, in the realm of memory research there is a fascinating, and surprisingly little reflected upon, confluence between the two, since the most recent scientific breakthroughs in discovering how the brain works more or less parallel the conclusions of the "constructivist" nature of autobiographical memory held by literary critics. I shall return to this matter soon, but here suffice it to say that contemporary neuroscientists' understanding of memory as reconstructive and influenced by retroactive context and motivation supports the literary theorists' emphasis on the active role of the autobiographer in self-construction. As a result, not only have the genre of autobiography and the degree of reliability of the contents of countless autobiographies been minutely dissected and deconstructed, the very building blocks of autobiography—what and how an author remembers and how he or she chooses to relate these memories in narrative form—have been called into question in fundamental ways that do not permit us any longer to look at autobiographies as unproblematically reliable first-person accounts of lives lived and stories told or as unmediated sources of truth.

It is not surprising that almost none of this flurry of scholarship on autobiography has affected the broad public, or even the broad reading public. "Tell-all" works by famous men and women—politicians, celebrities, and writers, either living, recently deceased, or long gone—are enormously popular, filling expensive prime shelf space at bookstores around the country and the best-seller lists of the *New York Times* and Amazon.com. The reason for this is not difficult to discern: we love to read about the lives, loves, successes, and failures of famous or infamous and sometimes ordinary men and women, for both benign and not so benign reasons, whether to learn how to emulate them and thus improve our lives, or simply to find out whom they loved, hated, or cheated on. Our television screens are filled, from early morning to late at night, with figures both well known and hitherto obscure, revealing (or purporting to reveal) their most intimate secrets, desires, fantasies, and furies to a seemingly insatiable audience. On some level, we know that much of what we hear and read in this vein is, in fact, not true; that the most outrageous talk shows blatantly employ actors to pretend to be who they are not, to erupt and explode over scripted insults, to the mounting delight of the studio audience chanting wildly for the next punch or kick to the groin. On a higher level, we know that celebrities and politicians reveal only parts of their lives to us even when they are not hiding behind obvious lies and covered-up scandals; in other words, that there is a distinction between what we are told and what we are not told even in tell-all books, and that line is constantly shifting. Periodically the public is scandalized when it turns out that an autobiographer has not told the truth, that a politician, actor, or famous writer has lied about or hidden essential aspects of his or her life in a book that purports, by definition, to reveal the true, factual story of that life. But the appetite for, and credulity in, the next tell-all volume is hardly diminished.

What is far more interesting to me as a professional historian is that the vast critical literature on autobiography has made very little impact on the historical profession, both within and outside the academy. Pick up a historical or biographical tome that uses autobiographical or memoiristic sources, and the chances are excellent that you will find the author relying quite unselfconsciously on these writings as unproblematically reflective of historical truth. This is true, as well, of works on Jewish history, in which memoirs and autobiographies continue to be used as unmediated factual accounts, even on the part of highly sophisticated and erudite scholars, either to reconstruct individual lives or to be mined for factual information about historical processes and events that they discuss.

The reason for this disjuncture between historians and literary theorists is also not difficult to discern. In general, despite the huge amount of theoretical (and pseudo-theoretical) debate on this subject over the last decades, most historians operate with a more or less unselfconsciously positivistic approach to the dilemmas of facticity and historicity, and (for good reason) have come to be exceedingly suspicious of the fads and fashions of literary scholarship in the last several decades that have caused an acute crisis in English and other literature departments across North America. Even my late Columbia colleague (and controversial autobiographer) Edward Said, the progenitor of much of avant-garde literary theory in American literary criticism, recently lamented, as president of the Modern Languages Association, the "disappearance of literature itself from the . . . curriculum" and denounced the "fragmented, jargonized subjects that have replaced it."[4]

Though I share in this lament, I think that historians pay a very high price for our collective inattention to the critical scholarship on autobiography, for the very nature of our enterprise and discipline demands that we use autobiographies and memoirs consistently in our research, writing, and teaching. More subtly, we have come to appreciate that the boundaries between history writing and autobiography are extraordinarily hazy, in both directions. Autobiographers and memoirists implicitly and explicitly are writing histories of their times, and it is a truism—noted long before the spread of postmodernism—that all historians bring their own autobiographical experiences to their history writing. Even those of us who stubbornly persist in believing that historians can and must strive for "detachment" in their history writing, if not pure objectivity, understand that historical interpretation is intimately and inextricably linked to and affected by our lives, experiences, and the interests and obsessions of our culture. The questions historians ask today, whether about ancient Japan or contemporary Zimbabwe, are fundamentally reflective of our cultural moment. To some extent, pondering the extent to which historical or autobiographical writings are non-veridical "constructions of selves" does serve to derail the possibility of our ex post facto reconstruction of the story of an individual life or a culture as a whole; as with so many other corollaries of self-consciousness, what we gain in precision we all but give up in the loss of narrative coherence. But this does not, to my mind, efface the possibility of an accurate depiction of the past or of an epistemology that distinguishes neutrally between fact and fiction. On the question of truth-telling I am far from a Nietzschean or Foucauldian denier of the very possibility of objective truth, believing that truth is in fact obtainable, if elusive, that it exists as an ontological goal, if not a preexisting metaphysical reality, and is discernible to us, if remarkably difficult to ascertain, through hard work and a close self-conscious study of reality, whether past or present.

These essays are hardly the first to ponder the problem of the dynamics of Jewish autobiographical writing, which has been a topic of academic study virtually since the rise of Wissenschaft des Judentums. In 1945, the Israeli scholar Shmuel Werses, who would later become the most important student of the Jewish Enlightenment movement as a whole, published a seminal essay entitled "The Modes of Autobiographical Writing in the Period of the Haskalah"[5] and his work has been followed, to cite only the most recent English-language examples, by studies such as Alan Mintz's *Banished from their Father's Table: Loss of Faith and Hebrew Autobiography*[6] and by Marcus Moseley's pathbreaking doctoral dissertation at Oxford on the beginnings of literary autobiography in Hebrew and Yiddish.[7] While both Mintz and Moseley were specialists in literature, soon thereafter four excellent historians—Mark Cohen, Jacob J. Schacter, Elisheva Carlebach, and David Ruderman—began to study early modern Jewish autobiographers, and the fruits of their important and erudite labors have begun to be published.[8] Moreover, the renowned French historian Natalie Zemon Davis dedicated a third of her 1995 book, *Women on the Margins: Three Seventeenth-Century Lives,* to one of the most famous Jewish autobiographers of all times, Glikl of Hameln, to whom I shall return below.[9]

My goal in these essays, then, is to build upon this scholarship by analyzing a small number of autobiographies written by Jews from antiquity to our time, pondering to what extent literary theory (and to a lesser extent, the new cognitive neurosciences) can help elucidate these texts, perhaps contributing to solving some of the extant problems in their interpretation, and finally, and to me most importantly, reflecting upon their problematic nature as sources for historical reconstruction. By no means do I attempt here even a capsule history of Jewish autobiography. Rather, I shall subject a small number of autobiographies written by Jews to two of the central questions posed by Pascal forty years ago and refined and reformulated by theorists over the intervening decades: first, what is the "design" of the autobiography or life-story at hand, and secondly, what is the relationship of this text to historical truth (without quotation marks)? In accord with Olney and others, I am not at all interested in revisiting the question of the genre distinctions between autobiographies, memoirs, life-stories, and the like; the taxonomic question is not only moot, it is circular: one proposes a seemingly canonical definition of autobiography based on Augustine or Rousseau or Proust and then decides if other texts either fit into this frame or not. Rather, "design" here is meant to interrogate the literary structure of a work, its purported audience, and most significantly, the view of self each author fashions and hopes to convey through telling his or her tale. On the question of facticity, I take as my starting point the assumption that every author I analyze has constructed a version of his or her life meant from the start to tell not the truth, the whole truth, and nothing but the truth, but a story of her or his life that conforms with an overriding sense of self, mediated by and refracted through the peculiar dynamics of autobiographical/memoiristic writing. In the event, conscious processes such as selection of which material to include and which to omit combine with the largely unconscious and still—despite the advances of neuroscience—mysterious psychic, somatic, and chemical dynamics of remembering and forgetting to yield a narrative that is, by definition, factually problematic. The challenge to the historian, as opposed to the literary critic, is to decide how to use such inherently problematic texts as historical sources. What can we learn from such compromised sources about the lives they open up and share with us, the time or place they depict, the societies they so eloquently describe?

My challenge here, moreover, was to decide which autobiographies to subject to these questions. Over the last five years I have read, at times at the madly obsessive rate of one per day, several hundred autobiographies and memoirs written by Jews in Hebrew, Yiddish, Russian, French, German, and English and found dozens that I thought merited a detailed analysis in these pages. But in the essays that follow I have limited myself to a mere handful of such texts and make no claim that those I discuss are representative either of Jewish autobiographies or of "autobiographical Jews" throughout the centuries. My primary principle of selection here was that the texts I discuss be of compelling interest—first to me, and then, I hope, to my readers—because like most readers of autobiographies, I, too, want most of all to read a good story, to learn about a fascinating life, even as we analyze and decode the complex relationship of these stories to the more mundane world of factual truth. While recognizing that the boundaries between seemingly factual autobiographies and autobiographical fiction is exceedingly hazy, I have nonetheless limited my discussion here to works that present themselves as the former, and I have not at all engaged with the equally challenging and fascinating genre of autobiographical verse. Moreover, I have very deliberately not included in this book any autobiographies written by victims or survivors of the Nazi ghettos, concentration camps, and death camps—a huge and still growing literature that has been analyzed by many other scholars. This is mostly because I have not (and probably never will) resolve for myself the profound moral dilemmas associated with subjecting the murder of European Jewry to the self-consciously detached scholarly methodology to which I am committed.

Before I turn to the texts I shall analyze, two excursions are necessary: first, on the relationship between autobiography, "self-fashioning," and Judaism; and second, a brief review of what we can learn from the new scientific studies of the brain that are relevant to the study of autobiography.

In his above-cited book, Alan Mintz asserted that the recently discovered flurry of autobiographical writing among Jews during the Renaissance was an "utter novelty" in the annals of classical Hebrew literary creativity, in sharp contrast with the "rich and continuous tradition of autobiography in classical and Christian Europe" from Augustine to Montaigne and thence to Rousseau. To explain this phenomenon, Mintz speculated that if

> the urge to self-portraiture is universal, then Judaism must impose upon this generalization considerable constraints. In the classical tradition the individual is so firmly imbedded within communal, legal, and historical structures that his or her separate inner drama is simply not viewed as a significant source of meaning for the tradition as a whole. . . . The relative alienness of autobiography in Jewish culture . . . results from the secondary status of the individual in Judaism. Although the individual is responsible for his actions, the meaning of his life is absorbed in collective structures and collective myths. With the partial exception of mystical testimonies in the kabbalistic tradition, Judaism, unlike Christianity, does not know the deeply personal experience of conversion nor the nuanced inner drama of individual salvation.[10]

Objecting to these generalizations, in an essay on *Megillat sefer*, the astonishing autobiography of Rabbi Jacob Emden, one of the preeminent Talmudists of the eighteenth century, Jacob J. Schacter wrote:

> It seems to me . . . that the reason [for the lack of Jewish autobiographies] lies elsewhere, not in the individual-communal dichotomy, but rather in the acknowledged hierarchy of values within the individual himself or herself. What I believe we have here is an expression on the individual level of the general phenomenon noted by Yosef Hayim Yerushalmi on the national level. . . . The repetitive, cyclical, and ahistorical nature of liturgy and ritual overshadowed and ultimately marginalized the details of the historical realm. The larger issue of the Jewish people's relationship with God mattered; the smaller issue of the story of that people's history did not.
>
> Writing the story of the group (history) is, in this regard, parallel to writing the story of the individual (autobiography). Just as concern with the Jewish nation's relationship with God made historiography irrelevant for the people as a whole, so did the Jew's personal quest for that relationship make autobiography irrelevant for the individual. What was important for the premodern Jew was not the specific details of his or her personal life but rather the larger metaphysical issues of his or her relationship with God and with His divinely revealed Torah. It was the quest for spirituality rather than the daily mundane experiences of life that served as the ultimate focus of both national and personal Jewish endeavor. As a result, the most significant aspect of a life was not what made it different and distinct from others—that is, the details of the particular events specific to that life—but rather, on the contrary, what that life had or expected to have in common with other lives. Hence, no story of one's own life was a story worth telling.[11]

I read the evidence—or rather, the lack of evidence—in a different way from Mintz and Schacter. First, a seemingly pedantic but to my mind crucial point. Long before the Renaissance or modern Hebrew literature there was committed to writing a crucially important autobiography written by a Jew: Josephus's *Life*, more commonly known by its Latin title, the *Vita*.

Although written in Greek and not in Hebrew by a famously controversial ancient Jew, it would be rash to generalize about the relationship between Judaism and autobiography without taking Josephus into account. I shall return in great detail to the *Vita* soon. More recently, the autobiography of a medieval German Jew was discovered by the Israeli historian Israel Yuval in a manuscript in the Bodleian Library,[12] and it is impossible to guess how many more such documents are buried in thus-far untapped archival and family collections. Moreover, it is inarguable that the autobiographical impulse, the need for individuation, self-justification, and self-fashioning did exist in rabbinic and medieval Jewish culture: there is abundant evidence of autobiographical self-presentation in genres as diverse as the ethical will, introductions to legal and homiletic works, and perhaps most profoundly, in poetry written both for liturgical and what we would call secular expression. It is rather that, as far as we know, the *genre* of autobiography seems to have remained basically foreign to Jews throughout the centuries, and it is only in the early modern period that we have the first appearance of an array of self-conscious and self-standing autobiographies written by Jews.

Thus, I am infinitely less confident than others that we can safely generalize from the absence of preserved Jewish autobiographies to a claim that they were never written, and that this was so because of some inherent phenomenological predisposition either of "Judaism" or of "premodern Jews" en masse. Here, as in so many other cases, we see what we may call the synecdochial nature of much of Jewish history writing, the substitution of one small part for the whole. While it is true that most streams of rabbinic Judaism attempted to subordinate the focus of eschatological speculation from the realm of individual salvation to that of national redemption, and that the autonomous Jewish community—like all political communities before and since—attempted to subordinate individual behavior to collective constraints, we are in absolutely no position to posit that the result was a uniquely Jewish constriction of individual self-examination, an absorption into collective structures and collective myths of millions of individuals' conceptions of the meaning of their lives. Similarly, despite its pervasiveness, there is absolutely no evidence to sustain the claim that for all, or even most, premodern Jews the quest for God, Torah, and spirituality rather than the daily mundane experiences of life served as the ultimate focus of their personal endeavors. Put simply, this claim confuses not only the prescriptive with the descriptive, but the prescriptions of a tiny, male, literary-clerical elite for the reality of millions upon millions of ordinary people over two millennia—male, and, not incidentally, female—whose inner lives, aspirations, and obsessions we know virtually nothing about. Moreover, even within the preserved writings of that male elite we have countless expressions of individuality, individuation, and richly idiosyncratic interiorities not circumscribed by their views of God and Torah—no one could confuse Maimonides' interior life with Judah Halevi's, or the Vilna Gaon's with the Baal Shem Tov's.

In general, I am highly suspicious of any and all a priori assumptions of Jewish "uniqueness." Upon examination, when not merely examples of the well-worn nominalist fallacy—all discrete phenomena are on some trivial level "unique"—they usually reveal themselves to be based not upon a rigorous comparative analysis, textual or anthropological, but on nationalist or theological axioms not subjected to scholarly scrutiny. Thus, I am by no means claiming here that there is a taxonomically separate genre called "Jewish autobiography" with its own dynamics distinguishable from life-stories written by non-Jews. Similarly, I am exceedingly skeptical of the currently fashionable academic orthodoxies about the innate differences between Western and non-Western societies (and am always confused about where the Jews fit into this dichotomy); thus for example, I do not for a moment subscribe to the claim made by Georges Gusdorf, that autobiography "has not always existed nor does it exist everywhere" but "expresses a concern peculiar to Western man," that it is dependent upon and symptomatic of an "involution of consciousness" which "is not possible in a cultural landscape where consciousness of self does not properly speaking exist," that "unconsciousness of personality" is characteristic of "primitive" or "traditional" societies.[13] To cite but one famous example, what, then, of the *Baburnama*, the memoirs of Babur, prince and emperor of sixteenth-century Hindustan, recently labeled "the first autobiography in Islamic literature" by Salman Rushdie?[14] Rather, with Stephen Greenblatt, the analyst of English Renaissance self-fashioning, I believe that in every age and place "fashioning oneself and being fashioned by cultural institutions—family, religion, state [are] inseparably intertwined" and am intrigued by his hypothesis that "self-fashioning occurs at the point of encounter between an authority and an alien, that what is produced in this encounter partakes of both that authority and the alien that is marked for attack, and hence that any achieved identity always contains within itself the signs of its own subversion or loss."[15]

This is not to say that the appearance of Josephus's *Life*, the sudden proliferation of Jewish autobiographies in the early modern period, and their explosion in the modern age were not in highly complex ways connected to specific historical stimuli, circumstances, and contexts. On the contrary, as a historian I believe as if by definition that the specific contexts of these individual constructions of selves are precisely where we must start in analyzing the texts that ensued. But at the same time, I believe that their attempts to portray their private and public struggles, anxieties, successes, and failures were, at the start and in the end, expressions of a basic drive for selfhood which is both timeless and time-bound, universal and culturally specific.

This complex imbrication of individuality and universality has led me, moreover, to immerse myself in the current scientific literature about precisely how our autobiographical memory works. This strikes me as absolutely crucial, since before we can attempt to analyze to what extent autobiographers—Jewish or Japanese—are manipulating the truth about their pasts, we must attempt to understand how we actually process, store, and retrieve our memories. Indeed, in the last several decades, these questions have returned to the forefront of neuroscientific and cognitive psychological research. As the historian David Gross has noted, the "epistemological deflation" of memory began in the late nineteenth century, when psychologists including William James began to argue that memory was not always as veridical as had been previously assumed, that

the processes of memory involve so much selecting, editing, revising, interpreting, embellishing, configuring, and reconfiguring of mnemonic traces from the moment they are first registered in the mind until the moment of retrieval that it is almost impossible to think of memory as a trustworthy preserver of the past. What is remembered is usually more distorted than people realize, since it is derived . . . from a more or less accidental combination of impressions. In fact, much late nineteenth-century research was intent on showing how often purported memories were actually "confabulations," that is, memories of occurrences that never happened at all.[16]

Following in these footsteps, Freud argued (as the last two autobiographers I study here well knew, and which has of course become the subject of a huge controversial literature) that childhood memories, in particular, are more often than not falsified, incomplete, or have undergone spatial or temporal displacement, not because of faulty memory but because of "intervening biases." Thus, while retaining a belief in the classic "storage model" of memory, he posited that repression, screen memories, latent dream content, the return of the repressed, and the like account for the ways in which fixed memories, however distorted and incomplete, manifest themselves and affect our present view of the world.[17] At the same time, he conceded that there may be a biological basis for what we remember and what we forget, but that "we know nothing about" those biological processes.[18]

Just a little later, the British psychologist Sir Frederic Bartlett argued, more broadly, that what we recall (as adults as well) is not what we actually experienced, but a reconstruction thereof that is consistent with our current goals and our knowledge of the world. As he put it, "Remembering is not the re-excitation of innumerable fixed, lifeless, and fragmentary forms. It is an imaginative reconstruction, or construction, built out of the relation of our attitude towards a whole active mass of organized past reactions or experiences."[19] At the time, this view was rejected by most psychologists but has been resurrected in recent decades as most neuroscientists and cognitive psychologists have come to reject the so-called "storage model" of memory, in which everything one learns or experiences is thought to exist somewhere in the mind, whether or not one can access it. This has been replaced by a belief that memories are ever changing because they are reconstituted in different ways each time one remembers—not only that memories are unstable and transient, effected or transformed by beliefs and emotions, but that there are even striking differences between the brain regions and chemical processes activated during the "encoding" task and those activated during the "retrieval" task.

Fundamental to this new view of memory is a distinction between two different kinds, and ultimately two different systems, of memory: a) implicit (also called non-declarative) memory, and b) explicit (or declarative) memory. Implicit or non-declarative memory is memory about how to perform something, memory for reflexive motor or perceptual skills: how to lift a pen, ride a bike, or read Hebrew or Hindi. This form of memory is entirely unconscious and may well be the only kind of memory available to invertebrate animals because they do not have the brain structures to support declarative memory. Explicit or declarative memory, on the other hand, is memory of factual information about people, places, and things, and what these facts mean, and it is recalled by deliberately conscious effort. It is then subdivided into semantic memory (memory for facts) and episodic memory (memory for events and personal experiences). Although no true consensus obtains as yet about which parts of the brain and which chemical processes are involved in the storage and retrieval of any sort of memory, the accepted textbook wisdom is that there is no general memory store, as we used to believe: memory, whether semantic or episodic, declarative or non-declarative, is not stored in a single region of the brain. Rather, each time knowledge about anything is recalled, the recall is built up from distinct bits of information, each of which is stored in special dedicated memory stores.[20] Most important for us here, retrieval of episodic memory involves bringing different kinds of information together that are stored separately in different storage sites and reassembling the information into a coherent whole. Retrieval of memory is thus much like perception; it is a constructive process and therefore subject to distortion, much as perception is subject to illusion. Depending on the cue or the reminder that is available, only some fragments of the encoded data may be activated; if the cue is weak or ambiguous, what is reactivated might even differ from what is stored, and it is eminently possible to confuse the thoughts and associations caused directly by the cue with the stored memory content evoked by the cue. Most of us know that when we try to recollect a story we often make creative errors, deleting some parts of the story, fabricating other parts, and generally trying to reconstruct the information in a way that makes sense. In general, neuroscientists now argue, autobiographical memory works by extracting the *meaning* of what we encounter, not by retaining and then accessing a literal record of it. What is stored in memory can be modified by the acquisition of new interfering information, as well as by later rehearsal and retrieval episodes. As a result, errors can be introduced into memory at any point: during encoding, during storage, as well as during the act of retrieval. Perhaps the most dazzling and destabilizing conclusion of this new view of memory is that it is very possible to re-member something that never happened—as one of the leaders in this field, the cognitive neuroscientist Daniel Schacter, has demonstrated, under controlled experimental conditions false memories are accompanied by high confidence levels and a sense of detailed recollection, and the newest technological advances in neuro-imaging document that the same patterns of brain activity are observed during true and false recognition.[21] Hence the current controversy over retrieved childhood memories, and far more broadly and central to our judicial system, the rethinking of the accuracy and hence the utility of eyewitness testimony in courts of law.[22]

Though as a human being I am rather discomfited by these conclusions, as a student of autobiography I have in many ways felt liberated by them, for after the first rush of schadenfreude it is not pleasant to devote one's time to decoding other people's conscious lies. Rather, the challenge to the student of autobiography—what the novelist and literary scholar A. S. Byatt has aptly termed "that most evasive and self-indulgent of forms"[23]—is to attempt to unravel the conscious from the unconscious distortions in these texts, to regard autobiographies as artifacts of individuals' quests, tempered by the constraints of our all-too-human embodiment, to make sense of their lives, first and foremost for themselves and then, if possible, for their readers. If none of us can truly produce an "objectively true" account of our lives, how can the historian approach the resultant texts as trustworthy documents of the past?

1 / Josephus's Life

I am by training and inclination a historian of modern Jewry, but I should like to begin my investigation in a time, place, and culture in which I have no first-hand experience, ancient Rome, and with a text not usually dealt with by the few other scholars of Jewish autobiography, Josephus's *Life*. I approach this work with much trepidation, primarily because I cannot read this text, as opposed to the others I shall be treating in these pages, in its original language, first-century Greek, and must rely on the many translations of the *Vita* into Latin, English, Hebrew, and German that I have consulted. Secondly, there is a vast and erudite scholarship on Josephus and his writings that I make no claims to controlling: the classicist Louis Feldman has recently noted that since the beginning of 1992, twenty-one books devoted to Josephus have been published in English alone![1] But how can a Jewish historian interested in the intersection between design and truth in Jewish autobiography *not* begin with Josephus's *Life*, which is by all accounts not only the first Jewish autobiography ever written but very possibly the first extant complete pre-Christian autobiography *tout court?*[2] Moreover, Josephus was of course the first, and certainly the most influential, historian of the Jews before the nineteenth century, and scholars have long realized that a huge amount of what we know, or think we know, about ancient Jewish history is dependent upon Josephus's accounts of that history, but that these accounts—most importantly, his *Antiquities of the Jews* and *Wars of the Jews*—are shot through with both overt and covert autobiographical details and agendas. The specific problem that the huge literature on Josephus's *Vita* has focused on is the complex relationship between that work and *Wars of the*

Jews, since these two accounts contradict one another in crucial and fundamental ways.

Before addressing this problem, let me introduce the text: written in Rome near the end of its author's life, sometime between 96 and 100 C.E., Josephus's *Life* is a short book, eighty-eight small-sized pages in the standard Loeb Classical Library edition. It begins with the author's genealogy, childhood, youth, and education, continues with a long narrative about his first trip to Rome at the age of twenty-six, and gives a description of the revolutionary situation in Jerusalem upon his return there. Then, in the main and by far the largest section of the book, we follow our hero to Galilee, where his mission was to convince the rebellious Jews to lay down their arms against Rome, but where he soon became one of the generals who led the moderate forces in the rebellion and—equally importantly— outfoxed the Jewish zealots and brigands who were mistreating their compatriots, until he was captured by the Romans and forced to accompany them as they attacked and laid waste to Jerusalem and destroyed the Temple. The *Life* then ends with a short summary of Josephus's departure from Judea, first to Alexandria and then with the imperial forces to Rome, where he was treated with much dignity by the emperors, housed in one of their palaces, and granted Roman citizenship and a pension, as well as lands back home that provided him with a fixed income for the rest of his life. Roughly two-thirds of the way through the main action, we encounter a short but very strongly worded attack on another Galilean ex-general turned Greek-Jewish historian, one Justus of Tiberias, who, Josephus insists, was not only a traitor to the Jews but a terrible and deceitful historian, unlike our author, who is pledged to tell the truth, the whole truth, and nothing but the truth.

The problem, as already noted, is that in countless places this "truth" contradicts the "truth" of Josephus's other account of the same events in his much longer *Wars of the Jews*, written some twenty years earlier. Most famously, in the *Vita* Josephus maintains that he was first sent to Galilee by the elders of Jerusalem to put down the rebellion and only later became a military leader, whereas in the *Wars* he is elected a general by those very same leaders *before* he departs for the north. Though many ancient, medieval, and modern readers were not troubled by these and other contradictions between these two texts, from the rise of German classical scholarship in the late eighteenth century to today, scores of scholars and experts have pondered the problem and have attempted to sort out which version is true; in the words of one recent scholarly article by an Israeli expert, "Where was Josephus Lying—in his Life or in the War?"[3] This expert, like many others, chose the *Life* over the *War*, on very learned grounds, though an almost equal number of Josephus scholars have argued the opposite, on equally erudite grounds. In the process there have been advanced many highly inventive and in turn controversial hypotheses about the origin and sources of the *Vita*, most famously a speculation that it was based on an earlier document—either a so-called *Rechenschaftsbericht* (a brief biography submitted to one's military or civilian authorities), or a *hypomnena* (an outline of a historical work submitted by ancient writers to the authorities before a final draft was penned). The latter hypothesis was made most forcefully by the ancient Jewish historian Shaye Cohen in his *Josephus in Galilee and in Rome*, published in 1979. Here, Cohen subjected the *Vita* to a minute analysis, comparing its historiographical method with that of the *Antiquities* and the *Jewish Wars*, and not incidentally for our purposes, demonstrated that from the start of the *Life* to its close, Josephus misrepresented the facts of his life, as discernible in retrospect. Thus, the very opening of the autobiography is hugely problematic:

> My family is no ignoble one, tracing its descent far back to priestly ancestors. Different races base their claim to nobility on various grounds; with us a connexion with the priesthood is the hallmark of an illustrious line. Not only, however, were my ancestors priests, but they belonged to the first of the twenty-four courses—a peculiar distinction—and to the most eminent of its constituent clans. Moreover, on my mother's side I am of royal blood; for the posterity of Asamonaeus, from whom she sprang, for a very considerable period were kings, as well as high priest of our nation. . . . With such a pedigree, which I cite as I find it recorded in the public registers, I can take leave of the would-be detractors of my family.[4]

Cohen comments:

The genealogy has two problems: 1. The chronology is impossible; 2. How does the list document Josephus's ancestry on his mother's side? If the list is genuine, either it is lacunose or Josephus has misunderstood what he excerpted from his documentary sources. . . . In any event, Josephus' Hasmonean ties are probably bogus. When he wrote [*Jewish Wars*] he claimed only priesthood . . . , but in [*Antiquities* and *Vita*] we suddenly discover his Hasmonean forebears.[5]

As a result, Cohen concludes that Josephus's detractors "apparently had some basis for their charges." Similarly, after discussing his lineage, Josephus continues:

> Brought up with Matthias, my own brother from both parents, I made great progress in my education, gaining a reputation for an excellent memory and understanding. While still a mere boy, about fourteen years old, I won universal applause for my love of letters; insomuch as the chief priests and the leading men [of Jerusalem] used constantly to come to me for precise information on some particular in our ordinances. At about the age of sixteen I determined to gain personal experience of the several sects into which our nation is divided. These, as I have frequently mentioned, are three in number—the first that of the Pharisees, the second that of the Sadducees, and the third that of the Essenes. I thought that, after a thorough investigation, I should be in a position to select the best. So I submitted myself to hard training and laborious exercises and passed through the three courses. Not content, however, with the experience thus gained, on hearing of one named Bannus, who dwelt in the wilderness, wearing only such clothing as trees provided, feeding on such things as grew by themselves, and using frequent ablutions of cold water, by day and night, for purity's sake, I became his devoted disciple. With him I lived for three years and, having accomplished my purpose, returned to the city. Being now in my nineteenth year I began to govern myself by the rules of the Pharisees.[6]

Cohen responds, "The impossible chronology in this section may be a sign not of textual corruption but of mendacity: Josephus had three years to study with Bannous because his tour of the academies was imaginary. His claim of adherence to Pharisaism, part of *V[ita]*'s religious apologetic, is probably false too."[7]

This line of inquiry was continued by many other scholars, who have subjected virtually every line and verse of the *Vita* to detailed forensic dissection, and the consensus that has emerged is hardly sympathetic to Josephus or to his scrupulousness either as a historian or as an autobiographer: "the story [of the *Vita*] is narrated with little concern for cohesiveness or logical development, and, as a result, the reader often becomes confused . . . he was not a meticulous and articulate craftsman"; the *Vita* is "literarily wretched," its author "more gifted as flatterer than classicist"; as a whole Josephus demonstrated "unusual sloppiness in historical detail," and the *Life* is "careless" as well as "tendentious."[8] In sum, as Seth Schwartz recently put it, "[t]here are those of us who have made a cottage industry of detecting Josephus' biases,"[9] and one scholar—Gohei Hata—has recently even tried to reconstruct what Josephus was hiding in the *Life* and the *War*, in a paper entitled "Imagining Some Dark Periods in Josephus' Life."[10]

But what of the *Vita* as an autobiography? The one scholar to address this question most frontally is Per Bilde, who, in his 1988 book *Flavius Josephus between Jerusalem and Rome: His Life, His Works and Their Importance*, wrote the following about the genre of what he terms "this curious little book":

In theory, there are two possibilities. . . . [e]ither *Vita* is not a true autobiography, but rather something other than what it pretends to be, or *Vita* should be understood to be an autobiography of a very special nature in which everything of importance is centred around a decisive climax [*sic!*] in the life of the author. The first possibility is the one most frequently taken into consideration and preferred in the history of research. According to scholars like Laqueur, Drexler, Schalit, Migliaro and Rajak, *Vita* is only ostensibly and on the surface an autobiography. In reality, the book is something entirely different, namely an apology written for the purpose of defending Josephus against accusations made to him by Justus of Tiberias. . . . [But] *Vita* contains far more material than that which pertains to the con-

troversy between Josephus and Justus, and this material receives no expla-
nation in this hypothesis. . . . Therefore, we must consider the other possibility that *Vita* can be looked upon as what it purports to be, namely, an autobiography. If so, then an autobiography of a very special kind, one which
is concentrated on the decisive events in the life of the author. . . . Thus *Vita*
no longer stands as an obscure appendix to Ant[iquities], an incomplete autobiography, let alone as an apologetic excursus which is difficult to understand. Then, *Vita* comes forth as a genuine autobiography, albeit an autobiography of a very special nature, since it is dependent upon the unusual
history of the author's life and his writings which the biography will serve
to elucidate and justify.[11]

I should like to agree with Bilde's main thrust but to refine it by rejecting the rather bewildering, if rather Platonic, notion that the first
specimen of a literary genre can be said to diverge from a preexistent
norm. On the contrary, I see the *Vita* not as an "autobiography of a very
special kind" but precisely the opposite: as an exemplar of a genre (or series of connected genres) in which an author's life-story is crafted by a
highly partial, both conscious and unconscious, selection of which
episodes of his or her life to retell, refracted through an ever-changing
sense of selfhood. Thus, to the extent that we can understand it, Josephus's selfhood was suspended between Rome and Jerusalem, Hellenism
and Hebraism, sedition and collaboration, and, most importantly for our
purposes, between his interior need for self-fashioning and his desire to
tell the historical truth, at least from the vantage point of a Judean general turned Roman loyalist. I would submit, therefore, that many if not
most of the differences and contradictions between Josephus's various
writings are caused, first and foremost, by this tension between the hugely
contrasting, if not inevitably contradictory, narrative imperatives of his-
toricism and self-fashioning, both compounded by the biologically based
reality that memories are ever changing because they are reconstituted in
different ways each time one remembers, that memories are unstable and
transient, effected or transformed by beliefs and emotions, and hence
by the contexts and cues that evoke these memories even before they are
articulated in words and then in writing. Seth Schwartz has reasonably

speculated that when Josephus came to Rome he had brought no files with him from Judea or Galilee, and thus depended in large measure upon his memory, and only his memory, for much of what he later reported.[12] To my mind, then, it is not cynical but utterly realistic to propose that the question "Where was Josephus lying, in his *Life* or in his *Wars*?" is, as the French say, *une question mal posée* (a wrongly posed question), answerable equally plausibly by "both" and "neither"!

The far more relevant question is, how did Josephus attempt to fashion himself in his *Vita*? What image of himself, which memories of his life—true, partially true, or false but nonetheless remembered or claimed—did he pass on to us in his autobiography?

In an important recent article entitled "An Essay in Character: The Aim and Audience of Josephus's Life," the historian Steve Mason ingeniously explains the *Vita* as an exercise in Roman rhetoric whose basic aim is the demonstration of an author's character, beginning with genealogy and education and following with politics and war, and necessarily rebutting a counter-case—thus Josephus's seeming obsession with Justus's attack.[13] While I find this argument compelling, I would extend it beyond a structural analysis to claim that the time has come simply to cease using the *Vita* as a source for the facts of Josephus's life-story—an enterprise which even the most skeptical readers of the autobiography have engaged in, if often *faute de mieux*. Rather, we should approach this text simply as the literary record of Josephus's last, retroactive self-fashioning. Moreover, I would argue, at the core of this last self-fashioning was Josephus's attempt to present himself as both a loyal Jew and as a man imbued with and defined by the Roman conception of *virtus*—as what we might call a Jewish *vir virtutis*.

In *Tusculan Disputations*, Cicero famously defined the Roman conception of virtue as follows:

> Though all right-minded states are called virtue, the term is not appropriate to all virtues, but all have got the name from the single one that was found to outshine the rest, for it is from the word for "man" that the word "virtue" is derived [*ex viro virtus*]; but man's peculiar virtue is fortitude, of which there are two main functions, namely scorn of death and scorn of pain. These then we must exercise if we wish to prove possessors of virtue,

or rather, since the word for "virtue" is borrowed from the word for "man," if we wish to be men.[14]

Thus, what is most remarkable to me about the *Vita*, given its juxtaposition to contemporary rabbinical writings in which a life devoted entirely to study is exalted as the ultimate summum bonum, is the extent to which Josephus, while in exile in Rome, seeking to justify himself both to himself and to posterity, remembered himself as a man whose life was marked by spectacular acts of physical courage, military brilliance, *and* utter devotion to the service of his God and His people. This seamless synthesis, he insisted, had already in his lifetime been misunderstood and misrepresented, and therefore must be corrected. Thus, throughout the autobiography he recounts episodes in which he escaped from life-threatening dangers through a combination of physical strength, nimbleness of mind, and probity of spirit, all of which were marked and defined by dedication to the God of Israel.

A few examples will suffice:

1. At the start of the autobiography, after detailing—and undoubtedly fictionalizing—his genealogy, he relates that when he was twenty-six he learned that other priests were "on a slight and trifling charge" sent in chains to Rome by the Judean procurator and even there, did not forget the pious practices of their religion and ate only figs and nuts so as not to contravene the laws of kashrut. He therefore set off to Rome to join these valiant heroes:

   > I reached Rome after being in great jeopardy at sea. Our ship foundered in the midst of the sea of Adria, and our company of six hundred souls had to swim all that night. About daybreak, through God's good providence, we sighted a ship of Cyrene, and I and certain others, about eighty in all, outstripped the others and were taken on board.[15]

2. This combination of manly physical fortitude and dedication to the laws of the Torah reasserts itself four years later, early on in his mission

to Galilee, when he was confronted with next "peril" to his life. The people of Galilee were totally loyal to him and worried more about his own safety than the fate of their wives and children taken into slavery. But his first major opponent, the brigand John of Gischala, son of Levi, came to Tiberias to try to induce the inhabitants to abandon their allegiance to him and join the rebellion. Hearing of this threat, Josephus mustered two hundred men and marched all night long to Tiberias, where, on reaching the stadium, he dismissed his troops, except for one bodyguard and ten soldiers; standing on a high parapet he addressed the crowd, trying to convince them to remain loyal to him:

> I had not completed my speech when I heard one of my men bidding me to come down, as it was no time for me to be thinking of my own life and how to elude my foes. John, on hearing that I was left isolated with my personal attendants, had selected the most trustworthy of the thousand armed men at his disposal and sent them with orders to kill me. They duly arrived and would have done their business, had I not instantly leapt from the parapet, with James, my bodyguard, and had been further aided by one Herod of Tiberias, who picked me up and conducted me to the lake, where I seized a boat, embarked, and escaping thus beyond all expectation from my enemies, reached Tarichaeae.[16]

3. At Tarichaeae, the inhabitants, on hearing of the treachery of the Tiberians, urged Josephus, he then claimed, to attack Tiberias and to reduce all its men, women, and children to slaves, a position shared by his friends who had escaped from there. But, being both a martial hero and a man of peace, and, above all, dictated by loyalty to his people, "I could not assent to their proposal: I was horrified at the thought of opening a civil war." He therefore made his way to Sepphoris, to preach his moderate position. The inhabitants of Sepphoris, however, had decided to remain loyal to Rome and paid Jesus, a brigand chief, to kill Josephus; soon, however, Josephus learned of this plot, tricked the brigand into submission, and showed him clemency—thus proving two other aspects of his virtue: cunning and forgiveness. But soon his

old enemy John of Gischala appeared again and spread vicious rumors that Josephus had stolen money meant for defense of the Jews, and that he was planning to betray the country to the Romans. A mob then came upon him and demanded that he come to the hippodrome to face charges of sedition; leading the crowd was one Jesus, son of Sapphias, the chief magistrate of Tiberias, "a knave with an instinct for introducing disorder into grave matters and unrivaled in fomenting revolution," who, with "a copy of the Law of Moses in his hands," incited the crowd further and hurried, with some soldiers, to the house where Josephus was lodging, intending to kill him:

> I, quite unaware of what was coming, had from fatigue succumbed to sleep before the riot. Simon [his aide], who was entrusted with the charge of my person and had alone remained with me, seeing the citizens rushing towards me, awoke me and, telling me of my imminent peril, entreated me to die honorably, as a general, by my own hand, before my foes arrived to force me to such action or to kill me themselves. Such were his words, but I, committing my fate to God, hastened to go forth to the people. Changing my raiment for one of black and suspending my sword from my neck, I proceeded by another road, on which I expected no enemy would encounter me, to the hippodrome; where my sudden appearance, as I flung myself on my face and rained tears upon the ground, aroused universal compassion. Observing the effect produced upon the people, I endeavored to create dissension among them before the soldiers returned from my house. I admitted that, according to their view of the matter, I was guilty, but craved leave to inform them for what purpose I was reserving the money obtained by the raid, before, if they so ordered, I was put to death. The crowd were just bidding me proceed, when the soldiers appeared and at the sight of me, rushed forward to kill me. At the people's order, however, they stayed their hands.[17]

At once like Isaac spared from Abraham's knife and like a true Roman orator swaying the crowd with rhetorical brilliance, Josephus recalled saying, "My countrymen, if I deserve to die, I ask no mercy, but before my death, I desire to tell the truth." Enraptured, the crowd attended to every word he spoke, and gave him leave to return home. But:

> I was not long left in peace. The brigands and the promoters of the disturbance, fearing that they would be called to account by me for their proceedings, again visited my residence, with six hundred armed men, to set it on fire. Apprised of their coming, and considering it undignified to fly, I decided to risk a course requiring some courage. Ordering the house-doors to be closed, I ascended to the upper story and invited them to send some of their number to receive the money, thinking thus to allay their anger. They sent in the most stalwart among them, whereupon I had him soundly scourged, ordered one of his hands to be severed and hung about his neck and in that condition dismissed him to his employers. Panic-stricken and in great alarm, supposing that I had indoors a force outnumbering their own, and fearing, if they remained, to meet the same fate themselves, my opponents made off in haste. Such was the stratagem by which I eluded this second plot[18]

—one might say, a combination of Roman manly courage and a *yidisher kop*. And not just a yidisher kop but a pious one at that.

4. A short time later, the citizens of Tiberias, still loyal to the king, sent him a letter asking him to send troops to protect their territory, but, hedging their bets, at the same time asked Josephus to build fortification walls to protect them. This he started to do, but a few days later Roman troops were spotted en route to Tiberias, and this caused great joy in Tiberius and hence alarm to Josephus, fearing that this major city would be lost to the rebellion. But what could he do, since he had sent his own soldiers home for the Sabbath, on which they were not supposed to fight, and even if he had summoned them, he could not ask them to bear arms, "such action being forbidden by our laws, however urgent the necessity." He therefore, once more, "had recourse to a ruse." He posted his most trusted guards at the gates of his house, but sneaked off with other supporters, launched many boats on the Sea of

Galilee, and tricked the Tiberians into believing that these were vessels of war capable of taking the city. Since the Roman troops that had been seen on the road were not, in fact, headed for Tiberias, the natives begged for clemency from Josephus, who cast anchor far off shore so that the lack of armed forces on the sea could not be noticed. He then secured Tiberias for the Jewish side, took many prisoners from the leaders of the city, and once more had the hand of one of the leaders cut off, and in an ingenious way. When he ordered his bodyguard to do this act, the man was afraid, for a large crowd had gathered; Josephus then called forth the prisoner and said:

> "For such base ingratitude to me you deserve to lose both hands. Act as your own executioner, lest if you refuse, a worse punishment befall you." To his urgent request to spare him one hand I grudgingly consented, at which, to save himself the loss of both, he gladly drew his sword and struck off his left hand. His action brought the sedition to an end.[19]

5. A final text, from the end of the *Life*: after being captured by the Romans Josephus had to accompany them on their pacification of Judea as a whole and Jerusalem in particular:

> From Alexandria I was sent with Titus to the siege of Jerusalem, where my life was frequently in danger, both from the Jews, who were eager to get me into their hands, to gratify their revenge, and from the Romans, who attributed every reverse to some treachery on my part, and were constantly and clamourously demanding of the emperor that he should punish me as their betrayer. . . . When, at last, Jerusalem was on the point of being carried by the assault, Titus Caesar repeatedly urged me to take whatever I would from the wreck of my country, stating that I had his permission. And I, now that my native place had fallen, having nothing more precious to take and preserve as a solace for my personal misfortune, made request to Titus for the freedom of some of my countrymen; I also received by his gracious favor a gift of sacred books. Not long after I made peti-

tion for my brother and fifty friends, and my request was granted. Again, by permission of Titus, I entered the Temple, where a great multitude of captive women and children had been imprisoned, and liberated all the friends and acquaintances whom I recognized, in number about a hundred and ninety; I took no ransom for their release and restored them to their former fortune. Once more, when I was sent by Titus Caesar with Cerealius and a thousand horses to a village called Tekoa, to prospect whether it was a suitable place for an entrenched camp, and on my return saw many prisoners who had been crucified, and recognized three of my acquaintances among them, I was cut to the heart and came and told Titus with tears what I had seen. He gave orders immediately that they should be taken down and receive the most careful treatment. Two of them died in the physicians' hands; the third survived.[20]

Many scholars of Josephus have wondered, pondering this account, what happened to the rest of Josephus's family—perhaps even his parents, his other brothers and sisters? We do not know not only because Josephus does not tell us, but because we do not know whether what he did remember actually happened, and whether he forgot things he did not want to remember.

In sum, anything that departs from Josephus's self-fashioning is omitted in the *Vita* not simply because it doesn't fit Roman rhetorical principles or a counterfactually preexisting normative notion of autobiography, but because Josephus—like all earlier and later autobiographers—committed to writing only a selective redaction of his memories, partially conscious and partially not, that served to ratify and document his particular self-presentation. In Greenblatt's terms, Josephus's encounter between Judean authority and the Roman alien produced a self-fashioning that partook of both that authority and that alien, and hence his "achieved identity" contained within itself the signs of its own subversion. In the *Vita*, Josephus desperately tried to make sense of that self-subverted identity: not a "Roemling" as patriotic Jewish historians would later term him, but a Jewish *vir virtutis*, a Pharisaic warrior, a pious general, true at once to his God and people and to the "manliness" the rabbis later found so problematic and repugnant.

Given what we now know about the vagaries of autobiographical memory and autobiography writing, we cannot continue to reconstruct Josephus's life-story on the basis of the *Vita*. But this autobiography remains an extraordinary historical document, a superbly evocative testimony to its author's unrelenting and never resolved struggle to fashion himself at once as a loyal Jew and a loyal subject of Rome. In this way, Josephus personifies in a way he never possibly could have intended, the constituent dilemma not only of first-century Judean Jewry, but of Jewry as a whole in the millennia between the years 70 and 1948—as his far more famous (perhaps fictional and certainly fictionalized) contemporary put it, how to render unto Caesar what was Caesar's, and to God what was God's.

2 / In the Culture of the Rabbis

ASHER OF REICHSHOFEN AND

GLIKL OF HAMELN

Despite his abundantly fertile imagination, Josephus could not possibly have imagined the shape Judaism would take in the centuries, not to speak of millennia, after his death. Although he remains our best, if extraordinarily problematic, source about the Pharisees and the response of the rabbis of his day to the destruction of the Temple in Jerusalem, he could not have foreseen the phenomenon we call rabbinic Judaism, the all-encompassing civilization invented and refined from the second century C.E. to our days. To be sure, from the start of that enterprise to this moment, those committed to its principles and modus operandi believe in its utter, indeed ineffable, seamlessness and its unimpeached and unimpeachable continuity with biblical Judaism and indeed with the Sinaitic revelation itself. Historians' insistence on the novelty and discontinuities of the rabbinic system, its dependence on Greek and Roman hermeneutical, legal, and social categories, and hence its defining departures from pre-Mishnaic Judaism are fundamentally and profoundly irrelevant to its adherents, who revel precisely in the fact that wherever they live, whatever language they speak, whatever trade they ply, they engage in an ontologically and epistemologically timeless and context-neutral conversation with Abraham, Isaac, and Jacob; Moses, Joshua and Isaiah; and Rabbi Akiva and Rashi. But, as discussed above, it does not follow from the above that we can presume to know exactly what went on in the hearts and minds of millions of actual, living and breathing Jews, male and female, from late antiquity to the present, or how they reacted to the vicissitudes of daily life while adhering to one extent or another to the rabbinic system and its categories of thought and exegesis. We must be exceedingly careful not to confuse prescriptive texts with lived lives, or the writings of a highly articulate minority with the feelings and experiences of the largely voiceless majority.

But this axiom, if not cliché, of late-twentieth-century historiography does not mean, as is often assumed, that the voiceless *necessarily* dissented from the strictures of the vocal elites, or that they created a culture separate from, and in conscious opposition to, that elite. On the contrary, we are better off thinking of rabbinic Judaism in terms borrowed from the historian of medieval Christianity John Van Engen, as a continuous—if gendered—spectrum of religious culture, shared both by the voiceless majority and the articulate minority.[1] As Peter Brown, the preeminent historian of late-antique Christianity, put it in his *The Cult of the Saints*:

> We must set aside the "two-tiered" model. Rather than present [popular Christianity] in terms of a dialogue between two parties, the few and the many, let us attempt to see it as part of a greater whole—the lurching forward of an increasing proportion of late-antique society toward radically new forms of reverence, shown to new objects in new places, orchestrated by new leaders, and deriving its momentum from the need to play out the common preoccupation of all, the few and the "vulgar" alike, with new forms of the exercise of power, new bonds of human dependence, new, intimate hopes for protection and justice in a changing world.[2]

And, I might add, new genres of literary and spiritual creativity, which in the case of Judaism were primarily legal, exegetical, homiletic, and liturgical and not, as in the case of Christianity, autobiographical as well. Thus, not only do we not have a Jewish parallel to Augustine's *Confessions* or Teresa de Avila's *Libro de la Vida*, we do not have *any* extant autobiographies or memoirs written by Jews in the medieval period except for the one German-Jewish autobiography discussed by Yuval. Why self-standing autobiographies written by Jews begin to appear in the early modern period we do not yet fully comprehend, though it stands to reason that this must have something to do with the efflorescence of autobiographical writing in Christian Europe, itself a function of the newfound centrality of individualism in Renaissance, and especially humanist, culture, and the concomitant new emphasis on the self, and hence on self-fashioning, in these centuries, "an increased self-consciousness about the fashioning of human identity as a manipulable, artful, process."[3]

Vi es kristlt zikh, azoy yidlt zikh, says the Yiddish proverb, which we may render: whatever happens in the Christian world soon happens in the Jewish world, if with a time delay. Thus, it is not entirely surprising that the first and best-known extant Hebrew autobiography comes from Renaissance Italy—Leon de Modena's *Life of Judah,* expertly studied by the historians Daniel Carpi, Mark Cohen, and others.[4] Modena was born in 1571 and died in 1648, and wrote his autobiography in installments from 1617 to a few weeks before he died. It remained unknown to scholars until the mid-nineteenth century, and an Italian summary of its contents was first published between 1863 and 1865. Only in the 1960s did the autograph manuscript come to light, and the first real scholarly edition appeared in Hebrew in 1985.

A roughly similar fate befell the most famous first extant Yiddish autobiography, Glikl of Hameln's *Zikhroynes.* Glikl was born in 1646 and died in 1724; her memoirs were first published in 1896 and were soon translated into German and English and later into Hebrew and modern Yiddish.[5] While there is a substantial scholarly literature on Glikl and her *Zikhroynes,* we are still awaiting the first scholarly edition of the autobiography, being prepared by Chava Turniansky of the Hebrew University of Jerusalem.

Far less known, however, is a remarkable Hebrew autobiography written by an Alsatian Jew, Asher ben Eliezer Ha-levi, whose life was almost contemporaneous with Modena's and was eerily connected through family ties with Glikl. Apart from his autobiography, we know of Asher Ha-levi only as the copyist of a manuscript of one of the chronicles depicting the massacres of Jews in the Crusades.[6] He was born in 1598 and died sometime in the mid-seventeenth century; we do not know precisely when because all we know of his life-story comes from his *Sefer zikhronot* (Book of memoirs), whose entries chronicle his life from birth to the age of thirty-seven, when he and his family were engulfed in the chaos and misery of the Thirty Years' War. This short but trenchant autobiography was published only once, in 1913, in the original Hebrew and a bowdlerized German translation;[7] although cited in footnotes by a handful of modern scholars interested in the history of Jewish autobiography, its contents have virtually been ignored in the literature on Jewish autobiography.[8]

What I propose to do in this chapter, then, is to compare and contrast Asher Ha-levi's presentation of self with that of Glikl of Hameln, his far more famous posthumous relative-by-marriage. I have chosen these two particular early modern texts for two reasons. First, because they come not from Italy, where the dynamics of influence from Renaissance culture have been well charted, if often vastly exaggerated, but from the heartland of rabbinic Judaism in these centuries, Ashkenaz, where the possible influence of humanist individualism is difficult, if not impossible, to imagine, much less to chronicle. Second, although close in geographical and chronological contexts, these two autobiographies present fascinating contrasts, if not antinomies: male versus female; Hebrew versus Yiddish; poor versus rich. But despite these differences, both Asher and Glikl (I will use their first names here to counter the norm that insists on calling women by their first names but men by their family names, and "Hameln" would be a preposterous substitute for "Glikl" since she never used that appellation) were not part of the rabbinic elite of Rhineland Jewry: Glikl, because she was a woman and hence automatically excluded; and Asher because he simply was not part of that elite. He studied with some of the leading rabbis of his time and gained enough traditional learning to serve intermittently as a ritual slaughterer and circumciser, but not enough to be ordained as a rabbi; he earned his living, such as it was, by dealing in wine and grain. Thus, to the extent that any autobiographer can be regarded as representative of the society he or she describes, Asher and Glikl appear to me to be better candidates than the handful of rather quixotic rabbis who penned the other extant early modern Jewish autobiographies. But it is absolutely crucial to understand from the very start that although they were part of the normally voiceless "silent majority" of early modern Jewry, Asher and Glikl were not to any extent dissenters from the religion of their rabbis. On the contrary, they were pious Jews, deeply committed to their faith, never for once doubting its eternal veracity and its requirements that they live entirely bounded and defined by its norms, laws, and strictures. Indeed, one of the shared central themes of both their works is their personal, intimate failings in living up to those norms and those strictures—their struggles with desire and lust, pride and envy, bereavement and joy. We can be certain that neither Asher nor Glikl ever read Augustine's *Confessions* or Modena's unpublished manuscript, and so we cannot dismiss their confessions of sin and declarations of faith as mere literary tropes, just as we ought not confuse their expressions of angst and doubt as "arguing with God" as Natalie Zemon Davis does in an insightful but deeply flawed chapter on Glikl in her *Women on the Margins*. For whatever reason, on some level profoundly unknowable to us, these two devout and yet all-too-human Jews decided to put pen to paper to record their lives for posterity. How did they do so, and how, given all we know now about autobiographies and the vagaries of individual memory, can we use their memoir books as sources for Jewish history?

The story of how Asher ben Eliezer Ha-levi of Reichshofen's memoirs were preserved is, to say the least, bizarre. It was published and annotated by the Jewish scholar Moses Ginsburger, who received the manuscript from Elie Scheid, a late-nineteenth-century historian of Alsatian Jewry, who found the manuscript in one of the antiquarian bookshops on the banks of the Seine in Paris. It was bound together with a parchment page of a Latin New Testament and an excerpt from Erasmus.[9] Neither Scheid nor Ginsburger seems to have pondered the contents of these pages, which in fact give us a fascinating hint about the identity of the person responsible for cobbling together this strange collection.

The New Testament text is 1 Corinthians 5: 9–13:

I wrote you in my letter not to associate with sexually immoral people. In no way did I mean the immoral of this world, or the greedy and swindlers and idolaters, since you would then have to go out of the world. But now I am writing to you not to associate with anyone who bears the name of brother and sister who is sexually immoral, or greedy, or an idolater, or verbally abusive, or a drunkard, or a swindler. Do not even eat with such a person. For what do I have to do with judging those outside? Are you not to judge those inside? But God will judge those outside. Drive out the evil person from among you.

The Erasmus is equally compelling: these pages were part of his *Convivium profanum* (The profane feast), in which he discusses, inter alia, the benefits of abstinence and fasting, and along the way has one of his characters, appropriately named Christian, say:

> In many matters it's not the fact but the intention that distinguishes us from the Jews. They used to abstain from certain foods as if from unclean things that would defile the mind. We, though we know that to the pure all things are pure, nevertheless deny nourishment to the lustful flesh as if to an unruly steed, so as to render it more obedient to the spirit. Sometimes we discipline our excessive use of delicacies by the vexation of abstinence.[10]

My hypothesis, then, is that Asher Ha-levi's autobiography may well have been preserved by a Christian Hebraist—possibly a convert from Judaism?—who was preparing an attack on Jewish vices, including alcoholism and sexual concupiscence, two of the sins Asher confesses to in his text. Be that as it may, Asher's confessions of these and other vices are, I think, essential to his text, if not its only raison d'être. That, he tells us, in the opening words of the autobiography, is:

> To turn my thoughts to and set in memory the events and experiences that affected me and my family from the day that God brought me forth from darkness to light, into the travails of this lowly world; may it come to pass that the day of my death be the same as the day of my birth, without sin and cleansed of all iniquity. Therefore, I have taken it upon myself to engrave with an iron pen the memory of everything that happened to me, good and bad, in order to praise and give thanks for it all, just as we bless the good so we must bless the bad, and I have appended to the end of this book everything that happened to my children, and I shall testify to all both firsthand and with the names of other witnesses to these events, as required by the Law . . . and I have appended as well a chronology of all that happened in my day to the People of Israel, and I shall start from the day of my birth, Friday, the third day of the month of Elul 5358 [4 September 1598].[11]

Thus, in sharp contrast both to Modena and, as we shall see, to Glikl, both of whom claim to have written their memoirs for the sake of their children, Asher's purpose is at once confessional and historicist: the former provides a crucial counterexample to the oft-stated claim that unlike Christians, Jews did not write confessional autobiographies; the latter runs counter to our expectations about traditional sixteenth-century Jews and their sense of history. Unfortunately, his second volume has not been preserved, but from the frequent cross-references to this book in his memoirs proper we can be sure that it included detailed explications of the battles of the Thirty Years' War, accounts of the expulsions and persecutions suffered by European Jews in the early seventeenth century, information about rabbis in the major communities of Ashkenazic Jews, their major works and years of death, and perhaps most intriguingly, precise descriptions of the economic history of the Rhineland in these decades—all issues that are interwoven throughout the autobiography, as well as a large number of poetic elegies, in typically cumbersome early modern rabbinic *melizah*. Asher's Hebrew prose, on the other hand, is crisp, clear, almost entirely grammatical—a true rarity in his day—and virtually devoid of the Aramaisms and allusions to Talmudic dicta that were (and still are) the mark of the educated rabbinic elite and render rabbinic prose so unfathomable to outsiders, including native Hebrew speakers. To be sure, biblicisms abound in Asher's text, but this is not the work of a Bible scholar. Rather, Asher's prose style seems to accord with the person and curriculum vitae it records: he tells us that he was born in a small town in Alsace in 1598, at the age of six was taught to read Hebrew at home by his father, and then sent to a cheder or two until, at the age of twelve, he began to study the Talmud along with the *Tosafot*; two years later he set off to Prague to study with the great rabbis of that metropolis, and remained there intermittently—interrupted by the outbreak of the plague and several highway robberies to which he fell victim—until he reached the age of seventeen, when he moved on to a nearby yeshiva where he was awarded the pre-rabbinic title "bakhur" and learned the laws of kosher slaughtering. After visiting Vienna and Frankfurt am Main he returned to Alsace and headed for the nearby yeshiva in Metz, where he studied and was certified as a ritual slaughterer. He then served as a *melamed* in several small nearby towns, until, at the age of twenty-four, he married Malka, the fifteen-year-old daughter of a middling merchant in the village of Reichshofen, where the new couple established their home, soon had two children, and tried to make ends meet by dealing, as noted above, in wine, wheat, and other agricultural produce. All of this is recorded in astonishingly precise detail: every significant event in his life is dated by his age at the time, including day, week, month; if one were so inclined, one could attempt to study the weather patterns, commodity markets, and cycle of communicative diseases in early seventeenth-century Alsace and Lorraine through Asher's detailed listing of rain- and snowfall, the rising and falling prices of grapes and grain, and the steady outbreak of the plague. Given the obscurity of most of this data, it is difficult, if not impossible, to assess its degree of accuracy. Ginsburger carefully compared Asher's dates of deaths of famous rabbis with independent documentary sources and found only a tiny number of factual errors in Asher's account; it is striking that his notations about the battles that overwhelmed Alsace-Lorraine in the Thirty Years' War are all precisely on target, and for this and other reasons it is a true shame that his second, more self-consciously historical volume is not extant.

Consider the following extract, late in the book, when the invading Swedish army faces the forces of Emperor Ferdinand II, and we are given both a precise chronology of the battles that ensued and an insight into the behavior of the Jews in the midst of the action:

> At that time there was war and great suffering in this region and land, and because of my fear already in the late summer of 1632 I sent my wife and children and almost everything I owned to [the village of] Oberborn, but after three days I myself returned home. The Swedes arrived on Sunday [28 October], and besieged the town. Thank God they were roundly defeated, for the townsmen pursued them and attacked them, and on Wednesday [31 October], I returned to my home and prayed to the Redeemer to save me, my family, and my brethren. For the siege of Hagenau, see part two where you will find a detailed description of what happened there on Tuesday [23 October 1632], when the Swedish forces arrived there

and then the Emperor's army came in stealthily and captured it on Saturday [15 January]. . . .

At that time there were billeted here in Reichshofen one hundred cavalrymen from the Emperor's army, and they captured two important Swedish officers who then sent me to Metz to arrange for their ransoming. On Tuesday [3 May 1633], I arrived there with great difficulty and in much danger, but by the by I bought a good deal of merchandise there and out of fear I went home in a roundabout way. . . . When I arrived, on Wednesday [11 May], past Puetllingen, near the village of Reich, five cruel imperial soldiers attacked me and stole from me everything that I had; thank God, the messenger who had my merchandise got away and I wasn't physically attacked, thank the Lord who protects the faithful.[12]

What is most intriguing about this autobiography is not such fascinating episodes but the continuous and gripping pathos of Asher's struggle with himself, his attempt to use the literary device of autobiography, so seemingly foreign to his culture and training, to record and confront his failings and thus to become a better human being, which, in his terms, was synonymous with becoming a better Jew. His most often recorded sins—as my hypothesized Christian Hebraist preserver of his text well knew—were drinking and gambling. He repeatedly records taking vows to stay away from taverns in which lowlife Jews and non-Jews cavort together, drinking and gambling, and seems (like Modena, too) to have been most addicted to the games of dice and cards in which he regularly lost substantial amounts of money, and which he feared would bring disgrace to his name and his family. As a pious Jew he knew that vows taken so solemnly cannot be broken. As a somewhat learned Jew he pored through the rabbinic codes to find legal ways to nullify these vows, only to renew them again and again when he strayed back to the gambling dens he found so appallingly irresistible. Similarly, he vowed to abstain from nonkosher wine, which he reports was imbibed by Jews of all types throughout his region, despite the rabbinic prohibition, a reality we know from other sources. In a wonderful paragraph he describes how he built his house to keep him more devout:

The house that I built and bought, with God's help and dedicated to His glory and His Torah, included three things: first, a small room for regular prayer and study of Torah, and to house my sacred books, which I shall list later on [alas, this part of the memoir is missing]; second, a small oven to bake matzo, and this Passover [1631] was the first time that I was able to fulfill this commandment according to the custom of the Rokeah, baking three matsot on the eve of Passover, and on Thursday, the fifth day of Passover, another three; this same small oven was used to bake challah for every sabbath for the blessing over bread, and to warm the *cholent* for the sabbath day; third, a small bathhouse behind the stove of the winter house, for several reasons, and most importantly because there is a bestial custom in these parts, that the Gentiles bathe together with their wives in one bathhouse, and Jews and their wives do the same, mixing with the Gentiles and their wives, and I fought for the honor of the Lord and built myself a special room in my house to bathe in on Sabbath eves, in the event I need bloodletting, and for women's ritual purification.[13]

This is immediately followed by a recording of an incident about another form of ritual impurity that speaks volumes about the nature and setting of this text, and the life it describes. We know from multiple scholarly studies that notions of sexuality, privacy, and what is appropriate to discuss in the public realm were far different in early seventeenth-century Alsace than in early twenty-first-century America; thus, Asher writes:

Here in Reichshofen there gathered together a minyan of neighbors for Rosh Hashanah and Yom Kippur, and I served without compensation as their prayer leader, standing on my feet all Kol Nidre eve and the entire day of Yom Kippur. But God caused me to have a nocturnal emission on the night of Kol Nidre, and I was not unaware of the talmudic discussions on these matters (which would prohibit me from leading the services); this happened between one and two in the morning, and I rose from my bed, went to my wife's room, and tearfully told her what had happened; we both cried, and I resolved to immerse myself in a ritual bath before sunrise, since I was the only cantor in these parts; I checked the legal codes to see whether

nine cubits of water were sufficient for immersions after nocturnal emissions, and in my research I discovered that immersion was not, in fact, required in a case such as this, that simply cleaning up was sufficient, since
the quantity was so small. So I immediately rose from my sleep and calmed
down; and I put my trust in God and implored him to have mercy on me,
on account of my forefathers and my little children, and I pledge to search
through my misdeeds and commit myself anew to His service, and He, the
Creator, will do what is just in His eyes—thus signed, Asher Ha-levi.[14]

And poor Asher, the very same thing happened to him again two years
later on Kol Nidre night, which he recorded again, with a broken heart, in
the midst of one of the worst battles of the Thirty Years' War.[15]

From the wording of these paragraphs we see that like a good part of
the autobiography as a whole, they were originally composed as diary-like
entries inscribed immediately after they happened; then, at some later
point, they were redacted to adhere to a more linear and coherently retrospective narrative form. This procedure is crucial to our understanding of
Asher's autobiography as a whole: what began as an intimate, confessional
diary, meant to record one man's sins in order to goad him into self-
improvement, was later revisited and redrafted by this same man for
frankly literary purposes. In other words, his self-study was gradually
transmuted into a self-conscious self-fashioning, an autobiographical narrative that tried to make sense of Asher's life and times first for himself and
then, in some way, for us, though we cannot know whether and in what
ways Asher expected his words to be read by anyone else. In a paradoxical
way, then, Asher's very ignorance of the Gentile genre of autobiography led
him to pen an autobiography that was essentially unmediated by the
screens and artifices of that genre and hence in many ways more directly
reflective of his lived experiences than other more stylized accounts.

But this still does not mean that we can be as delightfully naive as he
was, and blithely use this autobiography as a source for the social history
of early modern Jews, confidently generalizing from its anecdotes "facts"
about Christian-Jewish interactions, Jewish marital and dowry customs,
learning patterns, and the like in early modern Alsatian Jewry. Given what
we know about the constructive nature of episodic memory, here un-

doubtedly intertwined with the confessional purposes of the recollections, I for one would abstain from generalizing from the specifics of
Asher's life-writing to his society as a whole, until and unless we find
many more contemporaneous documents that allow us to check his re-
constructions against independent evidentiary sources.

But this in no way diminishes the historical importance of Asher's
Sefer zikhronot, whose abiding power consists not in what Asher shared
with his fellow seventeenth-century Alsatian Jews, but in what was singular and remarkable about him, the first ordinary Jew we know of—
learned, but not a rabbi; small-town Ashkenazic as opposed to worldly
Italian or Sephardic—who wrote his autobiography in the heyday of, but
apparently oblivious to, the renewed Renaissance self-consciousness
about individual identity. At the same time, though Asher was entirely devoted to the religion of the rabbis and the "collective structures and
myths" of rabbinic Judaism, he did not believe that the precise recording
of the details of his life-story was irrelevant because of those myths and
structures. On the contrary, he conceived of his life as a highly individu-
ated struggle for self-betterment in which self-awareness, and a literarily
self-conscious manipulation of that self-awareness, were crucial. In this, I
do not believe for a moment he was alone among premodern Jews, despite the paucity of literary evidence of parallel constructions of self.

Asher's autobiography ends in the winter of 1634–35, when, around
Hanuka time, the frost was so severe that he and his comrades feared that
the Rhine would freeze over and the Emperor's troops could cross over
and reinvade Alsace. But, he tells us in his typically precise way, the rains
came and the ice melted, and then another frost began on January 16,
1635.[16] Here the chronicle of his and his family's life comes to an end, and
Asher's last literary act is appropriately devotional: a genealogical record
of the births, marriages, and deaths of his extended family members for
several generations before him. Appended to his text is an addendum
written some three decades later, in 1671 and 1674, by his brother-in-law,
Jonah ben Simhah Ha-cohen of Metz, who, inspired by Asher's genealogical lists, recorded the history of his own family. Jonah refers to Asher as
his deceased brother-in-law,[17] but fails to record when it was that Asher
Ha-levi of Reichshofen died. Thus, his fate, and that of his wife, daughter,

and son, after the cold January days of 1635, remain unrecorded and un-known to us.

But we do know a good deal about the later history of one branch of Asher's extended family mentioned in his genealogical account—the wealthy Levi family of Metz, into which none other than Glikl of Hameln married in 1700, at the age of 54. At this point Glikl had probably already written a good chunk of the first draft of her own autobiography, the final version of which was preserved by her family for generations after her death in 1724 and, as already noted, was first published in its original Yid-dish 172 years later in 1896, by the renowned scholar David Kaufmann.[18] It was Kaufmann who dubbed her "Glückel of Hameln"—a designation she had never borne in her lifetime, though her first husband was oft referred to as "Haim Hameln" after the town of his birth. We do not know what she called herself or, for that matter, her autobiography,[19] since the original manuscript has never been located: the only extant manuscript is a copy made by one of her sons after her death; another copy made by a grand-nephew was available to Kaufmann but is now lost. The loss of the auto-graph manuscript is a terrible shame, since it prevents us from seeing— quite literally—how the book was composed: Glikl tells us that she began writing it in 1690, after the death of her first husband, and continued working on it until 1719, periodically going over and correcting her text, but it would be immensely useful for our purposes to see exactly how this editorial process proceeded and how much and to what extent she revised her words—and her memories—over these three decades of composition.

The original text is very different in almost every relevant respect from the terrible and unreliable English version edited by Marvin Lowenthal as *The Memoirs of Gluckel of Hameln*.[20] Lowenthal translated Glikl's words not from the Yiddish original but from a poor 1913 German translation which itself left out huge sections of Glikl's work. Lowenthal then made matters even worse by rearranging the order of Glikl's chapters, expur-gating additional sections of the text, and rendering it into an artificially archaic and pedantic English that in no way conveys to the reader Glikl's tone, style, and, to some extent, her worldview. (Another English transla-tion, by Beth-Zion Abrahams, is far more accurate, though itself riddled with many errors and omissions.[21]) Glikl's worldview, moreover, has for

understandable reasons often been hitched to ideological causes as foreign to Glikl as the twenty-first century is to the late seventeenth and early
eighteenth, presenting her as a Yiddishist or a feminist *avant la lettre,* or,
as I already mentioned above, as one who argued with God or questioned
basic Jewish religious law.[22] But my purpose here is not to quarrel with
these appropriations of Glikl; rather, I should like to pose the same questions to Glikl's text that I did to Josephus's and then to Asher's: what is the
design of the work, what purposes did it serve for its author, what is the
level of facticity in the text, and then, most important, how and in what
ways can we continue to use it as a historical source?

To answer the first question one must first assess Glikl's writing style,
which, like so many other aspects of her life and work, has been rather ro-
manticized in the literature. First and foremost we are dealing here with a
very long text—333 printed pages in the Kaufmann edition—divided by
Glikl's own design into seven books, which vary from 22 to 80 printed
pages. But unlike most early modern Yiddish texts, Glikl's does not have
either paragraph markers or even breaks between sentences. Each book
therefore reads like one long—often excruciatingly long—sentence. Although here and there commas appear between some clauses, the reader
is essentially forced to punctuate the text on her or his own, a challenge
made even more difficult by Glikl's habit of interspersing throughout her
narrative long folk stories taken from a variety of sources, probably
mostly—as Chava Turniansky has demonstrated—from other early modern Yiddish storybooks.[23] The result is an extraordinarily difficult and
dense text to read, and one is hard-pressed to imagine anyone but a
scholar of Jewish autobiography or seventeenth-century Jewish history
actually sitting down and doing so.

Then there is the highly complex issue of the nature of her Yiddish,
which has been the subject of scholarly scrutiny and erudite controversy
for the last ninety years, primarily because it includes a very large number of Hebrew and Aramaic terms, most of which are incomprehensible
today to native speakers of Yiddish not tutored in traditional Hebrew and
Aramaic. Indeed, when Glikl's memoirs were translated into modern Yiddish in the mid-twentieth century for the Buenos Aires–based series
"Masterpieces of Yiddish Literature," the editor had to append a long

glossary of these terms for his readers,[24] and most recently there appeared a 204-page German monograph devoted exclusively to an analysis of these Hebraisms.[25] The philological conundrum is at once gendered and circular: to what extent this degree of usage of Hebrew and Aramaic in Yiddish was typical or atypical for a seventeenth-century German-Jewish woman depends on one's evaluation of the extent of traditional learning among seventeenth-century German-Jewish women, and the best source for this is none other than Glikl's autobiography itself.

Which leads to the related question of the typicality and representativeness of Glikl herself. While often presented in popular sources as an "ordinary woman," Glikl was in fact extremely non-"ordinary" in socioeconomic terms: her father, she tells us, was the second richest (Ashkenazic) Jew in Hamburg in his day, paying the largest dowry ever known in the community to the husband of her sister Hendele. More reliably, the extant tax records of Hamburg-Altona reveal that her husband, Haim, was the fourth richest Jewish householder in that community in the next generation, and Glikl and Haim arranged matches for their children with even wealthier members of the tiny Jewish mercantile elite: their eldest son married a daughter of Eliyahu Balin, the third richest Jew of Hamburg; their younger son married a daughter of Moses ben Nathan, by far the richest Jew in the community; and their oldest daughter married a son of Elias Gompertz of Cleve, who was said to be worth 100,000 Reichstaler, an immense fortune at the time.[26] And when she left Hamburg to marry Cerf Levi in Metz, Glikl's socioeconomic status rose even further, as the Court-Jew-like, French-speaking Levi clan were far wealthier and more politically connected than any of the Jews in Hamburg-Altona at this time. Her memoirs are filled, then, with detailed and fascinating descriptions of the extensive business dealings she was engaged in, both during and after her first marriage, the protracted negotiations concerning the marriages of her children, and all the events and circumstances that surrounded and conditioned these intersecting and intertwined commercial and domestic affairs.

To what extent this highly atypical woman can be said to be representative of anything, I shall address soon; before then, I want to ponder more closely the connection between this anticipated rise in economic and social status attendant upon her second marriage and what Roy Pascal called the "design" of the autobiography itself. Glikl tells us, in the very opening of the book, that she began to write her memoirs as a result of the depression she suffered after the death of her first husband, whom she loved dearly. In my own translation these passages read as follows:

> In the year of creation 5451 [i.e., 1690–91] I begin writing this out of many worries and troubles and with an aching heart, as will follow later. May the Lord make us rejoice as often as He has afflicted us and send our messiah and redeemer speedily, Amen.[27]

And roughly three pages later:

> My dear children, I began writing this, with the help of God, after the death of your pious father, to give me some respite when melancholic thoughts came to me and out of deep distress, for we were strayed sheep that lost our faithful shepherd. I spent many sleepless nights and feared falling into a melancholia, and so I often arose in the wakeful hours and spent the time writing this.[28]

Although these sentences have—like everything else Glikl wrote—been taken as unproblematically accurate by all commentators on this text, I propose that we must be exceedingly careful before we take her words as factual. First, and self-evident, we must make sure that we translate her words correctly: my translation above differs from Lowenthal's and Abraham's (and from those into German and Hebrew) by insisting on rendering precisely the tense used by Glikl in these passages. The above-translated opening passage presents us with a linguistic conundrum that will become typical of the text as a whole: Glikl writes, "*Shnas 5451 askhil likhtov zeh mirov daygos vetsaros u-makhovey lev vi vayter folgn vert.* . . ." It is hard to know for certain why Glikl chose to begin the text with such a macaronic Hebrew-Yiddish sentence—possibly to seem more learned than had she begun in straightforward Yiddish? And what did she mean, precisely, by using *askhil*, the Hebrew first-person future of the verb "to begin"? My supposition from the context is that she meant "I begin" rather than "I shall begin." Far more relevantly, in the latter passage she used the Yiddish past perfect rather than the present or the past continuous—"I began" and "I spent" rather than "I have begun" and "I have spent," as the other translations render these lines. In other words, these sentences—and most of the text as a whole—were written by Glikl not at the time of their action or immediately thereafter, but retrospectively. More importantly, in between these two passages come two long pages which Lowenthal (following the German translation he was working from), Abrahams, and A. S. Rabinovitz, who rendered Glikl into Hebrew (based on the same poor German text[29]) omitted entirely, but are crucial to an understanding of what I take to be Glikl's fundamental motivation in composing this autobiography as a whole. These passages begin with what seems to be simply a conventional homily on God's mercy:

> [We are taught in Hebrew:] *kol mah shebara hakadosh barukh hu lo bara ela likhvodo vehaolam be-hesed yivneh*—Everything that God created he did so for His honor, and the world was created in mercy. [This means that] we know that God created and did everything out of great righteousness and mercy, for He has no need of any of his creatures, but He created them all for His honor and in righteousness and mercy, and for the benefit of us sinful people, for everything He created has utility for us humans, even if we cannot discern how this is so.[30]

But Glikl's thoughts soon turned to a meditation on the fundamental problem of theodicy: how and why does God permit evil to exist, and evil people to thrive while the righteous suffer? First she gives the conventional rabbinic answer that this life is short and true reckoning comes only after death, but this does not totally satisfy her, and so she continues:

> The poor man who has lived all his days in pain and suffering dies peacefully, for death is what he prayed for all his life, since he died a little bit every day, but had constant faith that God would reward him with a better life in the hereafter. . . . But the evil rich man who lives happily and with much money and seeks nothing other than what is good, and he and his children have only the best, nothing bothers them at all—when the time

comes for him to depart from this world, and he knows what and how much he is leaving, but in his last thoughts ponders how much God has rewarded him with, how he has to abandon his riches and power, and has to give a reckoning to God about how he handled himself in this world— the journey is much harder for him than for the poor man. I need not say more.[31]

These words make little or no sense in the context of the immediate aftermath of Haim Hameln's death, since Glikl repeatedly stressed only what a wonderful and righteous man he was. But they make eminent sense if composed in the aftermath of the death of her *second* husband, Cerf Levi, who lured her to Metz with promises of great wealth and honor, all of which came to naught when, almost immediately thereafter, he lost his fortune through bankruptcy and his family as a whole was disgraced in the greatest scandal to befall Metz Jewry in the early eighteenth century: the arrest and imprisonment of Samuel Levi, Cerf Levi's son and formerly chief rabbi of Alsace and latterly chief financial officer to the Duke of Lorraine.[32] After Levi's death in 1712, Glikl records, she was for the first time in her life reduced to utter poverty, forced to live in one room with her maidservant, and then to move into her daughter's home and become entirely dependent upon her children for sustenance. The proud, previously independent business woman who was raised in wealth and honor, who for decades had been an equal partner with her first husband in a thriving commercial enterprise and after his death carried on the business with great success, trading alone in the main mercantile markets of northern Europe, was now a shamed, poor widow, unable to live the life she was accustomed to from birth.

My hypothesis, then, is that although Glikl may have begun the autobiography after the death of her first husband in order to banish depression and to lift her spirits, the version we have before us was, from its first page to the last, redrafted years later with far different emotions at its core: bitterness, guilt, anger. For understandable reasons, the lionizing late nineteenth- and early-twentieth-century translators of her words into German, English, and Hebrew felt it necessary to omit many passages expressing these emotions, or to downplay others by under-translation.

Since we now know that emotions at the time of retrieval of episodic memories have a defining, indeed biochemical, effect on the nature and content of those memories, we cannot for a moment assume that her retroactively recorded memories were either factual or untouched by what neuroscientists call "retrospective bias."

To be sure, this is so even if my hypothesis about the precise time of the composition of the first part of Glikl's memoirs is incorrect. Under any circumstance, we must consider Glikl's recording of her life-story as a constructive literary act of self-representation, rather than a reliable, so-called "factual" account of what she experienced. This leads to my second hypothesis about this autobiography: that it is not only a literary self-representation but essentially a self-justification, an attempt to detail for her children how she spent her whole life dedicated to their father and to them, suffering for their benefit and through them. Even her marriage to Cerf Levi was effected, she insistently and repeatedly claims, so that she could secure her future and theirs, and especially not have to be dependent on them in her old age. This turned out to be a tragic mistake, she conceded: she should have focused on marrying off her youngest daughter rather than herself, and then moved to the Land of Israel where she could have lived out her last years as a pious Jewess. Instead, she succumbed to lust and greed, and God has punished her accordingly. But Glikl never expresses anger at God for this punishment; on the contrary, she insists, time and time again, that He treats His creatures fairly. She is angry at herself, at her own sins and shortcomings that led her astray and into the clutches of an "evil rich man" who promised her greater wealth and honor than she ever had, but died a death worse than any pauper's.

For the most part, Glikl tries not to appear vengeful in her account of her life with Cerf Levi. But in one particularly poignant passage, describing none other than their wedding and its immediate aftermath, her wrath at her second husband seeps through:

The wedding took place on Thursday, Rosh Hodesh Tammuz 5460 [18 June 1700]. In the morning I was taken from my daughter's house to my husband's neighboring home where I stayed till after midnight, when my husband betrothed me with an expensive wedding ring weighing an ounce. I

was led under the huppah, which was set up in the courtyard of our summer house by the Rebezzin Breinele and the wealthy Mistress Yafet. I was
then brought to our handsomely furnished room near the office, and was
served specially prepared wedding foods, as is the custom throughout Ashkenaz. Although I had fasted all day long I could not eat, since my heart was
so heavy, I had wept so many tears with my daughter Esther, as befit our
mood that day. My husband then took me into his office and showed me a
large box filled to the brim with bracelets and rings—but neither then nor
ever after did he give me even one gold or silver ring, and so I was hardly
the cause of his later financial ruin![33]

Then, in a Gothic scene virtually foreshadowing Daphne du Maurier's
Rebecca arriving in Manderley, Glikl describes being all but trapped in a
luxurious home presided over by a Mrs. Danforth–like housekeeper, who
excluded her from management of her own house and insisted on run-
ning the show as she had under her previous mistress. Worse, Cerf Levi's
children constantly complained of how Germanically frugal Glikl was,
compared to the lavish French ways of their dearly departed mother, and
laughed in her face when she sent gifts and special Sabbath fruits over to
their homes, remarking at how measly they were in comparison with
those their mother had lavished upon them. No wonder, then, that Glikl
ended this passage with the remark: "I put up with such things for a long
time, but nonetheless thanked God, thinking that my long sad widow-
hood had not been in vain, even it was, [as the Psalmist put it] 'joy mixed
with fear and trembling.'"[34]

As I hope these passages make clear, even more than with Asher Ha-
levi, what began as self-justification became a decidedly literary self-
fashioning: as already noted, it was Glikl herself who decided to divide her
autobiography into seven books, and she self-consciously extended some
stories to even out the length of the shorter books. She quite obviously
delighted in retelling tales of yore she had read or heard, molding their
plots to fit into her own life story. Given the length of the autobiography
and the massive amount of detail it includes, it is not surprising that the
chronology is often out of sync[35]—dead people are listed as still living,
and vice versa—and that the text ends rather jarringly with a curious and

unexplained episode that happened in her seventy-third year. But on the whole Glikl's *Zikhroynes* is a moving and extravagantly thick description of her life and times, a supremely controlled narrative in which the author is fully conscious of how to manipulate the telling of her own tale, and of how she wants her children—and perhaps us, her readers—to regard and remember her.

Thus, the facticity of her account—hitherto taken for granted and therefore not seriously addressed in the scholarship—is highly questionable. A handful of scholars compared her version of facts with those of documentary sources such as gravestones and tax records and found a small number of errors, like those of Asher Ha-levi;[36] more revealing of her economic class, she misrepresented her tax evasion upon her departure from Hamburg for Metz.[37] Turniansky, more interested in the literary sources of Glikl's retold folktales, noted that she often incorrectly attributed the sources of these stories, including claiming nonexistent biblical sources for some of them and not noticing the scriptural source of others.[38] No one I know of has cared to pay heed to her constant practice, like Josephus and so many memoir writers before her and since, of recounting verbatim conversations that took place outside of her presence and to which she could not possibly have been privy. My favorite example among many, is the following tale about one Mordecai, a Polish Jew who worked for her and her husband and decided, against the latter's advice, to travel from Hamburg to Germany proper to buy wine:

> Mordecai set out on his journey carrying with him about 600 Reichstaler. This money he handed to my brother-in-law Lipman when he reached Hanover, to be forwarded to those places where he bought wine. From there he had to go to Hildesheim. Mordecai was a stingy man who grudged the money that taking the post-wagon would have cost him. He made the distance from Hanover to Hildesheim, three miles, on foot. When he was about a third of a mile from Hildesheim, he came face to face with a highway robber who said to him: "Jew, give me money for a drink, otherwise I will shoot you." Mordecai laughed at him, for he knew that the highway between Hanover and Hildesheim is far safer than that between Hamburg and Altona. The poacher addressed him again, "You Jew carcass! Why do

you think so long? Say yes or no," and took his gun and shot him in the head. Mordecai fell dead immediately. . . . He had not lain long wallowing in his young blood when people coming from Hildesheim found him in this miserable plight.[39]

A wonderfully told story, with a novelist's touch for drama and dialogue—but one she obviously could not have witnessed.

And so, in the end, Glikl's self-fashioning is far more self-conscious than Asher's, and perhaps on a par with Josephus's. Indeed, the comparison with the latter is not so far-fetched as it may first appear, since, like the ancient Judean warrior-historian writing his memoirs in exile in Rome, Glikl too wrote hers in a sort of double exile—far from Hamburg, and far outside the elite stratum of Ashkenazic Jewish wealthy society she was born into and worked so hard to insure her children remain in.

But to end where we began, for all their self-conscious individualities, Glikl's and Asher's lives were lived entirely within the culture and religious faith of rabbinic Judaism in its early modern northern European mode. The world they confronted was, of course, neither static nor in reality easily circumscribed by the wisdom of the ancient—or, for that matter, contemporary—sages of the Jews. Thus, Glikl and Asher had to confront, each in her or his own way, what Peter Brown called "the common preoccupation of all, the few and the 'vulgar' alike, with new forms of the exercise of power, new bonds of human dependence, new, intimate hopes for protection and justice in a changing world."[40] But male or female, rich or poor, Asher and Glikl, for all their suffering and travails, never expressed any doubt whatsoever in the justice and mercy of the God in whom they trusted, or in His words and commandments as explicated and taught to them by their parents, teachers, and rabbis. Such doubts would indeed arise and be expressed, however, within less than half a century after Glikl's death in the very heartland of Ashkenazic Jewry, and would dominate Jewish autobiographical literature for the centuries to come.

3 / *Two Russian Jews*

MOSHE LEIB LILIENBLUM AND
OSIP MANDELSTAM

At first glance, it would be hard to find two modern Russian Jews so different from one another than Moshe Leib Lilienblum and Osip Mandelstam. The first, one of the most famous writers of the Hebrew Enlightenment, became an early leader of the "Love of Zion" movement in late-nineteenth-century Russia and hence a hero of Zionist history. The second, one of the most renowned Russian poets of all time, was profoundly ambivalent about his Jewishness and in fact underwent a formal conversion to Protestantism at the age of twenty. (Indeed, it may be argued that it is therefore inappropriate to include Mandelstam in a volume on "Autobiographical Jews"—a problem I shall discuss at some length below.)

Yet even before proposing a phenomenological parallelism between the two, it is important to point out their chronological and geographical congruity: Lilienblum was born in 1843 and died in 1910, and was thus still alive for the first nineteen years of Mandelstam's life—the latter was born in 1891 and died (in a Stalinist gulag) in 1938. Even more intriguingly, they hailed from surprisingly close backgrounds: Lilienblum was born in Kedainiai, a small town in central Lithuania barely sixty miles from Vilna, where Mandelstam's mother was born, and just a little farther in the other direction from Zhagory (Zagare), the northern Lithuanian town were Mandelstam's father's family was from (the oft-quoted misinformation about their Kurland roots notwithstanding). Lilienblum moved from Kedainiai first to nearby Vilkomir (now Ukmerge), where he was married, and then to Odessa, while Mandelstam's parents were married in nearby Dvinsk (now Daugavpils, Latvia) and moved first to Warsaw, where Osip was born, and then to St. Petersburg, where he was raised.

In other words, Mandelstam's parents were not only of the exact same background as Moshe Leib Lilienblum, but they—and especially his father—struggled at almost the same time, if with different results, with the same pushes and pulls of Orthodox Lithuanian Judaism, the Enlightenment challenges to that tradition, and the subsequent benefits and costs of Russification and embourgeoisement. Indeed, more thematically, both Lilienblum's and Mandelstam's lives were determined (or one might be tempted to say, "overdetermined") by their struggles with their fathers, each of whom was a perfect representative of successive cohorts of Russian-Jewish patresfamilias in the mid-nineteenth to the mid-twentieth centuries as they moved from traditionalism to modernity.

We know this, of course, from the astonishingly captivating autobiographies that each of them wrote: Lilienblum's *Hatot neurim* (The sins of my youth), first published in 1876 and then revisited in the 1890s,[1] and Mandelstam's *Shum vremeni* (The noise of time), written in 1923, published in part in 1925 and fully in 1928.[2] To be sure, dozens of memoirs and autobiographies were penned by Russian Jews, both professional writers and, to a lesser extent, ordinary folk, in these decades. I have chosen these two as paradigmatic both of the genre of the modern Jewish autobiography and of the problematics of using these works as sources for history because of their extraordinary literary power, albeit in radically different keys. Mandelstam's *Noise of Time* is a series of fourteen short, exquisitely crafted, and highly self-consciously literary vignettes about his childhood, written in a brilliant Russian prose at once pointillistically delicate, fiercely combative, and mockingly ironic. Lilienblum's *Sins of My Youth* is a three-volume deadly serious memoir in stolid if often gripping Hebrew prose, constructed out of citations from the author's diary and correspondence, tied together with brief retroactive interpolations; it is clear that the reader is meant to believe that the author has barely interceded in the narrative, which is presented essentially as a documentary history of the author's life from birth to the age of thirty-nine. Intriguingly and contrary to our usual expectations of autobiographers, both authors chose to write their life-stories when they were quite young: Lilienblum tells us that he began his autobiography on November 16, 1872—when he was just past his twenty-ninth birthday—and completed the first two volumes on November 10, 1873;[3] the third volume, *Derekh teshuvah* (The road of repentance) was written in the early 1890s—when he was in his late forties. Mandelstam left us no such precise dates, but we know that he wrote these pieces in 1923, when he was thirty-two, and had them published when he was thirty-four and thirty-seven—ironically, roughly the same age as Lilienblum was when the first volumes of his autobiography were published half a century earlier.

The unexpected parallels continue: as we shall see, Mandelstam uses the term "Judaic chaos" to describe his childhood, surely having no idea that Lilienblum's chapter on his childhood was entitled *Yimei ha-tohu*—"Days of chaos"![4]

Before embarking on an analysis and comparison of these two works, I must step back a bit and fill in some background information about Jewish autobiographies from the time of Glikl's death in 1724 to the publication of the first volumes of *The Sins of My Youth*. Indeed, these 152 years witnessed a veritable explosion of Jewish autobiographical and memoiristic literature. Although we possess several interesting autobiographies written by traditional Jews in the decades between Glikl's death and the publication of Jean Jacques Rousseau's *Confessions* in 1782—including the truly remarkable *Megillat sefer*, written by one of the giants of eighteenth-century Judaism, Rabbi Jacob Emden, and recently studied with great intelligence and care by Jacob J. Schacter[5]—there is no doubt that there is an obvious, if intricate, link between the efflorescence of the autobiographical genre among European Jews and the newfound centrality of the individual and fascination with the self in Enlightenment thought. Rousseau's *Confessions* mark a turning-point in the history of the genre as profound as that of Augustine's, a millennium and a half earlier. The first, and most studied, Enlightenment Jewish autobiography was that of Solomon Maimon, a quixotic and rather unruly Polish Jew who made his way to Berlin and to the forefront of the German philosophical world. As Marcus Moseley has recently demonstrated, Maimon's *Lebensgeschichte* (Life history), written in German and first published in 1796, was clearly modeled on Rousseau's *Confessions* as well as on contemporary German autobiographies and pseudo-autobiographies.[6] Soon after its publication, Maimon's book made a distinct impression on Goethe and

Schiller, and later on George Eliot; more relevant here, it served as the principal model for virtually all subsequent Hebrew and Yiddish autobiographies written in the Enlightenment mode. Thus, the first Eastern European Haskalah Hebrew autobiography, Mordecai Aaron Gunzburg's *Aviezer*, written in the late 1820s, was obviously influenced both by Maimon and by Rousseau in its graphic depiction of the travails of Jewish childhood and adolescence in Eastern Europe.[7] Gunzburg's overarching theme was the inescapable impotence—literal and metaphoric—of men reared in traditional Jewish homes that deny boys the right to be children rather than shorter versions of adult males, force them into early marriage before they are sexually mature, feminize them (and masculinize their wives), and in general deny and reject Nature in the name of a primitive and errant view of God's desires. As the first post-Rousseauian Hebrew autobiographer we know of, Gunzburg visibly struggled to convey his first-person intimate experiences in the Hebrew language, and his prose is hence not surprisingly stilted, tortuous, and at times unintentionally hilarious to modern readers, especially when he twists biblical locutions to convey sexual experiences not easily reproducible in a language he only knew from sacred tomes. Thus, the handful of specialists on modern Hebrew autobiography often comment on Gunzburg's description of his disastrous wedding night, conveyed in language so graphic that it offended the sensibilities of critics from the late nineteenth century to the late twentieth century, who condemned it as astonishingly crude and virtually pornographic.[8]

But I would submit that what is most relevant here—as with Asher of Reichshofen's earlier description of his nocturnal emissions—is the shifting and culturally specific boundary between the private and public realms, a subject exhaustively studied in regard to Western European and American societies but only now being critically examined in the case of Jewish history. In pre-twentieth-century Yiddish and Hebrew—as well as German and Russian, for that matter—there is no precise equivalent to the English word "privacy," which until the early nineteenth century largely meant "the state or condition of being withdrawn from the society of others, or from public interest; seclusion," as opposed to "free from public attention, as a matter of choice or right; freedom from interference or intrusion," as the term began to connote in English only in 1814.[9] One of the most subtle corollaries of the modernization of European Jewry was the gradual and largely unconscious acceptance of Western European norms of the appropriate line of demarcation between the public and private realms, including shifting boundaries in regard to public discussion of sex and sexuality. In an intriguing and little-noticed study, Julius Carlebach argued that even the *Tsenah Urena*, the Yiddish women's Bible used extensively in traditional Ashkenazic Jewish society, was progressively expurgated and bowdlerized, along Victorian lines, throughout the nineteenth century, gradually but crucially diminishing the discussion of sex and sexuality in its pages.[10]

Thus, for all its modernism, I would suggest, Gunzburg's *Aviezer* still partakes of traditional, pre-Victorian norms of the boundaries between the private and the public, soon to be rejected vociferously in later Haskalah polemics and autobiographies, which, as David Biale aptly put it, tend to "neutralize eroticism" in the name of the new virtues of Romantic love and the chaste bourgeois family.[11] A major topos crossing all genres of Hebrew and Yiddish literature becomes the enlightened young man who escapes from his sexually unattractive wife forced upon him in an early marriage, seeking greater freedom and openness away from home, but not to the extent of actually having sexual relations outside marriage.

The most extended and extensive example of the latter is the case of none other than Moshe Leib Lilienblum, whose *Sins of My Youth* is dedicated to a woman identified only by her initials, F. N., but who we know to have been Feige Nevakhovitch, whom Lilienblum fell in love with while a married man in Vilkomir, and with whom he carried on an epistolary relationship for many years. Indeed, much of the drama of the first volumes of the autobiography revolves around this tragic romance: our hero, married off at the age of fifteen to a woman hardly his intellectual or spiritual equal, finally meets the love of his life in his last few months in Vilkomir, when he is pursued with great zeal by Orthodox Jews because he has begun to doubt his faith and to seek Enlightenment. Only Feige understands him and gives him solace, but he is forced by the fanatics to abandon her, as well as his wife and children, as he escapes to Odessa and pursues the possibility of secular education. There, he suffers from poverty, loneliness, and a total inability to function in the modern world, all of which were caused, he continuously insists, by his father's rearing him in the backward and nefarious traditions of Eastern European Jewry.

For more than a century after its initial publication, Hebrew readers and highly sophisticated literary historians took Lilienblum's stirring autobiographical account to heart as unproblematically reflective of his life as it was lived. Thus, Yosef Klausner, a famous professor at the Hebrew University of Jerusalem and the author of the classic multi-volume *History of Modern Hebrew Literature*, wrote:

> The book is at once an autobiography and a confession. It is based not only on memoirs and oral knowledge, but also on citations from a diary and private letters, i.e. on written materials that are truly documentary in nature. In French belles-lettres at that time there then was the famous "Art Documentaire," and echoes of this literary trend reached Russia, as in Chernyshevsky's *What is to be Done?* which also has letters, citations from newspapers and diaries, etc. It is possible that this literary trend influenced the *form* of *Sins of My Youth* . . . which was also influenced by Mordecai Aaron Gunzburg's *Aviezer*, which Lilienblum praises and which he meant his book to complete in some way. Indeed, Lilienblum's book has the same honesty, even in regard to private matters, as we saw in *Aviezer*, although Lilienblum is far superior to Gunzburg in the depth of his understanding. . . . M. I. Berdichevsky called *Sins of My Youth* "a bill of divorce granted by one generation to another, by a new generation that seeks new paths to a generation imprisoned by the chains of an antiquated tradition." And there is much truth in this. For even though we have here an autobiography and confession of an individual, whose sufferings and struggles take on a central part of the story, this book is in essence a reflection of the lives of entire generations in Jewish Lithuania in particular and Russian Jewry as a whole. This book has the sort of simplicity, honesty, and openness that one finds only in Rousseau's *Confessions*, which perhaps Lilienblum read in their Russian translation. . . . Lilienblum almost does not hide from the reader any foolish thing he did, any coarse thing he did to his wife in order to be rid of her, any errant belief he held, yet at the same time does not indulge in false modesty

or overweening pride. . . . And this lively and bitter protest [against traditional Jewish life] found an enormous echo among the young generation of
Hebrew readers, and few Hebrew books were so influential as *Sins of My
Youth*. Its directness and inner truthfulness seized all hearts. And even today,
eighty-odd years after it was written, it is impossible to read this deadly serious book—despite its bitter satire—without deep emotions.[12]

Only in the late 1970s and early 1980s did this naively positivistic reading of Lilienblum begin to change, as the hermeneutic of suspicion began
to influence the study of Hebrew literature. Thus, Alan Mintz and the Israeli literary scholar Ben-Ami Feingold wrote excellent complementary
studies of Lilienblum's work, analyzing its avowedly literary nature and its
retrospective and ideologized "construction of self."[13] Feingold in particular compared some of the citations of correspondence and diary entries
in *Sins of My Youth* with the original letters and extant diary entries, noted
how the former differed from the latter, questioned the authenticity of
much of the alleged documentary material included by Lilienblum, especially the letters he claimed to have written to his wife, and offered a literary rationale for Lilienblum's curious decision to omit from *Sins of My
Youth* the heartbreaking story of the death of his son David, found in his
letters and diary fragments—a matter to which I want to turn soon. But
before then, I want to return in some detail to the Feige Nevakhovitch
matter: Mintz and Feingold both contributed useful and important literary analyses of Lilienblum's use of this relationship in his autobiography,
but neither noticed that in *Sins of My Youth* Lilienblum hid from his readers salient information about his relationship with Feige Nevakhovitch
that is included in the small part of his diary that has been preserved, and
from which extracts not included in the autobiography were published already in 1927.[14] Thus, we see in the diary not only that the correspondence
between Lilienblum and Nevakhovitch continued long after he tells us it
ended, but that he actually met her again face-to-face in an extremely
emotionally charged encounter when he and his family escaped from
Odessa to Vilkomir during the Russo-Turkish War of 1877. In *Sins of My
Youth*, Lilienblum referred to this trip only in the following words:

From my diary, part two: On 28 April [1877] I traveled with my family from [Odessa] and arrived with them in [Vilkomir] on 2 May. There I stayed about one month, since my three children came down with measles, and after they recovered, I traveled to [Kovno]. . . ; on 2 June I left [Vilkomir] again for [Kovno], left there early in the morning of 8 June, and arrived in [Odessa] on 10 June.[15]

The editor of the scholarly edition of the autobiography, published in 1970 in Jerusalem, tells us in a footnote that the manuscript of *The Sins of My Youth* contains the following text that was erased by Lilienblum himself:

Some readers, and especially female readers, will doubtless ask me: "Did you see the young woman N. when you were in [Vilkomir] and what did you say to her?" The answer to this question will only be known if the young lady herself ever writes her own autobiography and deals with this matter.[16]

But the same editor—usually scrupulous about alluding to diary entries not included in the published version—does not reveal what the extant diary extracts shows, that the entry for this date reads:

On 28 April 1877 I left Odessa with my family and on 2 May arrived in Vilkomir. On the very same day I saw Feige Nevakhovitch, whom I thought I would never see again for the rest of my life. On the 8th, she assailed me with strong condemnations

—alas, the rest of the sentence was crossed out later in another ink. But the entry continues:

On 10 May I cried my eyes out over her; on 23 May I wrote her a letter from Kedainiai; on 24 May I cried my eyes out again; on 28 May after

—again, the sentence is crossed out in another ink, followed by:

on 2 June I parted from her

—again, the rest of the sentence is crossed out.

On 6 June I wrote to her from Kovno. On 10 June I returned to Odessa and wrote to her again. On 17 June I started studying for the gymnasium and on 18 June I wrote to her again. On 22 June I received a letter from her and answered her on the 25th

and so forth.[17]

In other words, we have here not merely a selective presentation of diary materials on Lilienblum's part and a highly self-aware literary manipulation of this relationship, but a complex, almost entirely conscious and purposeful misrepresentation of the "facts" of that relationship, filtered through at least five layers of authorial intervention and obfuscation: first, the transition from reality to the original diary (without even pondering the unconscious neuro-psychological dynamics of the encoding of memories in Lilienblum's brain); second, Lilienblum's later censoring of the diary itself, clearly to hide embarrassing material; third, his partial selection of diary entries in the original manuscript of the autobiography, withholding the information about his meeting with Feige and their later correspondence; fourth, his titillation of his audience's curiosity about whether this meeting happened; and fifth, his decision to omit this titillation from the published version of the autobiography!

How, one may legitimately then ask, can we move back from this quintuple masking of the truth, to truth itself? Moreover, of course, we have only Lilienblum's side of the story, not Feige Nevakhovitch's; her only extant words are the ending of a letter written on May 3, 1895, eighteen years after the last traces of their correspondence in his diary: "My dear M. Leib: Please write to me again, but everything in more detail, which will delight your true, unending bosom-friend."[18] Alas, all we know—from her brother, the famous early Jewish socialist Morris (Nevakhovitch) Vinchevsky—is that she died unmarried and alone in Vilkomir, still pining for the love of her life, Moshe Leib Lilienblum.[19]

A similar dissonance between the "facts" of Lilienblum's life and his autobiographical representation pertains, as already noted, to another aspect of his personal life, which he pretended, Rousseau-like, to be fully revealing to us. While, to be sure, he continually harps on his unhappy marriage—including informing us that he suffered the same problem, i.e., impotence, as Gunzburg did on his wedding night, and even described his own nocturnal emissions, including one, like Asher of Reichshofen, on Kol Nidre night—he deliberately and continually muted mention of his children, to the extent that the reader cannot even follow how many children the Lilienblums had, and how many survived the ravages of infant mortality. At one point well into the narrative we learn that he had a four-year-old daughter—we are not told her name—but she is only summoned to make an obvious ideological point about the Jews' nonsensical and solipsistic belief that the world was created especially for them.[20] A few pages later, we are surprised to read that at this point (1863) he already had three living children, and one who died[21]—information one would have thought essential to a Rousseauian commitment to total disclosure, but here only revealed to emphasize his own incapacity to live life as an autonomous adult, itself caused by his own father's errant commitment to the traditions of Eastern European Jewish child-rearing. Indeed, since the overarching theme of the first two autobiographies was his progressive loss of faith in God and in traditional Judaism, the silence about the death of this child is quite remarkable.

But seven years later, in 1870, another one of Lilienblum's children died, a fact we learn about not at the time it actually occurred, but several months later, in a letter written to none other than Feige Nevakhovitch, in which he writes:

Much thanks from the depths of my heart for your condolences on the death of my son. You of course will understand that I do not ascribe such events to God or His providence. . . . But I truly do not know why this loss did not make as much an impression upon me as it ought to have. I would never have imagined that the death of my dear boy would have caused me to cry for two days and no more! Perhaps my departure is the cause of this, or perhaps because there is no going back from this. Even before I heard the news, I had intuited that a disaster might befall my son, and lost much sleep over this and was depressed; or perhaps because my heart is so wounded, it cannot be moved by any tragedy.[22]

What is so strange and important about these and similar passages is that they blatantly contradict the evidence about his profound love for his children recorded in the diary fragments still extant but not chosen by Lilienblum to be included in his autobiography. Thus, in the diary we read consistent laments about how terribly difficult it was for him to leave his children when he departed from Vilkomir; how often he pined for his children while he was in Odessa without them; and, most especially, how the death of his son David shattered his universe. I will cite only a part of the long wrenching lament he wrote in his diary on September 28:

I received a letter from my wife that tore my heart asunder and killed it, a letter that darkened the skies and the earth of my universe and left me utterly broken. This letter brought me the bad news that my most beloved son David died. My son! My son! Who will bring me close to you, who will take you out of your grave for a moment so that I can kiss you for the last time? My son! My son! I run through my house like a madman, back and forth, my face awash in the tears that I can barely wipe from all my pores, but which no one sees. Come here, my son! Come to me, I'll take you in my arms and pour my boiling tears on you, for you were my dear son, my favorite! O my poor son! You will no longer come to your sad father, who always carried you in my arms and sang songs to you! My churning tears, pouring forth on your untimely death, fall to the ground, trodden over by feet. My son! My son! Your eyes were closed, the grave swallowed you up, earth covered you, my eyes are no longer turned from you but are led by their tears all the way to cursed Vilkomir, to water the grass on your desolate tomb. My son's bones will nourish this grass, and how can his father's tears not mix in with his son's? But all in vain! My tears flow without cease but will stay in their place and never reach my son. . . . My son! My son! On Saturday, 14 Elul 1869, when you ran up to me and said: "Papa, see how I'm eating!" and my heart ached from the knowledge that I would soon be leaving you . . . and soon thereafter, on Tuesday, 24 Elul, when I kissed you over and over again as I left you, I didn't know that these would be the last moments and the last kisses I would have with you! My son! My son! . . . Farewell my son! Sleep in peace. This wound will never heal, I will never forget you, your eternal monument will be my broken heart, wounded forever.[23]

I do not think it possible objectively to reconcile the contrast between this searing lament and the stone-heartedness Lilienblum claimed in his autobiography, just as we cannot responsibly reconstruct the objective truth of his relationship with Feige Nevakhovitch. To be sure, one could propose varying psychological and literary explanations for this dissonance, but these would be unredeemingly tautological, based inevitably on the presumption of facticity of the rest of the autobiography. What is intriguing and crucial here is not only that Lilienblum's autobiography, like all autobiographies, was partial and self-selected, but that he used the conceit of total disclosure to veil his intimate life from his readers while brilliantly manipulating our perception that he was doing precisely the opposite.

And the purpose of this occlusion was neither psychological nor literary but, I would argue, fundamentally ideological: as Lilienblum himself often stated, the point of his autobiographical exercise was didactic, to teach readers not to follow his errant ways. Thus, his self-fashioning, his selection of which "memories" and "documents" to include and which to exclude and misrepresent, was determined by their ideological utility, even as the contents of that ideology shifted from dedication to the Enlightenment and secular education to Zionism. Thus, in the first two volumes, his overriding goal was to fashion himself as a true Enlightenment hero, a victim of his benighted society and upbringing who sacrificed all, and especially true love, on the altar of reason and self-improvement. He had to present himself, therefore, not only as a victim of his upbringing but, even more importantly, as a broken man, unyielding to the temptations of the flesh, or, for that matter, too emotionally shattered even to be perturbed by the death of his children. The tragic romance with Nevakhovitch was foregrounded, and fictionalized, in the first two volumes since it was central to his ideologized mask: in Hebrew *hatot neurim* is a rabbinic euphemism for masturbation, and thus the socially determined unconsummability of his relationship with Feige served Lilienblum as an extended synecdoche for his pathetic and unproductive life as a whole.

By the time the third volume of Lilienblum's autobiography was written, however, in the middle and late 1890s, he had come to reject his Enlightenment beliefs, and thus the autobiographical self-presentation had to conform to, and impose upon the "facts," an entirely different narrative trajectory. And so we learn that after years of attempting to learn enough Russian, German, Greek, Latin, and mathematics to enter university, our hero's dreams are shattered by the pogroms of 1881, but these lead him to the solution to his woes, and those of the Jewish people as a whole—Zionism. In this alternative heuristic account, Nevakhovitch is all but forgotten: for the first few years away from home he continues to write to her, but soon comes to realize that their mutual love is pointless, and he (counterfactually) ceases communicating with her, as he discovers first radical Russian thought and then Zionism. Romantic love is dismissed as but one of the affective disorders of the naive Enlightenment, replaced first by Realist criticism, and then by the most effective remedy of them all, Love of Zion.

And so we are not truly surprised when, in *The Way of Repentance*, another one of Lilienblum's children, his daughter Rosalie, dies, and the tragedy evokes only the following response:

> 14 July [1880], my wife returned to Odessa. How my heart has turned to stone! Even the death of my daughter Rosalia [on 13 Nissan/27 March] did not cause me to shed even one tear. During the month of July I studied for six and a half hours a day; my work hours were reduced because of the troubles I had because of the arrival of my wife.[24]

On the other hand, when he hears the reports of the pogroms raging through Ukraine in 1881 his stony heart is shattered and dissipates into utter despair. The narrative ascribed to diary entries for April 10 to April 28, 1881, is unbearably tense: the violence is nearing, the news is horrific— what horrors will follow? On May 5, we read:

> The situation is horrible, horrible, terribly frightening. It's as if we're in a fortress, the gates locked, from minute to minute we peer out of the holes in

the gates to see if the plunderers are pouncing on us out of the blue. All the household goods are hidden in cellars, we sleep in our clothes, without pillows or sheets (hidden in the cellars) out of fear that the attackers will come, so that we will be able quickly to take the small children, who also sleep in their clothes, and escape somewhere. But will they allow us to escape? And what will be the end of our suffering? Will they have mercy on our small children, who don't yet know they are Jews, but only that they are suffering, and not injure them? Horrible, so horrible! Until when, God of Israel?[25]

Finally, May 7:

It is good that I have suffered. The pogrom-mongers came close to the house in which I live. The women shrieked loudly and held their infants tight in their arms, not knowing where to flee. The men stood around astounded. We all thought, that in a few moments, all our efforts would be for naught. . . . But, thank God, the pogromshchiki passed us by and fled, out of fear of the soldiers, and nothing bad happened to us. It is good that I have suffered. At least once in my life I have been able to feel what our forefathers felt all their lives. For their whole lives were filled with fear and violence, and why should I not feel that horrible feeling that they felt all their lives? For I am their son, their sufferings are dear to me, and in their honor I too shall suffer. . . . How uplifted is my spirit, now, for I came to know and feel the sufferings of my people in their exile. . . . It is good that I have suffered.[26]

"It is good that I have suffered" (Tov li ki uneiti): the proof text, of course, is from Psalm 119, originally uttered in a radically different context:

The Lord is my portion, I have resolved to keep Your words. I have implored You with all my heart; have mercy on me in accordance with Your promise, I have considered my ways and turned back to Your decrees. . . . You are good and beneficent, teach me Your laws. Though the arrogant have accused me falsely, I observe Your precepts wholeheartedly. Their minds are thick like fat; Your teaching is my delight. It is good for me that I have suffered, so that I might learn Your laws.

But in accord with his newfound ideology, Lilienblum's repentance is not to the Lord or His Torah but to their nationalistic displacement, far more radical than that of the superseded Enlightenment.

Unfortunately, the latter portions of Lilienblum's diary have not been preserved, and so we are unable to check the text of *The Way of Repentance* against the actual diary entries. My suspicion is that, as with his romance with Nevakhovitch and his reaction to the death of his son, what we have here is not the contemporary documentary record it claims neutrally to reproduce, but a highly ideologized retroactive fictionalization. As Roy Pascal put it, "autobiography is . . . an interplay, a collusion between past and present; its significance is indeed more the revelation of the present situation than the recovery of the past."[27] Thus, whereas others confidently read Lilienblum's text as the most telling contemporary example of the reaction of Russian Jews to the pogroms of 1881, I cannot do so, for it is a good possibility that, like Theodor Herzl and Max Nordau's counterfactual linking of their conversions to Zionism with the Dreyfus Affair, and Jabotinsky's creative dissemblance about his own road to Zionism, Lilienblum—deeply committed to the Zionist solution when he wrote the last volume of his autobiography—retroactively embellished his account of the events of 1881–82. Be that as it may, one must be struck by the sharp contrast between his impassioned expression of vicarious suffering in the aftermath of communal attack and the complete absence of any actual suffering in response to the death of a third child, only months before.

In sum, for Lilienblum the mask of autobiographical veracity served only, if brilliantly, to occlude the private self in the name of an ideologically construed public self-fashioning. We have come a long way from Josephus, but, in the end, not that far at all.

Osip Mandelstam's autobiographical mask was even more elusive than Lilienblum's, and not only since his *Shum vremeni* is rhetorically a far more elliptical text than *Sins of My Youth*, or, for that matter, any of the other autobiographies I have discussed so far. Indeed, despite its slimness—merely forty-eight pages in the standard English translation[28]—so complex is this text that even its title has occasioned detailed confusion, given the difficulty of rendering the Russian word "shum" into English. As

Clarence Brown, its first translator—and, not surprisingly, Mandelstam's first English biographer—wrote: "The translation of *shum* is difficult out of all proportion to the miniature size of the word. My first choice was 'noise,' and it found favor with some, but there was impressive insistence that *shum* is best rendered by 'sound.'"[29] Vladimir Nabokov translated it as "hubbub" in his famously obtuse translation of Pushkin's *Eugene Onegin*, remarking, inter alia, that "it is at heart more of a swoosh than a racket," and, more importantly, that all its forms are "beautifully onomatopoeic."[30] My own preference would be either the paranomastic "rush of time," or better yet, the "sounds of time past"—grammatically imprecise, but, I think, more reflective of Mandelstam's variation on the Proustian conveyance of memory through sensory impressions—in this case, through the sounds and smells of childhood. For this autobiography—like Gunzburg's *Aviezer,* which Mandelstam was most certainly unaware of and unable to read—deals only with its subject from the age of three to fourteen or so, that is, not only before he became an adult, but before he became a poet. We hear nothing about Mandelstam's crucial stays abroad, in Paris and then in Heidelberg; nothing about his conversion to Christianity, nothing about his university years, nothing about his affair with Marina Tsetaeva, his first years as a poet, his crucial friendship with Nikolai Gumilev and Anna Akhmatova and their founding of Acmeism, nothing about the revolution, or even his marriage to Nadezhda Khazina.

Near the end of the story, in the opening of its penultimate chapter, we are told:

My desire is not to speak of myself but to track down the age, the noise and the germination of time. My memory is inimical to all that is personal. If it depended on me, I should only make a wry face in remembering the past. I was never able to understand the Tolstoys and the Aksakovs, all those grandson Bagrovs, enamored of family archives with their epic domestic memoirs. I repeat—my memory is not loving but inimical, and it labors not to reproduce but to distance the past. A rootless intellectual [*raznochinets*] needs no memory—it is enough to tell of the books he has read, and his biography is done. Where for happy generations the epic speaks in hexameters and chronicles I have merely the sign of the hiatus.[31]

These are lovely phrases, and, like the facts of the life the self-proclaimed *raznochinets* claims to present and then to ignore, have been taken as factually true by most commentators on Mandelstam. But as Charles Isenberg, one of the most sensitive students of Mandelstam, has noted, this disclaimer of the personal is both hyperbolic and ironic:

> The narrator of *The Noise of Time* does not in fact represent himself as a deracinated figure, formed by books alone. His search for identity reflects a twofold cultural displacement. Not only must he somehow come to terms with the cataclysmic disruption of prerevolutionary Russian culture, but he must also come to terms with the fact of his Jewish descent. The conflicting claims put forward by these two traditions put his identity under tension from two directions. The dislocating stresses that they create underlie the theme of the outsider with divided loyalties which pervades both *The Noise of Time* and Mandelstam's verse of the same period.[32]

Indeed, I would add, *The Noise of Time* itself rhetorically subverts its own abjuration of remembrances of things past—its first words are "I well remember" and, as one Mandelstam biographer well put it, its ending "proposes the art of retrospection as the only path for comprehending the present"[33] with the words:

> To remember not living people but plaster casts struck from their voices. To go blind. To feel and recognize by hearing. Sad fate! Thus does one penetrate into the present, into the modern age, as via the bed of a dried-up river. As you know, these were not friends, nor near ones, but alien, distant people! Still, it is only with the masks of other men's voices that the bare walls of the house are decorated. To remember—to make one's way alone back up the dried riverbed.[34]

For good reason, the scholarship on this astonishing autobiography—which Prince Dmitri Sviatopolk-Mirsky called "one of the three or four most significant books of our times"[35]—has been almost totally mesmerized by the power of its prose, and by its acceptance as a truthful account of Mandelstam's childhood and adolescence on the part of the ultimate authority on Osip Mandelstam, his widow Nadezhda Mandelstam, who, in her own wonderful and justly famous memoirs, regards everything her martyred husband wrote, including his autobiography, as sacred writ.

I read *The Noise of Time* in a totally different way: as a sardonic, and in some measure, parodic, highly fictionalized autobiography infused with outrageously deliberate, and increasingly risky, "political incorrectness," circa 1923. Indeed, even the troubled and tortuous meditations on what Mandelstam called the "Judaic chaos" of his childhood must be read, I propose, first as self-consciously literary self-fashionings rather than as unmediated reflections of autobiographical and historical truth. Moreover, they must be understood against the backdrop of the varied contexts in which they were written: first, the political and cultural history of the early years of the Soviet regime; second, the Mandelstam family and its internal dynamics; and finally, the century-long engagement of Russian Jews, and specifically upper-middle-class Russian Jews like the Mandelstams, with the Russian language, Russian culture, and Christianity. This is a rather tall order, and I will be forced to move in and out of the text of *The Noise of Time* and its many contexts in a way that I hope will not be too dizzying for the reader.

First, a bit of crucial background about its composition, about which not a word is said in *The Noise of Time* itself, or, to my knowledge, in any of Mandelstam's other writings or extant correspondence. All we know about the circumstances of its creation is from Nadezhda Mandelstam, who relates[36] that in 1923, Isay Grigorevich Lezhnev, (formerly Isaac Altshuler), the editor of the Bolshevik journal *Rossia* in which Mandelstam had recently published two prose pieces, commissioned Osip to write an autobiography for his magazine, which he did while they were on vacation in the Crimea. But Lezhnev then turned down the finished product after reading it. He had expected a totally different kind of childhood story, that of a Jewish boy from the shtetl who discovers Marxism—something like Chagall's memoirs, or those written by Lezhnev himself and published on direct orders from none other than Stalin. After this rejection, Mandelstam took his autobiography to several other publishers, but they all turned it down, as devoid of plot, story, class consciousness, or any kind of social significance. The only person to show interest was Georgi Blok, the cousin of the poet, who worked for Vremia, a private publishing firm already on its last legs, which put out the first edition of *Shum vremeni* in 1925, in a series that also included Mandelstam's translation of Lefebvre Saint-Ogan's *Toudiche,* as well as Russian editions of Stefan Zweig's *Brennendes Geheimnis*, Georges Duhamel's *Le prince Jaffar,* Panait Istrati's *Viata lui Adrian Zografi,* and Louis Paul Lochner's *Henry Ford America's Don Quixote*.[37] These admittedly rather obscure titles (except for the Zweig) reflect the cosmopolitan, if naturally leftist, range of literary possibilities still available to Soviet publishers and consumers in the early and mid-1920s, soon to be obliterated by the enforced turn to Socialist Realism even before the murderous horrors of High Stalinism began.

In regard to the years 1923 to 1928, we ought not take Nadezhda's understandable emphasis on Osip's ostracism from the Soviet literary elite too literally. Although, like everyone else, the Mandelstams had to make do in terrible material conditions, and Osip had enemies aplenty on the Left who recognized that his support for the revolution was reluctant, tepid, and highly idiosyncratic, his poetry was still being published in official publishing houses, and he would enjoy—and use for his and his family's benefit—the support of high party officials, especially Nikolai Bukharin. His second book of verse—entitled just that, *Vtoraia kniga*—was brought out by the State Publishing House in 1923, in sharp contrast to his first book of poetry, *Kamen'* (Stone) which he had to print at his own expense a decade earlier, under the mark of a nonexistent publishing house.[38] No longer (or at least so he thought) could he be vilified by the anti-Semitic rhetoric common in the tsarist years even among the literary elite—he had famously been referred to as Zinaida Gippius's "little Jew-boy"; now even Aleksandr Blok, no friend of the Jews, confided to his diary, "Mandelstam has grown a great deal. Gradually one gets used to the kike and sees the artist."[39]

But this is not to deny, for it would be silly to do so, that already by 1923 Mandelstam was fundamentally out of step with the regnant trends in Soviet life and culture. As the critic Omry Ronen explained, although Acmeism—the movement in Russian poetry initiated by Mandelstam, Akhmatova, and Gumilev—need not be regarded as a conservative return to neoclassicism, its self-referential aestheticism, its anti-symbolist but still highly metaphysical Christian symbolic core, and its insistence on being open to and part of Western European bourgeois culture—what Mandelstam himself, "to a hissing crowd of Soviet vulgarians," called its essential "longing for world culture"—rendered it highly suspect to orthodox Soviet critics and officials.[40] These would come to the fore in 1928, the year in which a second edition of *The Noise of Time* was published, and would lead in due course to Mandelstam's tragic end.

The Noise of Time begins: "I well remember the deaf years of Russia—the Nineties, their slow crawl, their unhealthy tranquility, their deep provincialism—a quiet backwater: the last refuge of a dying century."[41] I have rendered these words literally, to convey their deliberate complexity: as Brown pointed out, the "deaf" in "deaf years" can also mean "overgrown," "wild," "remote," or "desolate," and he is undoubtedly correct that there is here an intertexual opposition to Aleksandr Blok's "Those born in deaf [or remote or desolate] years do not remember their own path."[42] In contrast, Mandelstam well remembers his own path, or, as already cited, his own "dried riverbed," but chooses to convey memory mostly through sounds and smells:

> At morning tea there would be talk about Dreyfus, there were the names of Colonels Esterhazy and Picquart, vague disputes about some "Kreutzer Sonata," and behind the high podium of the glass railroad station in Pavlovsk, the change of conductors, which seemed to me a change of dynasties. . . . Locomotive whistles and railroad bells mingled with the patriotic cacophony of the 1812 Overture, and a peculiar smell filled the huge station where Tschaikovsky and Rubinstein reigned. The humid air from the moldy parks, the odor of the decaying hotbeds and hothouse roses—this was blended with the heavy exhalations from the buffet, the acrid smoke of cigars, a burning smell from somewhere in the station, and the cosmetics of the crowd of many thousands.[43]

Through these brilliantly evoked auditory and olfactory images the reader is immediately thrust back into a highly specific time and place: this cannot be otherwise than a late-nineteenth-century childhood of a highly cultivated—in both the aesthetic and horticultural senses—upper-middle-class Russian Jew. The juxtaposition of morning tea, talk of Drey-fus, Esterhazy, and Picquart, and disputes over "some" Kreutzer sonata—we know immediately that we are not on a Chekhovian noble estate but in the midst of the peculiar charms of the Petersburg Jewish bourgeoisie: dachas; worries about the anti-Semitism that may follow them from the Pale of Settlement they recently abandoned, and that hailing from the Paris they probably have not yet seen, but will soon send their sons (and not yet their daughters) to study in; casual extramarital affairs to fend off the boredom of proper but stultifying bourgeois marriages; the cult of classical music as the quickest path to Kultur; and fawning patriotism to the reigning great-grandnephew of the Christian tsar celebrated by Tchaikovsky while privately pining for Napoleon's heirs to win both at home and abroad.

Just as precisely, we are retroactively inducted into the author's secret world: he was repulsed, even at the age of seven or eight, by these hypo-critical adults who knew no more than he, read no more than he, the men concerned solely with business and anti-Semitism, the women—"that is the ladies with the bouffant sleeves"—hiring and firing servants, "sniffing them over" as in a slave market, accepting recommendations from gener-als' wives who would never admit these Jewish ladies anywhere near their homes, or from Père Lagrange, the Catholic priest in a shabby cassock on the Nevsky Prospekt, whom they came to consult with about French gov-ernesses "with their parcels in their hands straight from the Gostiny Dvor,"[44] the fancy emporium filled—then, as now—with imported ex-pensive wares vastly inaccessible to all but the truly rich and their aspir-ing fellow travelers among the haute bourgeoisie.

I do not know of any commentators on Mandelstam who have pointed out the parodic, indeed virtually comic, but still insistently anti-bourgeois nature of the opening of *The Noise of Time*—to my mind a crucial issue, given the circumstances of its publication. To parse this description of his milieu, we must interrupt the flow of *The Noise of Time* and step back to investigate the history of Osip Mandelstam's family, and through it, the century-long struggles of Russian Jews, and specifically upper-middle-class Russian Jews like the Mandelstams, with the Russian language, Rus-sian culture, and invariably, with Christianity as well.

In her memoirs, Nadezhda Mandelstam claimed first that the "found-ing patriarch" of the clan was "a watchmaker and jeweler [who] moved from Germany to Kurland at the invitation of Biron, the duke of this Baltic province, who was eager to attract craftsmen to the local popula-tion"[45] and later that in the late 1920s, in Yalta, she and Osip met a mem-ber of the extended Mandelstam family with genealogical records of the clan, who related to Osip that his family was a famous rabbinical clan.[46] These etiologies have been taken as fact even by usually scrupulous schol-ars, and hence we read several times that Osip's ancestors were "the ob-scure Kurland branch of the well-known Mandelstam rabbinical fam-ily."[47] In fact, there was no well-known Mandelstam rabbinic family anywhere, and the extant documentation contradicts the story of the Kur-land origin of the Mandelstam family. Osip's brother, Evgeny Mandel-stam, claims in his own recently published memoirs that his father's fam-ily hailed from Zagare, Lithuania, and this is verifiable from the surviving tax records of that town.[48] Zagare, known in Russian as Zhagory, in Pol-ish as Zagary, and in Yiddish as Zager, is today a rather impoverished and neglected town on the border between Lithuania and Latvia. But in the nineteenth century, it was a rather bustling market town, divided into two sections, known as Old and New Zhagory. At the beginning of the cen-tury, the population was about 3,000, roughly half of whom were Jews; by 1897 the population would rise to 8,628 residents, of whom 5,867 were Jews. Due to its proximity to the Kurland border, it became one of the first centers of the Haskalah movement in the Russian Empire, though it was also renowned for its two Talmudic academies, and later for being the birthplace of the famous Orthodox rabbi Israel Salanter.[49] Among the Jewish residents in Zagare at the turn of the nineteenth century were two Mandelstam brothers: Yosef (Osip), born around 1780, and Zundel, born in 1795—both of whom became the progenitors of large Mandelstam clans. The Mandelstams were not rabbis but well-heeled merchants (al-beit by small-town Lithuanian standards) enrolled in the merchant guilds of tsarist Russia. As was customary, both branches of the family named their children after deceased grandparents and other relatives, and hence the most common male names throughout the century were Yosef/Osip, Benjamin, Leib/Lev, and Ezekiel (Hatskl in Yiddish)—the latter westernized as "Emil" already in the 1830s. (Thus, the poet was Osip Emilevich; his father was Emil Veniamovich; Emil's father was Veniamin Osipovich.) The earlier Osip Mandelstam had three sons: two of them, Benjamin and Leon, are well known in Russian-Jewish history as the two most radical members of the early Russian Haskalah;[50] the third son, Ezekiel/Emil, was the father of Emanuel/Max, a famous professor of ophthalmology in late Imperial Russia, one of the founding fathers (along with none other than Moshe Leib Lilienblum) of the "Love of Zion" movement in the early 1880s, and a leader of Russian Zionism and then of the Territorialist movement in the early years of the twentieth century. Interestingly and ironically, one of Dr. Max Mandelstam's brothers, named Iosif (or Osip) Emelianovich Mandelstam, born in Zagare in 1846, attended Kharkov University and became professor of Russian Language and Slavic Studies at Helsingfors University; to qualify for this post he converted to Christianity, but he retained a lively interest in things Jewish, and published a series of popular and scholarly studies on such subjects as "Jewish Mythology" in the Russian-Jewish press of the 1880s.[51]

Emil Mandelstam's branch of the family seems to be have been far less flamboyant. In *The Noise of Time* Osip portrayed his paternal grandparents as pious and traditional Jews, living in Riga and unable to speak Russian. His account of traveling to visit these grandparents is almost Gothic, but also imbued with much humor—missed by many readers:

> When I was taken to Riga, to my Riga grandparents, I resisted and nearly cried. It seemed to me that I was being taken to the native country of my father's incomprehensible philosophy. The artillery of band boxes, baskets with padlocks, and all the chubby, awkward family baggage started upon its journey. The winter things were salted with coarse grains of napthalene. The armchairs stood about like white horses in their stable blankets of slipcovers. The preparations for the trip to the Riga coast seemed to me no fun. I used to collect nails at that time—the absurdest of collecting whimsies . . . they would take my nails away to be used in packing.
>
> The trip was alarming. At night in Dorpat some sort of *Verein* [society] returning from a large songfest would storm the dimly lit carriage with

their loud Estonian songs. They would stamp their feet and throw themselves against the door. It was very frightening.

My grandfather, a blue-eyed old man in a yarmulke which covered half his forehead and with the serious and rather dignified features to be seen in very respected Jews, would smile, rejoice, and try to be affectionate, but wasn't really able to—his dense eyebrows would tighten together. He wanted to take me into his arms, but I almost burst into tears. My sweet grandmother, with her black wig over gray hairs and a housedress with yellowish little flowers, walked with tiny steps over the creaking floor and kept wanting to feed somebody. She kept asking "pokushali? pokushali?" (have you eaten? have you eaten?), the only Russian words she knew. But I didn't like the spicy old-people's treats, with their bitter almond taste. My parents went off to town. My somber grandfather and sad, bustling grandmother tried to distract me with conversation and ruffled their feathers like old offended birds. I tried to explain that I wanted to go to Mama, but they didn't understand. Then I showed them what I meant by putting my index and middle figures through the motions of walking on the table.

Suddenly, my grandfather took out of the dresser a black and yellow silk cloth, put it around my shoulder, and made me repeat after him words composed of unknown sounds; but dissatisfied with my babbling, he was disappointed, shaking his disapproving head. I felt stifled, afraid. I don't remember how my mother arrived to save me.[52]

This wonderful scene—we can almost smell the cookies, the naphthalene, and the old tallies—has been quoted by many critics not only as factual, but as highly indicative of Osip's visceral rejection of Judaism. But these critics rarely realize that this is a brilliant variation on the set piece of generational estrangement found in countless Jewish autobiographies, in Eastern and Western Europe, North America and Israel. And more importantly, that it is followed immediately by:

My father often spoke of my grandfather's honesty as of some lofty spiritual quality. For a Jew, honesty is wisdom and almost holiness itself. The farther one went back among the generations of these stern, blue-eyed old men, the more honesty and sternness one found. Our forefather Benjamin once said: "I am closing down the business—I need no more money." He had exactly enough to last him till the day of his death—he did not leave a kopeck behind.[53]

I submit that one can only read these words against the specific background of the precise time they were written: the first years of NEP—Lenin's New Economic Policy—which, as a "temporary retreat on the road to Socialism," permitted small-scale private trade to be reestablished after the horrible years of War Communism, but still derided (often Jewish) "Nepmen" as capitalist exploiters, only a rung beneath the contemptible "kulaks." Particularly vicious in their attacks on these retrograde forces were the Jewish Communists, members of the Evsektsiia, who established special brigades of agitprop workers to work in the shtetls of the Pale to bring "revolution to the Jewish street." A major part of their propaganda work was venomous characterization of traditional Jewish small businessmen as "blood-sucking capitalists," part of the rabbinic Zionist-bourgeois conspiracy to exploit the hardworking toiling masses of Yiddish-speaking proletarians.

In the sharpest possible contrast, Mandelstam's description of the innate honesty and integrity of these "blue-eyed Jewish old men" is more than striking—it is, I would argue, deliberately provocative, even more so than his far more pro-Soviet contemporary and colleague Isaac Babel in stories such as "Gedali." This does not mean that Mandelstam was "positively" inclined toward Judaism or Jews, as other critics have claimed he became later in life, seizing on tidbits of his prose and poetry that are much less straightforward than this.[54] Rather, at one and the same time he could express total but sometimes tender alienation from the world of tradition which he visited only occasionally, bitter sarcasm about what he reviled as the preposterously pretentious Jewish upper-middle classes in which he grew up, and especially contemptuous hatred for the newest version of the fawning Jew, the official Soviet-sanctioned "Jewish Bolshevik."

Meanwhile, we have to return to his parents: Emil Mandelstam appears to have been a rather typically rebellious son of traditional Lithuanian-Jewish parents, much like his older contemporary Moshe Leib Lilienblum, if far more successful in business. In *The Noise of Time* Emil is characterized first by his sound:

> My father had absolutely no language; his speech was tongue-tied and lan-
> guagelessness. The Russian speech of a Polish Jew? No. The speech of a
> German Jew? No again. Perhaps a special Courland accent? I never heard
> such. A completely abstract, counterfeit language, the ornate and twisted
> speech of an autodidact, whose normal words are intertwined with the an-
> cient philosophical terms of Herder, Leibniz, and Spinoza, the capricious
> syntax of a Talmudist, the artificial, not always finished sentences; it was
> anything in the world, but not a language, neither Russian nor German.[55]

Already in 1973 Clarence Brown noted that this description was clearly
hyberbolic, and that the émigré poet Georgy Ivanov testified that Emil
"spoke excellent literary Russian without the least trace of accent."[56] And
yet, well into the 1930s, Emil continued to pen his own quasi-philosoph-
ical writings (and, it seems, his own memoirs, unfortunately not extant)
in German, which seemed rather idiosyncratic to his famous son and
daughter-in-law, but in fact was not at all uncommon among upper-
middle-class Jews of his background and generation, whatever their degree of fluency in other tongues.

But Osip's description of his father went beyond his tongue-tiedness:

> In essence, my father transferred me to a totally alien century and distant,
> although completely un-Jewish, atmosphere. It was, if you will, the purest
> eighteenth or even seventeenth century of an enlightened ghetto some-
> where in Hamburg. Religious interests had been eliminated completely.
> The philosophy of the Enlightenment was transformed into intricate Tal-
> mudic pantheism. Somewhere in the vicinity Spinoza is breeding his spi-
> ders in a jar. One has a presentiment of Rousseau and his natural man.
> Everything fantastically abstract, intricate, and schematic. A fourteen-year-
> old boy, whom they had been training as a rabbi, runs off to Berlin and
> ends up in a higher Talmudic school, where there had gathered a number
> of such stubborn, rational youths, who had aspired in godforsaken back-
> waters to be geniuses. Instead of the Talmud, he reads Schiller—and mark

you, he reads it as a new book. Having held out there for a while, he falls out of this strange university back into the seething world of the seventies in order to remember the conspiratorial dairy shop on Caravan Street, whence a bomb was tossed under Alexander, and in a glove-making shop and in a leather factory he expounds to the paunchy and astonished customers the philosophical ideals of the eighteenth century.[57]

What can we make of this runaway, virtually uncontrolled yet superbly funny parody, a brilliant variation on the theme, already stereotypical in Haskalah literature, of the powerless—indeed impotent—Jewish father? Evgeny Mandelstam's account, though clearly influenced by Osip's, seems to bring us closer to the ground:

> Father's childhood and youth were difficult. Using his intelligence and inquiring mind, he strived to escape from the closed world of the Jewish community. Without his parents' knowledge, he would study by candlelight in his garret at night. He sought knowledge, and studied not Russian, but German. The urge to master German literature and philosophy characterized the whole of Father's life, reflecting to some extent the ties which have historically linked the Baltic States with Germany. It was not long before Father found his home life too oppressive and he escaped to Berlin. Here, far from his family, he could freely immerse himself in the works of Schiller and Goethe, of Herder and Spinoza. His straitened circumstances, indeed downright hunger, soon drove him to abandon his studies, and to return to the Baltic in search of a living wage.[58]

Evgeny and Osip's mother, Flora Osipovna Verblovskaia, was born in Vilna to a middle-class Jewish family that, like many if not most middle-class Jewish families in Vilna in the latter decades of the nineteenth century, was thoroughly Russified. The Verblovskys were closely related to the Vengerov clan, which included the first woman autobiographer in Russian Jewish history, Pauline Vengerov, and her far more famous children, the renowned literary historian Semen Afanasevich Vengerov (who, Osip Mandelstam claimed in Noise of Time, "understood nothing in Russian literature and studied Pushkin as a professional task"[59]), Zinaida Vengerova, the literary critic, and Isabelle Vengerova, the famous professor of piano at the St. Petersburg Conservatory and then at the Curtis Institute in Philadelphia. Through several marriages, the Vengerovs were intertwined with the Slonimsky family, which hailed back to the first two scientists of the Russian Haskalah. About Flora Mandelstam's relationship to Judaism we know much less. Evgeny Mandelstam reports only that his mother completed her schooling at the Russian grammar school in Vilnius, a fact consistent with Osip's claim in *The Noise of Time* that the inscription in her schoolgirl's edition of Pushkin was inscribed "For her diligence as a pupil of the Third Form" and that she spoke excellent Russian:

> The speech of my mother was clear and sonorous without the least foreign admixture, with rather wide and too open vowels—the literary Great Russian language. Her vocabulary was poor and restricted, the locutions were trite, but it was a language, it had roots and confidence. Mother loved to speak and took joy in the roots and sounds of her Great Russian speech, impoverished by intellectual clichés. Was she not the first of her whole family to achieve pure and clear Russian sounds?[60]

Nadezhda added only that Flora was "a woman of considerable culture, a music teacher who gave her children a good education and brought [Osip] up to love classical music."[61] Of her relationship to Judaism nothing was said, but I think it fair to speculate that she was a typical second-generation bourgeois Russian Jew; her mother, who lived with the Mandelstams in St. Petersburg, communicated with her grandchildren in Russian. Jews like Flora Mandelstam, as I have explained elsewhere, lacked any intimate connection with or interest about the Judaism and Jewish culture of their grandparents. Foreign to them, as well, was the experience of their contemporaries (in this case, her husband) in the small towns of the Pale of Settlement, struggling firsthand with the Sturm und Drang of the confrontation between the Jewish tradition and modernity. To some extent, their Jewishness consisted in the social stigma attached to their origins, compounded and exacerbated by legal restrictions that made difficult, but far from impossible, their educational and social advance. While some sons and daughters of the Russian-Jewish middle classes became Jewish nationalists or revolutionaries, their numbers were outweighed by those who (not to speak of her son) were totally estranged from and ignorant of any form of Judaism, and who found their identities not in politics but in contemporary Russian literature and culture.[62]

In any event, Flora and Emil's wedding invitation—issued solely in Russian, a vivid marker of the degree of Russification of at least her family—documents that they were married on January 19, 1889 in Dvinsk; he was 33, she 23.[63] Soon thereafter they moved to Warsaw, where their two elder boys, Osip and Alexander, were born, before they moved to St. Petersburg, where Evgeny was born in 1898. Both these moves were undoubtedly motivated by Emil's business considerations: in these decades thousands of Lithuanian Jews moved to the more Westernized Polish provinces and especially Warsaw and Lodz, the mercantile centers of the former Polish kingdom, provoking widespread protests against the "invasion of the Litvaks," i.e., their economic competition and their Russian language, culture, and allegiance to the tsarist autocracy. At the same time, many upper-middle-class Russian Jews strove to move to the even more potentially lucrative St. Petersburg (and Moscow), residence in which was restricted to those with sufficient capital to enroll in one of the merchant guilds, or those with other professional, educational, or military qualifications. According to Evgeny Mandelstam, his father was enrolled in the First Merchant's Guild; if so, this would have required a truly substantial amount of capital, as this was the highest prestige social estate of non-nobles in the empire. Evgeny Mandelstam later recalled:

> The diploma from the First Guild decorated the wall of Father's study. This diploma, marking me as a merchant's son, almost caused me to lose my job in 1935, and it would have been difficult to find another after dismissal for such a reason. I turned for help to Korney Chukovsky, who as a friend of Osip's had been a frequent visitor at our home, and knew our family's circumstances. He wrote me a letter, saying that our family had always had difficulty making ends meet, that Osip never had any money and constantly borrowed money for his return trip from their house in Kuokkala or from Repin's house in Penates. In a postscript Chukovsky added: "I remember that some document, stating your father was a merchant in some

guild or other, used to hang in his study, but we all understood that this was simply protection against the Tsarist police." Chukovsky was right. Our father's actual circumstances were far removed from the world conjured up by that diploma. Apart from a few years, when Father owned a small glove factory, he never had his own business, nor was he likely too [sic]. Father spent virtually his entire life dealing with leather as a raw material. He never had the means to buy skins and resell them to leather factories, but usually remained an intermediary between tanneries and leather processors. Day by day, through the years and decades, Father worked from dawn to dusk in cold sheds and warehouses, applying all his knowledge and experience to this difficult and physically demanding work.[64]

It is difficult to know how much to credit this comment: As a loyal Soviet—much to his brother Osip's later disgust—Evgeny needed to mute his family's elite economic origins, as he himself testified, and Chukovsky's letter, even if authentic, would have been written at the height of the Stalinist terror, when a father's membership in the first merchant guild could well have led to a death warrant for his son. But without vouching for the veracity of Evgeny's memoirs, I think they do add an interesting alternative voice to the story of the Mandelstam household, which has heretofore been represented solely on the basis of Osip and Nadezhda's descriptions. Thus, for example, Evgeny's description of his mother is fascinating: it was she who insisted that Osip, and then his younger brothers, be sent to the Tenishev school, one of the most prestigious schools in the Russian Empire, which later counted Vladimir Nabokov among its alumni. It was Flora who tried to instill love for music in all three of her sons and took them along to concerts at the Club of the Nobility and to opera and ballet at the Mariinsky Theatre. She was never satisfied with their apartments in St. Petersburg, and

was prey to a passion for moving house. The reasons were of the most unlikely kind, but usually they began to appear towards spring, after the habitual move of the previous autumn. Either she did not like the floor, or it was too far from the children's school on Mokhovaya Street, or else the rooms received too little sunlight, or perhaps the kitchen was inconvenient.

By my reckoning, by the time of the 1917 February Revolution, we had moved seventeen times in St. Petersburg.[65]

As was typical of their milieu, the Mandelstams kept a dacha out of town, usually in Tsarskoe Selo, which had become a favorite summering spot for the Petersburg Jewish bourgeoisie, and periodically traveled to German spas to "take the waters." After the 1905 Revolution, Evgeny reported, Flora, who was always a "prey to worry," began actively to fear that a pogrom would break out against the Jews in St. Petersburg, and "sent us off to the suburbs, to Pavlovsk or to Tsarskoe Selo, where, it seemed to her, there was no chance of such excesses," while Emil kept on his bedside table "an elegant lady's revolver, to protect the family against any danger."[66] In general, Evgeny explained:

Our family was not an easy one. Its internal contradictions [a favorite Soviet cliché] could not fail to be reflected in its behavior. Father took no active part in family life. He was often gloomy, buried within himself. He scarcely bothered with us children, whereas we were the main reason for Mother's existence. He devoted all his time to work. With age, and no doubt as a result of his abnormal working hours and mealtimes, Father often fell ill, suffering from migraines and stomach pains. Arriving home, he would shut himself up in his study and lie there the entire evening. We spoke in undertones in the house, and laughter and music were heard there less and less.

According to Osip, however, Father was much more gregarious in his younger years. He used to talk about his youth, his parents and his brothers. By the time I was about seven or eight, there was hardly ever an opportunity to sit down and talk with Father. Sadly, I cannot remember him once taking us for a walk or to the theatre.

With the passing of time, all the acute conflicts between Father and Mother left their mark and reappeared in different guises in each of the three brothers. Our domestic troubles had a particularly strong effect on Osip. This was understandable considering the sensitivity and susceptibility of his temperament.[67]

Evgeny failed to mention the most acute of these conflicts, which we know about from Nadezhda: that, in 1916, at the age of fifty, Flora Mandelstam died of a heart attack after hearing that Emil was involved in an extramarital affair.[68]

Meanwhile, several years earlier, the couple had to face the problem of the boys' entry into university, given both the Jewish quota and the fact that Osip reportedly did not do very well in school—though his one extant school report, from 1906, records rather high grades. In any event, and again in line with the standard operating procedures of the Russian-Jewish upper-middle classes in this period, Osip was sent abroad to travel and to study, in this case, first to Paris. Evgeny reports that the trip to Paris was arranged by Flora as a precaution against Osip's getting involved with young revolutionaries (we will return below to his own reports of his youthful engagement with Marxism and the Socialist Revolutionary Party). In Paris he befriended Michael Karpovich, later professor of Russian history at Harvard, who left an oft-cited remembrance of Mandelstam that, inter alia, included the fact that

> about his family Mandelstam almost never told me anything, and I did not inquire about them. . . . Only on one occasion . . . he gave me to understand that his relationship with his parents was not altogether satisfactory. He even exclaimed: "It's terrible, terrible!" but since he was in general prone to overuse that expression, I immediately suspected him of exaggeration. And I still think that if Mandelstam's parents permitted him to live in Paris and occupy himself with whatever he wished they must not have been so indifferent to his wishes, and the family bonds did not lie so heavily on him.[69]

According to Evgeny, Osip had to return home after a year, but neither he nor Flora abandoned the thought of his continuing his studies at a European university, and at the first opportunity he went off again, this time to Heidelberg, where, as we know from the university's records, he studied Old French literature. In 1911, he returned to St. Petersburg, where he crammed for entrance to the local, highly prestigious university. His previous academic record was—again, reportedly—not sufficient to have him admitted under the regnant *numerus clausus* for Jews, even more re-strictive in the capitals than in the provinces. It was at this point that in Vyborg, Finland, Osip Mandelstam underwent a conversion to Christian-ity, an act that has occasioned much confusion in the literature. First and foremost, he converted not to Lutheranism, as Nadezhda recorded and after her many scholars, but to the small and rather obscure Evangelical Methodist Church.[70] Neither in his autobiography nor anywhere else did Osip mention this conversion; all we have is other people's reconstruc-tions of the meaning (or non-meaning) of this event, all of which were determined by their overarching position on his relationship to Judaism and Christianity. Nadezhda—who herself became a Christian in her later years—regarded Osip's conversion as merely a formal legal maneuver to gain entrance to the university, with no spiritual significance. On this point Evgeny concurred, getting the denomination—and the name of the pastor—correct:

> A certain Pastor Rozen in Vyborg, who belonged to a rather small episco-palian-methodist church, counting a worldwide community of about one and a half million people, helped Osip become a Protestant. Osip had no idea, of course, how the episcopolian-methodist church differs from other religious denominations. . . . The procedure to change one's faith was not complicated, involving only the exchange of documents and a small mon-etary fee. . . . Mother had nothing against such a solution, but for Father, Osip's baptism was a matter of extreme grief.[71]

The latter is entirely plausible, and I am certain that Mandelstam had no particular engagement with Evangelical Methodism. But this does not mean that his becoming a Christian had no spiritual significance to Osip. Only three years earlier, while in Paris, Mandelstam had written a letter to his former teacher at the Tenishev school, the symbolist poet Vladimir Vasilevich Gippius, which recorded his strivings for some religious prin-ciple in his life: "having been brought up in a milieu where there was no religion (family and school), I have long striven toward religion hope-lessly and platonically—but more and more consciously."[72] We have a rea-sonably reliable account, from several years later, that Osip was attracted first to Roman Catholicism and then to Russian Orthodoxy,[73] and it is inarguable that from the start to the end of his artistic career his poetry was suffused with Christian images and sensibilities, far outweighing the occasional Jewish metaphor and allusion.

I shall return soon to this fraught issue; but what is generally not well understood is the rather complex legal and social situation that this conversion rendered for Osip Mandelstam, not so much for the remaining six years of the tsarist regime, but, more importantly, for his twenty-one-year existence in Soviet Russia. Upon conversion to any denomination of Christianity in the tsarist empire, Jews were exempted from any of the restrictions incumbent upon them in matters such as residence and education; technically their civil status also changed, releasing them from compulsory membership in the Jewish community. (However, Jews inscribed in merchant guilds, such as the Mandelstams, were already released from membership in the Jewish community, and so baptism had no effect on their civil status.) The question of to what extent Jewish converts to Christianity continued to bear the social stigma of their Jewishness is a complex one, and certainly Mandelstam was still regarded as a Jew by many others in the last years of Romanov rule. More importantly, after the Bolshevik Revolution, religious affiliation had absolutely no civil status, which was based rather on class origins and nationality. Although the Bolsheviks did not truly believe that the Jews were a nation, they acceded to the Jews' demands that they be so recognized, and hence anyone with two Jewish parents—whether Osip Mandelstam or Leon Trotsky or many of the leading Old Bolsheviks—was automatically listed in all their internal and external documents as a Jew. Later, this designation of nationality—known in Soviet shorthand as "paragraph 5"—would be overwhelmed with anti-Semitic allusions and consequences, but this was not so in the early Soviet period. Thus, whether Mandelstam's conversion to Christianity was formal or not, and in the face of whatever religious sensibilities he maintained in his heart of hearts, Osip Mandelstam remained a Jew, not only in Soviet law and in the minds both of other Jews and non-Jews, but also, I would argue, in his highly complex self-understanding as well. Here it is important to contrast him with the small but significant number of thoroughly Rus-

sified Jews in the early Soviet Union who so wanted to distance themselves both from their Jewish origins and from Soviet culture as a whole
that they converted, after the revolution, to Russian Orthodoxy; or to a
figure such as Boris Pasternak, who persistently claimed to have been
baptized in the Russian Orthodox Church as a child—whether this was
true or not—and to the end of his life vociferously rejected any identification as a Jew.

To be sure, the subject of Mandelstam's complex relationship to Judaism and to Jewishness has been broached many times in the scholarship.[74] To make an extremely complicated story short, the literature on
this matter can be divided into four tendencies. The first, and most popular, sees him moving from an early hatred and disgust for his Jewish
roots and family, as expressed in *The Noise of Time*, to a more positive engagement with Judaism and Jewishness in the *Fourth Prose*, written in
1929 (not published until 1955 in New York, and in Russia only in 1988);
one scholar has even argued that by the end of his life, Mandelstam consciously and successfully became a "poet-Jew" writing "rejudaized poetry."[75] In sharp contrast, there is the view of Mandelstam as simply and
irretrievably a self-hating Jew—as the entry in the *Encyclopedia Judaica*,
written by the American Slavicist Maurice Friedberg, put it most tren-
chantly: "Both Mandelstam's verse and his poetry [*sic!*] demonstrate a
painfully neurotic self-hating awareness of his Jewish antecedents."[76]
Close to this line, but taking a different tack, is the interpretation of Mandelstam as a devout Christian poet, an exponent of authentic Russian,
and hence Russian Orthodox, spirituality. As Nikita Struve, the most prolific spokesperson for this viewpoint, recently put it: "after all that has
been said about the worldview of Mandelstam . . . it seems that the Christian core, the Christian foundation of his life's work, does not require any
further demonstration."[77] Indeed, the journal of the Russian Orthodox
Student Movement of Paris, *Vestnik RKhD*, sponsored a survey on this
issue which returned a "surprising unanimity" in favor of viewing Mandelstam as a pious Christian poet.[78] Finally, there is a rather shallow neo-
Romantic school of thought, heavily influenced by Nadezhda Mandelstam herself, which regards Mandelstam as rejecting any limiting ethnic
or religious filiations; as Robert Alter wrote in (of all places!) *Commen-*

tary magazine in 1974: "Let us keep ultimate distinctions clear. Osip Mandelstam did not believe either in Judaism or in Christianity: he believed in poetry."[79]

What all these commentators share, I think, is a vast overemphasis on Osip Mandelstam's "beliefs" about Judaism and Jewishness. First, as already noted, in the Russian context Jewishness was always as much an ethnic designation as a religious one, and this was incalculably more so in the Soviet period (and remains so today). More subtly, like so many other Jews in his day (not to speak of ours), Mandelstam's attitude to Jewishness was not primarily cognitive or ideational, but an inchoate mixture of hatred, love, pride, beliefs, reactions to anti-Semitism, and perhaps most importantly, the tangled web of family relationships—in his case, particularly his relations with his father, which changed significantly over the years, and for the better. Thus, on all levels, to pigeon-hole this complexity into any descriptive or prescriptive taxonomy is fundamentally to misrepresent what was for Osip Mandelstam an extraordinarily tangled web at the very core of his being.

This complexity begins to emerge in the second chapter of *The Noise of Time*, called "Childish Imperialism," whose very title indicated its utter political incorrectness: instead of the expected, Lezhnev-like description of a youthful dedication to revolution, Mandelstam delighted in his childlike fascination with things military, with the statue of Nicholas I on horseback, with the marine guards at the dock, with all of Dutch Petersburg which he

> regarded as something sacred and festive. I do not know what imaginary inhabitants the fancy of young Romans used to people their capital, but as for me, I filled these fortresses and squares with a sort of unthinkably ideal, universal, military parade. . . . I was in ecstasy when the lanterns were draped in black crepe and black ribbons were strung up on the occasion of the death of the heir to the throne. . . . I was delirious over the cuirasses of the Royal Horse Guard and the Roman helmets of the Cavalry Guard, the silver trumpets of the Preobrazhensky band; and after the May Parade, my favorite distraction was the regimental festival of the Royal Horse Guard on Lady Day.[80]

All of this celebration of tsarist militarism was outrageously on the cusp of what was deemed anti-Soviet, or worse, counterrevolutionary in a publication of 1925! And this was, I would argue, the point of the exercise—not a precise description of his childhood (and not only because there was, in fact, no funeral of an heir to the throne that he could have witnessed, as he well knew)! Rather, the point of his retroactive fictionalized militarism was not only its anti-Soviet flavor, but its related utility in juxtaposing himself to his family. Thus, the second chapter ends with the following words:

> All this mass of militarism and even a kind of police aesthetics may very well have been proper to some son of a corps commander with the appropriate family traditions, but it was completely out of keeping with the kitchen fumes of a middle-class apartment, with father's study, heavy with the odor of leather, kidskin and calfskin, or with Jewish conversations about business.[81]

This is the first time we hear the word "Jewish" in this autobiography; but before continuing on to his now admittedly Jewish family, Mandelstam intersperses yet another vignette, a chapter entitled "Riots and French Governesses," which pursues the antirevolutionary theme in even more dangerous directions:

> It was always known in advance when the students would riot in front of the Kazan cathedral. Every family had its student informer. The result was that these riots were attended—at a respectful distance, to be sure—by a great mass of people: children with their nannies, mamas and aunts who have been unable to keep their insurrectionists at home, old civil servants, and simply people who happened to be walking about.[82]

This comic representation of one of the *sancta* of Soviet life, the insurrections of the anti-tsarist revolutionary movement, as motored not by history and class struggle but by spoiled bourgeois schoolchildren, their French governesses, and retired civil servants, could not have been meant otherwise than to shock readers with its bold heterodoxy. Only now does he come to his own personal form of insurrection:

But what had I to do with Guards' festivals, the monotonous prettiness of the host of the infantry and its steeds, the stone-faced battalions flowing with hollow tread down the Millionaya, gray with marble and granite?

All the elegant mirage of Petersburg was merely a dream, a brilliant covering thrown over the abyss, while round about there sprawled the chaos of Judaism—not a motherland, not a home, not a hearth, but precisely a chaos, the unknown womb-world whence I had issued, which I feared, about which I made vague conjectures and fled, always fled.

The chaos of Judaism showed through all the chinks of the stone-clad Petersburg apartment: in the threat of ruin, in the cap hanging in the room of the guest from the provinces, in the spiky script of the unread books of Genesis, thrown into the dust one shelf lower than Goethe and Schiller, in the shreds of the black and yellow ritual.

The strong, ruddy Russian year rolled through the calendar with decorated eggs, Christmas trees, steel skates from Finland, December, gaily bedecked Finnish cabdrivers and the dacha. But mixed up with all this there was a phantom—the new year in September—and the strange, cheerless holidays, grating upon the ear with their harsh names: Rosh Hashanah and Yom Kippur.[83]

The "chaos of Judaism" as the unknown gloomy womb from whence he had issued, but from which he fled, always fled, juxtaposed against the ruddy Russian hard stone he vastly preferred: I am not aware of any psychoanalytically informed analyses of this jarring metonym, which could easily be reinforced with Nadezhda's confession that Osip always preferred non-Jewish women to Jewish ones, and several times came close to abandoning the only Jewish woman he ever was with—none other than Nadezhda herself!—in favor of more attractive *shiksas*.[84] But I hesitate—for conceptual rather than Puritanical reasons—to go further down this particular path, especially since I read this passage, as all others in *The Noise of Time*, with a presupposition of its deliberate ironic jocularity, despite the utter seriousness of its subject matter.

This intense seriousness is elaborated in the next chapter, entitled "The Bookcase," which begins with an extraordinarily strong image, moving, as

Mandelstam does consistently in *The Noise of Time*, from the auditory to the olfactory, and only then to the tactile:

> As a little bit of musk fills an entire house, so the least influence of Judaism overflows all of one's life. Oh what a strong smell that is! Could I possibly not have noticed that in real Jewish houses there was a different smell from that in Aryan houses? And it was not only the kitchen that smelled so, but the people, the things, the clothing.[85]

The truly attentive reader must now ask: Was the house he grew up in a "real Jewish house" in these terms? Did his parents, he, Nadezhda, smell different, smell Jewish? Or is he talking about his grandparents' "real Jewish house," which, he continues, "[t]o this day I remember how that sweetish Jewish smell swaddled me in the wooden house of my grandfather and grandmother on Klyuchevaya Street in German Riga." From here we switch back to Petersburg:

> My father's study at home was like the granite paradise of my sedate strolls: it led one away into an alien world, and the mixture of its furniture, the selection of the objects in it were strongly knitted together in my consciousness. First of all, there was the handmade oak armchair bearing the image of a balalaika and a gauntlet, and, on its arched back, the motto "Slow but Sure"—a tribute to the pseudo-Russian style of Alexander III. Then there was a Turkish divan completely overwhelmed with ledgers, whose pages of flimsy paper were covered over with the minuscule gothic hand of German commercial correspondence. At first I thought my father's occupation consisted of printing his flimsy letters by cranking the handle of the copying machine. To this day I conceive of the smell of the yoke of labor as the penetrating smell of tanned leather; and the webbed kidskins thrown about the floor, and the pudgy chamois skins with excrescences like living fingers—all this, plus the bourgeois writing-table with its little marble calendar, swims in a tobacco haze and is seasoned with the smell of leather.[86]

So it seems that it is not, in fact, the sweetish (female?) smell of Judaism that the adult Mandelstam recalls from his parental home, but, on

the contrary, the heavy (one must suppose, defiantly male) odors of to-
bacco, leather, and oak. Once more, in the Soviet context of 1923, the
phrase "to this day I conceive of the smell of the yoke of labor as the pen-
etrating smell of tanned leather" is rather incendiary in its identification
of labor—the now sacred *trud*—with bourgeois artisanry. But that is not
the main thrust here, which, contrary to the way this section of the autobiography is usually parsed, is not a condemnation of the "Jewish smell"
of his childhood home, but precisely the opposite: the masking of that
smell with the bourgeois/mercantile odors that relegated authentic Judaism to the past. This makes even more sense when we continue with the
narrative from the olfactory to the tactile and visual:

> And in the drab surroundings of this mercantile room there was a little
> glass-front bookcase behind a curtain of green taffeta. It is about this book-
> case that I should like to speak now. The bookcase of early childhood is a
> man's companion for life. The arrangement of its shelves, the choice of
> books, the colors of the spines are for him the color, height, and arrange-
> ment of world literature itself. . . .
>
> There was nothing haphazard in the way that strange little library had
> been deposited, like a geological bed, over several decades. The paternal
> and maternal elements in it were not mixed, but existed separately, and a
> cross-section of the strata showed the history of the spiritual efforts of the
> entire family, as well as the inoculation of it with alien blood.[87]

These last images are remarkably important: the paternal and the maternal were not synthesized into a coherent whole, the family was inocu-
lated with "alien"—i.e., Russian—blood:

> I always remember the lower shelf as chaotic: the books were not standing
> upright side by side but lay like ruins: reddish five-volume works with
> ragged covers, a Russian history of the Jews written in the clumsy, shy lan-
> guage of a Russian-speaking Talmudist. This was the Judaic chaos thrown
> into the dust. This was the level to which my Hebrew primer, which I never
> mastered, quickly fell. In a fit of national contrition they even tried hiring
> a real Jewish teacher for me. He came from his Torgovaya Street and taught

without taking off his cap, which made me feel awkward. His correct Russian sounded false. The Hebrew primer was illustrated with pictures that showed one and the same little boy, wearing a visored cap and with a melancholy adult face, in all sorts of situations—with a cat, a book, a pail, a watering can. I saw nothing of myself in that boy and with all my being revolted against the book and the subject. There was one striking thing about this teacher, although it sounded unnatural: the feeling of Jewish national pride. He talked about the Jews as the French governess talked about Hugo and Napoleon. But I knew that he hid his pride when he went out into the street, and therefore did not believe him.[88]

This is an astonishing paragraph that has been badly misinterpreted, I think, in the literature on Mandelstam, and not only because the standard editions misidentify the author of the Russian-language history of the Jews as Ilia Orshansky—the first Russian-language historian of the Jews, if only in one volume; the real-life author was Heinrich Graetz, the famous German-Jewish historian, whose best-selling *History of the Jews* was indeed translated into Russian already in 1900.[89] Far more importantly, the "Judaic chaos" is here defiantly not the regnant culture of his home, but the dustbin into which his bourgeois Jewish family thrust the authentic Judaism that they rejected. Here the precise language Mandelstam used is absolutely crucial to note: it was the *iudeiskii* not the *evreiskii* chaos, literally translatable in English as "Judaic" or even "Judean," but denoting even more conscious euphemistic distance from "Jewish" than the "Hebrew" of nineteenth-century Anglo-American and "israélite" in French or "Israelit" in German. Both in his poetry and in his prose, Mandelstam used *evrei* and *evreiskii* in an essentially negative tone, as connoting present-day and especially Sovietized Jews about whom he wrote two searing short poems in the mid- and late-1920s: The first is a parody of "a Jew, undoubtedly a Komsomolets," who attempts to paint a picture of the old noble way of life but is reduced to pitiful caricature. The second is a two-line epigram:

> Miaknul kon' i kot zarzhal—
> Kazak evreiu podrazhal.

(The horse meowed and the cat neighed—

A Cossack imitated a Jew)[90]

—a venomous, if hysterically funny, skewering of none other than Isaac Babel, then in favor with the regime for his stories of a Jew imitating a Cossack!

On the other hand, *iudei* and its adjectival form *iudeiskii* conjure up, in Mandelstam's poetry, either authentic Jews such as his grandparents, or Judeans of the ancient past. Related to but not synonymous with the Western Church's distinction between authentic Jews before the Crucifixion and perfidious Jews thereafter, in Mandelstam's cultural taxonomy, *iudeistvo* (i.e., authentic Judaism and its practitioners, *iudei*) were on a substantially higher plane than *evrei*—not coincidentally the term which appeared in his own passport as the sign of his ineradicable identity. Thus, the frequently argued case that in his *Fourth Prose* Mandelstam moved from an earlier negative attitude to Jews, Judaism, and Jewishness to a positive one, as embodied particularly in his statement that "writerdom, as it has developed in Europe, and above all in Russia, is incompatible with the honorable title of Jew, of which I am proud,"[91] is fundamentally erroneous, as that is emphatically not what he wrote: "the honorable title of *iudei* of which I am proud."[92] Moreover, the rhetorical context in which this statement occurred—an extraordinarily complex blend of experimental prose, phantasmagoria, and ideological diatribe—cannot under any circumstances be taken as a veridical autobiographical assertion. The conflation between the narrator of *The Fourth Prose* and the historical Mandelstam is speciously simplistic. But back to *iudei* versus *evrei*: as opposed to the highly negative use of *evrei* in the two sarcastic verses just cited, Mandelstam used *iudei* or its adjectival forms in five highly complex poems that have been much studied in the literature;[93] here I wish to cite only one of these poems, his searing lament on the death of his mother in 1916, which I translate as follows, leaving *iudei* in the original:

This night cannot be undone
But it's still day where you are.
At Jerusalem's gates
A black sun rises.

A yellow sun is stranger,
Hush, my baby, hush,
In the bright temple of the *iudei*
They buried my mother.

Without Grace
And without a priesthood
In the bright temple of the *iudei*
They prayed over her remains.

And over mother there rang
The voices of the Israelites
I awoke in my cradle,
Lit by the glow of a black sun.[94]

As Kiril Taranovsky and other have noted, Mandelstam consistently used yellow and black color imagery to evoke Judaism—the strange *tallis* his grandfather wrapped him in in *Shum vremeni*; here, the Christian apocalyptic image of the "black sun" is sharply contrasted with the even stranger, or more estranged, "yellow sun" lighting the temple. Though profoundly imbued with Christian symbolism, this poem does not have *evrei* presiding over the mother's funeral, but *iudei* (representatives of authentic Judaism), changed in the last stanza to *izrail'tian* (Israelites), presumably in order to rhyme with *osian* (the word meaning "lit" "or illuminated").

And so we return to *The Noise of Time*. The Hebrew teacher with the correct but somehow false-sounding Russian almost impressed the young Mandelstam with his potentially authentic Jewish national pride, here rendered *evreiskii* precisely because it was deeply inauthentic: "I knew that he hid his pride when he went out into the street, and therefore did not believe him."[95] In the next vignette we are transported to Finland, where Petersburgers drove, Mandelstam wonderfully put it, "in order to think to the end what could not be thought to the end in Petersburg"[96] — possibly an elliptical reference to his conversion to Christianity in Vyborg. In that town, he recalled, the Mandelstams used to visit their friends the Sharikovs, a family of merchants descended from the Jewish soldiers in the army of Nicholas I, "a fact that permitted them to reside legally in Finland, otherwise free of Jews." The Sharikovs

> ate so much that one could hardly rise from the table. Old Sharikov swam in fat, like Buddha, and spoke with a Finnish accent. One of his daughters—a plain, dark girl—sat behind the counter, and the other three, who were beautiful, ran away in turn with officers of the local garrison. Their house smelled of cigars and money. . . . After the thinnish atmosphere of Petersburg I rejoiced in this stable, oaken family.[97]

The "thinnish" atmosphere of Petersburg is but a passable rendering of the word Mandelstam used here—*zhiden'kii*—redolent of the Russian pejorative *zhid*; one is reminded of the possibly apocryphal story of the son of Daniel Chwolson, the most famous Jewish convert to Russian Orthodoxy in the nineteenth century, who as a professor of physics at Moscow University never discussed liquidity—*zhidkost'*—in class, so sensitive as he was about his family's tainted origins! Thus, Mandelstam here was playfully contrasting the healthy oaken atmosphere of Vyborg (once more, where he himself became a Christian) to the unhealthfully "Jewish" Petersburg. The Sharikovs, moreover, were not Russian Jews. Their sound was Finnish, they did not suffer from the pathology of Jews within the Pale of Settlement or their children, and their engagement with Russia was the oldest in Russian-Jewish history, stemming from the Nicholaevan conscripts who earned their right to free residence throughout the empire in the most unjewish method of them all: military service (which Osip Mandelstam himself evaded, of course, like any well-connected bourgeois Jewish boy, though he allegedly unsuccessfully tried to enlist in an orderly corps in the First World War, back in his birthplace, Warsaw).

In any event, this excursion to Finland is followed by the chapter entitled "Judaic Chaos," which begins with a small, revealing digression:

> There once arrived at our house a person completely unknown to us, an unmarried lady of about forty, in a little red hat and with a sharp chin and angry dark eyes. On the strength of her having come from the small town of Shavli, she demanded that we find her a husband in Petersburg. She

spent a week in the house before we managed to send her packing. From time to time wandering authors would turn up—bearded and long-skirted people, Talmudic philosophers, peddlers of their own printed aphorisms and dicta. They would leave us autographed copies and complain of being tormented by evil wives.[98]

Now that we know that the Mandelstams were from Zagare (and not Kurland), not at all far from Shavli, we can better understand why this unappealing woman would demand the Mandelstams' help in joining in their upward mobility—which Osip so despised for its eviscerating deracination. The decidedly less venomous sketch of the more authentically Jewish bearded authors from the Pale leaving signed copies of their works while complaining of their wives—one thinks of Moshe Leib Lilienblum!—is followed immediately by a description of his own ineradicable distance from Judaism as a religious system:

Once or twice in my life I was taken to a synagogue as if to a concert. There was a long wait to get in—one practically had to buy tickets from scalpers—and all that I saw and heard there caused me to return home in a heavy stupor.[99]

But before we come to the odiously bourgeoisified synagogue, we get yet another contrast with authentic, traditional Judaism:

There is a Jewish quarter in Petersburg: it begins just behind the Mariinsky Theater, where the ticket scalpers freeze, beyond the prison angel of the Litovsky Castle, which was burnt down in the Revolution. There on Torgovaya [Merchant] Street one sees Jewish shop signs with pictures of a bull and a cow, women with an abundance of false hair showing under their kerchiefs, and mincing along in overcoats reaching down to the ground, old men full of experience and love of their children.[100]

In sharpest contrast, there stands the Great Synagogue of the Romanov capital, which, with its conical caps and onion domes loses itself like some elegant exotic fig-tree amongst the shabby buildings. Velveteen berets with pompoms, attendants and choristers on the point of physical exhaustion, clusters of seven-branched candelabra, tall velvet headdresses. The Jewish ship, with its sonorous alto choirs and the astonishing voices of its children, lays on all sail, split as it is by some ancient storm into male and female halves. Having blundered into the women's balcony, I edged along stealthily as a thief, hiding behind rafters. The Cantor, like Samson, collapsed the leonine building, he was answered by the velvet headdress, and the awesome equilibrium of vowels and consonants in the impeccably enunciated words imparted to the chants an invincible power. But how offensive was the crude speech of the rabbi—though it was not ungrammatical; how vulgar when he uttered the words "His Imperial Highness," how utterly vulgar all that he said! And all of a sudden, two top-hatted gentleman, splendidly dressed and glossy with wealth, with the refined movements of men of the world, touch the heavy book, step out of the circle and on behalf of everyone, with the authorization and commission of everyone, perform some honorary ritual, the principal thing in the ceremony. Who is that? Baron Ginzberg. And that, Varshavsky.[101]

Though obviously brilliantly hyperbolic—the Jewish ship split by "some ancient storm" into male and female halves!—Mandelstam's description of the Petersburg Choral Synagogue is eerily precise; its architecture was a conscious blend of the Russian and the Moorish, and included a design feature, unique, to my knowledge, in the Jewish world: the front pews, originally reserved in fact for the Barons Ginzberg and the Varshavskys, had specially constructed doors leading directly out of their pews so that the barons and other plutocrats would not even have to move to the aisle and potentially mix with hoi polloi to receive their honors.

To be sure, Mandelstam's condemnation of the vulgarity, ostentation, and dedication to the twin bourgeois idols of wealth and civic loyalty, though breathtakingly vivid, is hardly unique in the annals of the writings of sons of bourgeois Jewish fathers who detest their empty faith. Only four years earlier, none other than Franz Kafka penned his famous *Letter to My Father*, which included the following parallel description of a visit to the Prague synagogue:

> Four days a year you went to the synagogue, where you were, to say the least, closer to the indifferent than to those who took it seriously, patiently went through the prayers as a formality, sometimes amazed me by being able to show me in the prayerbook the passage that was being said at the moment, and for the rest, so long as I was present in the synagogue (and this was the main thing) I was allowed to hang about wherever I liked. And so I yawned and dozed through the many hours (I don't think I was ever again so bored, except later at dancing lessons) and did my best to enjoy the little bits of variety there were, as for instance when the Ark of the Covenant was opened, which always reminded me of the shooting galleries where a cupboard door would open in the same way whenever one hit a bull's eye, except that there something interesting always came out and here it was always the same old dolls without heads. Incidentally it was also very frightening for me there, not only, as goes without saying, because of all the people one came into close contact with, but also because you once mentioned in passing that I too might be called to the Torah. . . . This was the religious material that was handed to me, to which may be added at most the outstretched hand pointing to "the sons of the millionaire Fuchs," who attended the synagogue with their father on the high holy days. How one could do anything better with this material than get rid of it as fast as possible, I could not understand, precisely the getting rid of it seemed to me the devotest action.[102]

As is well known, Kafka rebelled against what he deemed his father's sterile and vulgar upper-middle-class Judaism in ways both similar to and fundamentally different from his contemporary Mandelstam: both abandoned their fathers' bourgeois way of life and found refuge in literature, but to resolve his oedipal-cum-spiritual conflicts, Kafka soon turned to Judaism. Indeed, as he related later in *Letter to My Father*, his interest in Hebrew, Yiddish, and Jewish texts was abhorrent to his father, who complained that he was "nauseated by Jewish writings." This turn would have been well-nigh impossible in the interwar Soviet Union as opposed to

Czechoslovakia. But the phenomenological parallel to Kafka, and more elliptically to Lilienblum, is still insistent, not least because the foregoing devastating depiction of the St. Petersburg synagogue is followed immediately by a surprisingly positive description of the sounds of the language despised by Mandelstam's parents, as well as Kafka's:

> In my childhood I absolutely never heard Yiddish; only later did I hear an abundance of that melodious, always surprised and disappointed, interrogative language with its sharp accents on the weakly stressed syllables.[103]

This offhanded comment is noteworthy because of Mandelstam's hypersensitivy to sounds, since it immediately precedes the descriptions of his parents' speech patterns and visits to his Riga grandparents cited above, and since it foreshadows Mandelstam's extremely benign portrait of the Yiddish writer Solomon An-sky later in the autobiography.[104] To be sure, one ought not make very much of these fleeting passages: they merely reemphasize and bring to a rhetorical end the argument I have been making about how we should read the Jewish/Judaic motif in Mandelstam's fancifully creative reconstruction of his childhood. For after the chapter on the Judaic chaos, almost exactly halfway through the text, the Jewish sub-theme of the autobiography as a whole is now almost entirely dropped, replaced by rather nostalgic recollections of the concerts he attended as a child, the Tenishev school, and miscellaneous family friends, and then two rather bold chapters on his youthful political engagement, which chronicle his alleged movement from Marxism to Populism (and thence, as we know, but left unspoken in the autobiography, to Christianity and poetry.) This is precisely—and I think, deliberately—the opposite trajectory from the Orthodox Soviet childhood that Lezhnev had expected and commissioned, and contained much overt and hence dangerously anti-Soviet material. Thus, in the chapter entitled "The Erfurt Program" we read that young Osip got hold of Marx's *Das Kapital*, but "got burnt by it, and threw it away ... Marx's *Kapital* is the same as Kraevich's *Physics*. Surely no one can think that Kraevich leads to any new ideas."[105] Similarly, in the next chapter, on the (part-Karaite) Sinani family, Mandelstam boldly proclaimed: "I arrived in class a completely prepared and

finished Marxist, but a very serious opponent was waiting for me"[106]—
i.e., his friend Boris Borisovich, the son of the famous Boris Naumovich
Sinani, who led the young Osip to recognize the error of his Marxist ways
and to solidarity with the Socialist Revolutionary Party, one of the Bolsheviks' archest enemies. Just barely could one get away with such overt
anti-Bolshevism in 1925, not to speak of in 1928; only a few years later, a
similar parody, this time against Stalin himself, would lead to Mandelstam's first arrest and sentence to exile in the backwaters of Voronezh,
where, not incidentally, he wrote some of the finest poetry of his life.

Whether in these latter years Mandelstam's poetry became infused
with positive Jewish themes is a matter I must bracket here; but I would
hardly be surprised if a new analysis of this question, based on a subtler
knowledge of Jewish culture than that evinced in the scholarly literature
on Mandelstam thus far, would parallel my argument about the role of
Judaism and Jewishness in his autobiography.

It is only the last of the tragic ironies of Osip Mandelstam's life that the
prison records of the Far Eastern gulag where he died in 1938 at the age of
forty-seven (but looking seventy-five) defined him by the three lapsed
identities he described with such creatively fictionalized retrospection in
The Noise of Time: Osip Emilevich Mandelstam, *evrei*, son of a merchant,
and former member of the Social Revolutionary Party.[107] We will probably never know if there was any factual basis to the last, and potentially
most lethal, of these identities, the only source of which is Mandelstam's
own autobiography. In a horribly gruesome sense, then, his brilliant self-
fashioning, based only in a delicately fragile way on the mundane truths
of his life, led to his death.

4 / Autobiography as Farewell I

STEFAN ZWEIG

When Stefan Zweig's *Die Welt von Gestern: Erinnerungen eines Europäers* was first published in Stockholm in 1942, just a few months after his suicide in Brazil, it was immediately hailed as a masterpiece of autobiographical writing.[1] Less than a year later it was translated into English as *The World of Yesterday,* published by Viking Press in New York,[2] and fulsome reviews quickly appeared throughout the American and English press. Typical was the response of Irwin Erdman, a well-known Columbia University philosopher, who wrote in the *New Republic:*

> The very success with which this book evokes the beauty of the past and the fatality of its passing is what gives it tragic effectiveness. It is not so much a memoir of a life as it is the memento of an age, and the author seems, in his own phrase, to be the narrator at an illustrated lecture. The illustrations are provided by time, but his choice is brilliant and the narration is evocative.[3]

Such praise was, of course, nothing new. Zweig was an enormously popular author in the interwar years, and probably the most translated writer of the time, his works having appeared in over thirty languages, including Chinese, Catalan, and Marathi. The news of his suicide (together with his second wife, Lotte Altmann) on February 23, 1942, shook the entire Western literary world and was widely taken to be yet another tragic consequence of the war and the obliteration of German culture under the Nazis.

Among the few dissenters in the American press and in the émigré German community was Hannah Arendt, who launched a blistering attack against Zweig and all that he stood for:

In this his last book, Stefan Zweig describes a part of the bourgeois world—
the world of the literati, which had given him renown and protected him
from the ordinary trials of life. Concerned only with personal dignity and
his art, he had kept himself so completely aloof from politics that in retrospect the catastrophe of the last ten years seemed to him like a sudden
earthquake, in the midst of which he had tried to safeguard his dignity as
long as he could.[4]

Particularly galling to Arendt was Zweig's steadfast aversion to political engagement, which she—at this point still a convinced, if idiosyncratic, Zionist—identified as the defining pathology of bourgeois Diaspora Jews:

> Not one of Stefan Zweig's reactions during all this period was the result of
> political convictions; they were all dictated by his supersensitiveness to so-
> cial humiliation. . . . The Jewish bourgeoisie, in sharp contrast to their Ger-
> man and Austrian equivalents, were uninterested in power, even of the eco-
> nomic kind. . . . Had the Jews of western and central European countries
> displayed even a modicum of concern for the political realities of their
> times, they would have had reason enough not to feel secure.[5]

Thus, Zweig was to be doubly condemned, as an apolitical bourgeois
aesthete and as a self-denying Jew:

> The bourgeois Jewish man of letters, who had never concerned himself
> with the affairs of his own people, became nevertheless a victim of their
> foes—and felt so disgraced that he could bear life no longer. . . . When
> finally the whole structure of his life, with its aloofness from civic struggle
> and politics, broke down, and he experienced disgrace, he was unable to
> discover what honor can mean to men.
>
> For honor never will be won by the cult of success or fame, by cultiva-
> tion of one's self, nor even by personal dignity. From the "disgrace" of being
> a Jew there is but one escape—to fight for the honor of the Jewish people
> as a whole.[6]

On the "honor of the Jewish people" Arendt would, of course, significantly change her tune, if not her tone, later in her life, and her attack on Zweig foreshadowed the central motifs both of *The Origins of Totalitarianism* and of *Eichmann in Jerusalem*. As usual, though, Arendt's brilliant analytic acumen overwhelmed her mastery of mere "facts." In this case, it was specious, and probably consciously disingenuous, for her to maintain that Zweig had never taken a political position on the Nazis and the war or that he had never concerned himself with Jewish affairs. As she undoubtedly well knew, Zweig—unlike many of his Jewish-born colleagues in German and Austrian letters—had always publicly identified himself as a Jew, and a good number of his best-selling works had been written on Jewish themes, most famously, his early play Jeremiah, his stories "Rahel rechtet mit Gott," "Der begrabene Leuchter," "Die Legende der dritten Taube," "Im Schnee," and my favorite—and to my mind, one of the great Jewish short stories of the twentieth century—"Buchmendel," a remarkably sensitive tale of an Eastern European Jewish bookseller in Vienna, indebted, I would propose, to Y. L. Peretz's "Bontsche shveig," though tellingly, Zweig rejected Peretz's socialist-inspired harsh denunciation of the passivity and quietism of the traditional Jew. Arendt may not have known that already in 1933 Zweig had publicly condemned the Nazis' attacks on the Jews and called for the emigration of Jewish children to England and Palestine, but she could not have been entirely ignorant of his public abandonment of his previous world-famous pacifism before and during the war, in England, the United States, and Brazil. What was actually at stake here were the radically different, and hugely contested, stances both on politics and on Jewishness and Judaism held by Zweig and Arendt, as well as other Jewish intellectuals—a matter to which I shall return at some length below.

But Arendt was entirely on target in criticizing *The World of Yesterday*'s highly nostalgic description of the world in which he had lived before the Nazis' rise to power. His designation of the late Habsburg Empire as the "golden age of security" she found particularly absurd: "Naturally, the world which Zweig depicts was anything but *the* world of yesterday; the author of this book lived only on its rim. The gilded trellises of this reservation were very thick, depriving the inmates of every view and every insight that could mar their bliss."[7] How could Zweig not have known, she asked, that the Habsburg empire of his youth was mired in corruption, that the German empire—"the militarist and stupid regime of the Junkers"—was hated by the middle classes and the workers alike, that the French Third Republic was continuously gripped by political and economic crises, and that anti-Semitism rose to astonishing new levels in the very years he lauded as secure and even serene:

> In Germany the first antisemitic parties arose during the 1880's. . . . The turn of the century brought the Lueger-Schonerer agitation to Austria, ending with the election of Lueger as Mayor of Vienna. In France the Dreyfus affair dominated both internal and foreign policies for years. Even as late as 1940 Zweig could admire Lueger as an "able leader" and a kindly person whose official antisemitism never stopped him from being helpful and friendly to his former Jewish friends. Among the Jews of Vienna no one took antisemitism, in the amiable Austrian version Lueger represented, the least bit seriously—with the exception of the "crazy" feuilleton editor of the *Neue Freie Presse,* Theodor Herzl.[8]

Here, too, Arendt was imprecise, for as we shall see, Zweig did not in fact condemn Herzl as "crazy"—on the contrary, he found him personally quite brilliant and inspiring, and although he did not agree with Herzl's Zionism, he condemned those who unfairly and maliciously criticized Herzl both within and outside the Zionist movement.

Despite these gaffs, Arendt's essay on Zweig is immensely revealing, since it is by far the most negative appraisal of *The World of Yesterday* I have been able to locate, at least until the late 1980s, when a minor, if rather nasty, small-town variation on the Historikerstreit in Germany broke out in Austria over Zweig and his position on the Nazis.[9] But this hardly affected Zweig's overall popularity—among ordinary readers, if not academics—and that of his autobiography, which has continued to be republished in multiple editions in German, English, Russian, and many other languages, and to attract largely positive and often exceptionally laudatory critical responses. Although others, including Zweig's best and most influential biographer, Donald Prater,[10] and Leon Botstein,[11] have pointed out flaws in Zweig's representation of his life-story, the scholarship as a whole is remarkably uncritical not only of this autobiography but of its author as a man, thinker, and writer. To some extent this is the result, as the Israeli Zweig expert Mark Gelber has noted, of the domination of the field by Friderike Zweig, Stefan's first wife, who for almost thirty years after his death promoted her lionizing conception of Zweig as the modern cosmopolitan humanist par excellence[12]—an intriguing parallel to the case of Nadezhda Mandelstam discussed in the previous chapter. Moreover, like Osip Mandelstam's death in the Stalinist gulag, Zweig's death as a forced exile from Nazism contributed a great deal to the admiring stance adopted towards him in the scholarship, a tendency reinforced in the last several decades by the peculiar dynamics of the study of German-Jewish authors.

Be that as it may, *The World of Yesterday* presents itself as a rather unusual autobiography, since, as Zweig himself claimed, it was intended as a portrait of an age rather than a person, and is almost entirely devoid of information about Zweig's private life—even Friderike, his wife of three decades, is never mentioned in the book! It begins with the following demurral of interest in the self:

I have never attached so much importance to my own person that I would have been tempted to tell others the story of my life. Much had to occur, infinitely more events, catastrophes, and trials than are usually allotted to a single generation had to come to pass, before I found the courage to begin a book in which I was the principal person or better still, the pivotal point. Nothing is further from my thought than to take so prominent a place unless it be in the role of the narrator at an illustrated lecture. Time gives the pictures; I merely speak the words which accompany them. Actually, it is not so much the course of my own destiny that I relate, but that of an entire generation, the generation of our time, which was loaded down with a burden of fate as was hardly any other in the course of history. Each one of us, even the smallest and the most insignificant, has been shaken in the depths of his being by the almost unceasing volcanic eruptions of our European earth. I know of no pre-eminence that I can claim, in the midst of

the multitude, except this: that as an Austrian, a Jew, an author, a humanist, and a pacifist, I have always stood at the exact point where these earth-
quakes were the most violent.[13]

As we have seen so many times before, such a disavowal of self-impor-
tance has long been a commonplace—or as Pascal would say, "a necessary
condition"—of the autobiographical genre. But Zweig's strategy for con-
cealing his life while simultaneously revealing—and reveling in—it was
rather different from that of the other authors we have encountered. First
and most simply, his is by far the longest autobiography I shall analyze
here—493 pages in the German original; secondly, as the author of hugely
popular biographies of Verlaine, Balzac, Dickens, Dostoevsky, Rolland,
Casanova, Stendhal, Tolstoy, Marie Antoinette, Mary Queen of Scots,
Magellan, Erasmus, and Freud, among others, Zweig was well practiced in
the "life and times" genre. More subtly, as the author of a great deal of
semiautobiographical fiction, often in the form of first-person mono-
logues, Zweig was superbly adept at playing with the reader's credulity: in
these stories and novellas the reader is at one and the same time urged to
believe and not to believe that what is described in these stories actually
happened, that the characters depicted once lived and acted as they do in
the story, that the narrator is the same person as the author.

But this does not mean that Zweig's assertion of disinterest in his life
succeeded in rendering a depersonalized autobiography; on the contrary,
this is a highly self-absorbed and self-worshipping story in which the hero
never leaves center stage, chronicling his ever mounting public successes
in great detail while simultaneously stressing his discomfort with public
disclosure. Indeed, *The World of Yesterday* reveals just enough personal information for the reader to be drawn into Zweig's charmed circle of os-
tensible self-effacement. In a brilliant stroke, he even added a chapter entitled "Eros Matutinis" (Youthful sexuality) detailing what he, as a friend
and disciple of Freud, regarded as the unhealthy sexual mores and behav-
iors of the middle classes during his youth, while never writing a word
about his own erotic experiences. In sum, like so many others, Zweig ma-
nipulated the genre of autobiography and the story of his own political
and artistic development, set in the elaborately described context of the

politics and literature of his age, effectively to screen his innermost self from public view.

This was accomplished, first, by claiming that he wrote this autobiography entirely from memory:

> I am aware of the unfavorable circumstances, characteristic though they are of our time, in which I am trying to shape my reminiscences. I write them in the midst of war, in a foreign country, and without the least aids to my memory. None of my books, none of my notes, no friend's letters are at hand in my hotel room. Nowhere can I seek information, for in the whole world the mails from country to country have been disrupted or hampered by censorship. . . . I have nothing more of the past with me than what I have retained in my mind. All else at this moment is unobtainable or lost.[14]

This was—not surprisingly—not true: a good part of the section of *The World of Yesterday* dealing with Theodor Herzl, for example, was reproduced word-for-word from Zweig's essay "Erinnerung an Theodor Herzl," first published in the *Pester Lloyd* (the Budapest analog to the *Neue Freie Presse*) in 1929 and thereafter oft reprinted and translated;[15] I am certain that a sustained textual comparison of the autobiography as a whole and Zweig's massive oeuvre would determine that this was hardly an isolated incident. Moreover, Prater reported that Zweig's move to Ossining, New York, in the summer of 1941 was determined "primarily by the fact that Friderike, whom he wanted to be able to consult frequently over the book, had moved there some weeks before; installed nearby, he could readily tap her own memories;"[16] and in her own memoirs, Friderike Zweig confirmed her active participation in the writing process.[17]

Moreover, still in the preface to the autobiography, Zweig had claimed:

> It is quite possible that the loss of documentation and detail may actually be an advantage for my book. For I look upon memory not as an element which accidentally retains or forgets, but rather as a consciously organizing and wisely exclusionary power. All that one forgets of one's life was long since predestined by an inner extinct to be forgotten. Only that which wills to preserve itself has the right to be preserved for others. So choose and

speak for me, ye memories, and at least give some reflection of my life before it sinks into the dark![18]

While this was, of course, bad Freudianism—the master long held that
the exclusionary power of remembering and forgetting was largely unconscious—it was a brilliant literary strategy (adopted some ten years before
Nabokov's *Speak Memory*) for relinquishing responsibility for inaccuracies
in the text: it was his memories, not he, that spoke here! Donald Prater has
pointed out the most important "lapse of memory" in the autobiography:
Zweig's claim that as a convinced pacifist he opposed World War I from the
start was "scarcely born out by the facts."[19] Zweig's letters from the early
part of the war reveal enthusiasm for the German-Austrian cause, a passionate desire to defeat "the France that one must chastise because one
loves her" and England, who was fighting "for her moneybags." Prater char-
itably explains that already in 1922 Zweig had "forgotten" his position at the
beginning of the war, and believes that by the time Zweig came to write his
autobiography, he "had convinced himself that his pacifism (or, more accurately, his opposition to the war) had dated from its very outbreak."[20]
Given what we know about the brain's ability to substitute ex post facto
politicized interpretations for stored memories, the latter may well be true.

Similarly, although the topic of Zweig's Jewishness has been the subject
of a great deal of commentary in the literature on him—although not so
extensive and controversial as the parallel literature on Mandelstam—
most of what has been written on this score has taken Zweig's retroactive
fashionings on these matters in *The World of Yesterday* as unproblematically factual, although, as we shall see, they were hardly so. Only a tiny
number of critics have reflected critically on the problem of Zweig's retrospective self-fashioning, and, inter alia, on the Jewish aspects of this autobiographical self-presentation and its relationship to the extant documentary record. As we have already seen, Zweig identified himself as a Jew
on the very first page of the autobiography, and immediately in the first
chapter on "the world of security" of pre-1914 Habsburg Austria dealt extensively with his family background. Identifying his parents as wealthy
members of the "gute jüdische Bürgertum that gave so much of value to
Viennese culture,"[21] he described his father's ancestors as typical Mora-

vian Jews who "lived in small country villages on friendly terms with the peasants and the petty bourgeoisie" and were "entirely free both of the sense of inferiority and of the smooth pushing impatience of the Galician or Eastern Jews."[22] While this was not precisely factual, it was indeed the self-conception of many formerly Moravian Austrian Jews, and we cannot expect Zweig to have known any better. More problematic is his characterization of his forefathers' quickly discarded Judaism: "early emancipated from their orthodox religion," he wrote, "they were passionate followers of the religion of their time, 'progress,' and in the political era of liberalism they supported the most esteemed representatives in parliament." While this depiction of their political attachments was undoubtedly entirely on the mark, the historian Leo Spitzer has documented that Zweig's grandparents, on both the paternal and maternal sides, were far more traditional Jews than Zweig himself allowed: his paternal grandfather, Hermann Zweig (1807–1884), was an overseer of the Jewish community of Prossnitz, where he also served as a Judenrichter—a judge in internal Jewish disputes—and remained "observant of Jewish religious practices, supportive of Biblical, Talmudic, and Hebrew instruction for the young, and involved in organizations concerned with aid to the poor and infirm."[23] It is of course entirely typical of his time and place that his son Moritz (1845–1926) was far less traditional and involved in Jewish concerns than his father, especially since he was also far wealthier. In Zweig's generation (as in ours) there is a rigorously predictable proportionate relationship between socio-economic status and engagement in Jewish religious practices. In the autobiography, Zweig says nothing about his father's Jewishness, or, for that matter, most other aspects of his life. The portrait we are permitted to see is that of a thoroughly honest businessman whose greatest pride was that he never signed a promissory note or was in debt to his bankers (the Rothschilds, of course); who permitted himself only small luxuries even when he became extremely wealthy, "even by international standards"; who always traveled second-class, smoked cheap cigars, and never felt comfortable in the Sacher Café, preferring a less aristocratic setting.[24] Most importantly, we are told that although "he was better educated than most of his colleagues—he played the piano excellently, spoke both French and English," Zweig senior persistently refused any honor or office offered to him, and this was his "secret pride" that he "never asked anything of anyone, that he was never obliged to say 'please' or 'thanks' to anyone." And this, his son tells us, was transmitted to him from his father:

> Inevitably there comes into the life of each one of us the time when, face to face with our own being, one re-encounters his father. That trait of clinging to a private, anonymous mode of life now begins to develop more strongly in me from year to year, even though it stands in marked contrast to my profession, which, to some extent, forces both name and person before the public eye. And it is out of the same secret pride that I have always declined every external honor; I have never accepted a decoration, a title, the presidency of any association, have never belonged to any academy, any committee, any jury. Merely to sit at a banquet table is torture for me. . . . But it is my father in me, and it is his secret pride that forces me back, and I may not offer opposition; for I thank him for what may well be my only definite possession—the feeling of inner freedom.[25]

I shall come back to this psychological self-portrait, but here want merely to contrast this depiction of Moritz Zweig with that in Friderike Zweig's memoir:

> Stefan's father was the prince consort in this marriage. A slow, deliberate man, he helped to maintain a dignified equilibrium. According to his own account, he was more devoted to his sons than was his fashionable wife. Assuredly the latter, too, cared for them in her own way, but it was the father who watched at their bedside when they were sick.[26]

Of his mother, Stefan Zweig wrote only:

> My mother, whose maiden name was Brettauer, was of a different, more international origin. She was born in Ancona, in the south of Italy, and spoke Italian as well as German as a child. . . . From my earliest youth I was familiar with risotto and artichokes . . . and later whenever I went to Italy, I always felt at home from the first moment of my arrival.[27]

It is difficult to know what to make of the elementary geographical error here: Ancona is on the same latitude as Florence—hardly the south of Italy!—and one wonders what "tricks" Zweig's memory was playing in depicting his flamboyant mother as a "hot" southerner rather than a "cold" northerner. In any event, he continued:

> But my mother's family was by no means Italian, rather it was consciously international. The Brettauers, who originally owned a banking business had—after the example of the great Jewish banking families, though on a much smaller scale—early distributed themselves over the world from Hohenems, a small place near the Swiss border. Some went to St. Gall, others to Vienna and Paris, my grandmother to Italy, my uncle to New York; and this international contact gave them a better polish, wider vision, and a certain family pride. There were no longer any small merchants or commission brokers in this family, but only bankers, directors, professors, lawyers, and doctors. Each one spoke several languages, and I can recall how natural it was to change from one language to another at table in my aunt's house in Paris.... My father was respected because he was an industrialist, but my mother, although she was most happily married to him, would never had allowed his relatives to consider themselves on the same plane with her own. This pride in coming from a "good family" was ineradicable in all the Brettauers, and when in later years one of them wished to show me his particular goodwill, he would say condescendingly, "You are really a regular Brettauer," as if to say, "You fell out on the right side."[28]

What Zweig does not mention, but we know from Spitzer's research, is that his Brettauer grandparents—including his grandmother, who moved into the Zweig family home after the death of her husband, just around the time of Stefan's birth, with whom he was very close, and who left him a sizable inheritance while he was still relatively young—had also been observant Jews and active members of the Jewish community (in this case, Hohenems, Austria) before their departure for business reasons to Ancona and then their move to Vienna in the 1870s.[29] Thus, while Zweig's depiction of the trans-European cosmopolitanism of the Brettauer family was entirely accurate, this did not come at the expense of active involvement in Jewish religious and philanthropic concerns—at least not until the cohort of Zweig's mother, Ida, who was born in 1854 and died in 1938.

Stefan Zweig gives us no further description of his mother, but Friderike gives us a rather more ample picture of her (former) mother-in-law:

> His mother, one of the old school, was a woman of marked personality. In her later years she was able to give up her opulent mode of life with only great difficulty. Her uncurbed, unrestrained vitality, undiminished even in old age, often caused much suffering to her son. . . . In later years, the mother was tenderly attached to her sons. It seemed unnatural that Stefan should still remain critical and resentful of this deaf, old woman, thus robbing him of the joy of having a mother. She . . . never differentiated between Jew and non-Jew . . . and never objected to her sons' marriages to women of other faiths. . . . How often she told me with what difficulty she had tamed this usually gentle child . . . what already emerged in his early years were outbreaks of such willfulness that they confronted those about him with a truly elemental force. The otherwise gentle and tender boy was suddenly transformed into a savage little being. . . . And how should this fashionable mother have managed a boy who, when strictly ordered to put on one of the stiff collars then in vogue, resisted by locking himself in his hotel room and refusing to budge? Later it was the mother's turn to be locked in by her son, whom she disturbed while he was immersed in his work. . . . Once, when spending the holidays with his mother in Vienna, and watching her trim a small tree for the maids, Stefan said to me, full of bitterness, "It would have been nice if she had done the same for her children." . . . The way in which he reacted to the memory of childhood experiences by adopting an opposite course had almost a mathematical precision.[30]

One is intrigued by the sharp contrast between Zweig's depiction of his youth as a period of utmost "security" and these hints of a profoundly unhappy and troubled childhood. Stefan seems to have suffered from depression already as a youth, as well as frequent uncontrollably wild tantrums, much to the distress of his all-too-proper and aloof mother. We know that throughout his life Stefan Zweig suffered from very severe and recurring bouts of depression, alternating at times with periods of near manic obsession with work (and, it seems, womanizing), amid constant fear and avoidance of public performance. Although there have been several attempts posthumously to diagnose Zweig's emotional problems, none is very convincing, given the dearth of reliable evidence at our disposal. Far less speculative is the fact that while intensely resenting his mother well into his adulthood—and "adopting an opposite course" from everything she did with "almost a mathematical precision"—he strove throughout his life to emulate her cult of aristocratic cosmopolitanism, while rejecting the all-too-typically Viennese-Jewish bourgeois mode of life of his father, continued by his older brother, Alfred, who for decades was angered by Stefan's cavalier attitude to money and the Zweig factories while living off their substantial benefits. We also know that some of his less fortunate acquaintances regarded the young Zweig with distaste, as a spoiled rich boy affecting aristocratic hauteur while exemplifying the all-too-bourgeois lifestyle of the parvenu Viennese Jewish rich.

Interestingly, by the time he came to write his autobiography, Zweig felt it necessary to insist, immediately after describing the social-climbing snobbery of his mother's family, that this obsession with pedigree on the part of Jewish families for whom "it was merely a matter of fifty or a hundred years earlier or later that they had come from the same ghetto" was actually one of the "most profound and secret tendencies of Jewish life":

> It is generally accepted that getting rich is the only and typical goal of the Jew. Nothing could be further from the truth. Riches are to him merely a stepping stone, a means to the true end, and in no sense the real goal. The real determination of the Jew is to rise to a higher cultural plane in the intellectual world. Even in the case of Eastern orthodox Jewry, where the weaknesses as well as the merits of the whole race are more intensely manifested, this supremacy of will to the spiritual over the mere material finds plastic expression. The holy man, the Bible student is a thousand times more esteemed within the community than the rich man; even the wealthiest man will prefer to give his daughter in marriage to the poorest intellectual than to a merchant. . . . Subconsciously something in the Jew seeks to escape the morally dubious, the distasteful, the petty, the unspiritual, which

is attached to all trade, and all that is purely business, and to lift himself up to the moneyless sphere of the intellectual, as if—in the Wagnerian sense— he wished to redeem himself and his race from the curse of money.... They all obey the same subconscious impulse, to free themselves of cold money-making, that thing that confines Jewry; and perhaps it expresses a secret longing to resolve the merely Jewish—through flight into the intellectual— into humanity at large. A "good" family therefore means more than the purely social aspect which it assigns to itself with this classification; it means a Jewry that has freed itself from all its defects and limitations and pettiness which the ghetto has forced upon it, by means of adaptation to a different culture and even possibly a universal culture. That this flight into the intellectual has become disastrous for the Jew, because of a disproportionate crowding of the professions, as formerly his confinement in the purely material, simply belongs to the eternal paradoxes of Jewish destiny.[31]

Although this was clearly meant as a defense of the Jews, reading these words written in German in late 1941 is still a rather chilling experience, and one can appreciate Arendt's ire even as one tries to maintain scholarly detachment. But as we shall see, Zweig's notion that Jews have a "subconscious" desire "to resolve the merely Jewish into humanity at large" was to become the leitmotif of his writings on the Jewish Question over several decades. As he put it soon thereafter in *The World of Yesterday,*

Nine-tenths of what the world celebrated as Viennese culture was promoted, nourished, or even created by Viennese Jewry. For it was precisely in the last years—as it was in Spain before the equally tragic decline—that the Viennese Jews had become artistically productive, although not in a specifically Jewish way; rather, through a miracle of understanding, they gave to what was Austrian, and Viennese, its most intensive expression.... They felt that their being Austrian was a mission to the world; and—for honesty's sake it must be repeated—much, if not most of all that Europe and America admire today as an expression of a new, rejuvenated Austrian culture, in literature, the theater, in the arts and crafts, was created by Viennese Jews.[32]

Though such a description of Viennese culture is by now a well-hackneyed cliché (at least outside of Vienna!) it was not decidedly so when Zweig penned these words in 1941. Beyond this rather idiosyncratic take on the highest spiritual activity of the Jews over the millennia, as Arendt noted, Zweig's retroactive view of the Vienna he grew up in was on the whole rather astonishingly naive:

> One lived well and easily and without cares in that old Vienna. . . . Rich and poor, Czechs and Germans, Jews and Christians, lived peaceably together in spite of occasional chafing, and even the political and social movements were free of the terrible hatred which has penetrated the arteries of our time as a poisonous residue of the First World War. In the old Austria they still strove chivalrously, they abused each other in the news and the parliament, but at the conclusion of their ciceronian tirades the selfsame representatives sat down together in friendship with a glass of beer or a cup of coffee, and called each other Du. Even when Lueger, the leader of the anti-semitic party, became burgomaster of the city, no change occurred in private affairs, and I personally must confess that neither in school nor at the University, nor in the world of literature, have I ever experienced the slightest suppression or indignity as a Jew. . . . Lueger was modest and above reproach in his private life. He always maintained a certain chivalry towards his opponents, and his official anti-semitism never stopped him from being helpful and friendly to his former Jewish friends.[33]

David Lowenthal has famously quipped that "nostalgia tells it like it wasn't," and certainly Zweig's portrait of the absence of anti-Semitism in pre-1914 Vienna and the entirely benign nature of Lueger's Jew-hatred was extraordinarily one-sided, even (or especially) recognizing that it was written in the face of Nazism and Zweig's forced flight from his motherland. In sharp contrast, his totally negative appraisal of his gymnasium education as entirely a waste of time seems to have been more intense in retrospect than it was at the time, and the chapter that follows it, entitled "Eros Matutinus," as I have already mentioned, is a bizarrely impersonal diatribe against the repressive sexuality of Viennese society. It seems, then, that Zweig's nostalgia about Vienna was tied mostly to his counterfactually idyllic representation of its supposedly unproblematic openness to and cultural dominance by universalistic Jews just like him.

Matters get a bit more complicated, though, when we come to his next chapter, on his university years and his first publications. Here we learn that he had his first short stories and essays published while still at the gymnasium, and that his first book of poems, entitled *Silberne Saiten,* appeared when he was but nineteen, under the imprint of the prestigious German publisher Schuster and Löffler—poems that he would never allow to be republished.[34] And then, in 1901, he had the temerity to offer his works to the "oracle of my fathers," the *Neue Freie Presse,* whose feuilleton editor was none other than Theodor Herzl. As I have already mentioned, much of the long passage about Herzl that follows in *The World of Yesterday* was copied from Zweig's "Erinnerung an Theodor Herzl," first published in the *Pester Lloyd* in 1929 and immediately translated into English as "Konig [sic] der Juden" in a memorial book to Herzl issued by the Zionist Organization of America in New York[35] (the German original was later included in Zweig's *Begegnungen mit Menschen, Büchern, Stäten,* published in 1937). But despite the substantial overlap between the original essay and that portion of it included in the autobiography, there are significant differences between the two, which merit a detailed discussion here.

Before we come to these texts, it is crucial to note that neither version of Zweig's rendition of his first meeting with Herzl can be checked against their diaries or correspondence, both of which contain no record of this meeting; only one letter from Herzl to Zweig is extant, and none from Zweig to Herzl. That one letter, dated November 2, 1903, roughly two years after their first encounter must have occurred, reads as follows:

My dear Zweig,

How young you are! I am sending your letter back to you, so that in twenty years you will be amused reading it again. Particularly, the entry way to the beautiful woman will give you much joy. One is not proud in the face of beautiful women.

To the main point: for a long while I have for various family reasons—

illnesses, etc. —been out of the office, and do not yet know when I shall return. Reclaim your piece directly from the editorial offices.

You have not lost my sympathies—young branch [a pun on "zweig"],
quite the contrary.

With best wishes.[36]

Alas, Zweig's letter that occasioned this response has not been preserved,
and we cannot entirely parse this intriguing exchange.

In *The World of Yesterday* Zweig introduced Herzl as "the first man of
world importance whom I had encountered in my life—although I did
not then know how great a change his person was destined to bring about
in the fate of the Jewish people and in the history of our time."[37] Herzl was
then the darling of Vienna, Zweig relates, because of his enchanting plays
and essays, and of course because he served as the feuilleton editor of the
Neue Freie Presse, the high temple of Viennese bourgeois culture. When
Herzl became a Zionist, however (and here Zweig repeats Herzl's own
counterfactual claim that it was the Dreyfus Affair that made him into a
Zionist), he became the laughing stock of the Viennese bourgeois Jews,
who thought it preposterous that they should be asked to abandon their
palatial homes on the Ringstrasse for Palestine, their beloved German
language for Hebrew. Rabbis thundered against him, Karl Kraus wrote a
mocking pamphlet about him called "The King of Zion," and when he entered into a theater, people whispered sneeringly, "His Majesty has arrived!" Zweig, on the other hand, encountered a truly regal figure, with
"natural majesty," who immediately read the young writer's feuilleton and
accepted it for publication in his newspaper: "It was if Napoleon had
pinned the Knight's Cross of the Legion of Honor upon a young sergeant
on the battlefield."[38] This kindness and generosity was repeated by Herzl
until his death, including in a final encounter in the Stadtpark some few
months before the latter's premature death, when he graciously invited
his young protégé to his home, an invitation Zweig did not accept.

All this is faithfully transcribed from the original 1929 essay, with three
highly significant changes. First and probably most telling, in *The World
of Yesterday* Zweig wrote that despite Herzl's early championing of his
work, "it was difficult for me to determine—ungratefully, it might seem—

not to join his Zionist movement actively and in the responsible position that he would have wished." That was because, he continued,

> The right relation never presented itself. I was estranged above all else by the disrespect, of a kind hardly comprehensible today, with which his own party associates treated Herzl. Those of the East charged him with not understanding Judaism and not even knowing its customs; the economists looked down upon him as a feuilletonist; each one had his own objection and they were not always the most respectful. I realized how important and necessary it would have been to Herzl to have persons and particularly young people around him who were completely submissive, but the quarreling and dogmatic spirit, the constant opposition, the lack of honesty, hearty subordination in this circle, alienated me from the movement which I had only approached curiously for Herzl's sake.[39]

In the 1929 essay, Zweig's attitude to Zionism was represented rather differently:

> My gratitude to [Herzl] personally had also made me attach significance to the idea that was occupying him more and more. I began to follow the Zionist movement, and sometimes attended, as a spectator, the little meetings that usually were held in the basements of various coffeehouses. There, as well as at the University, I met, more and more frequently, the noblest of his disciples, Martin Buber, who at twenty-one was far superior to all of us in seriousness and knowledge and in maturity of view.
>
> But I was actually unable to ally myself with the Zionists of that day. The students to whom the ability to defend themselves was, somehow, still the nucleus of Judaism, were alien to me; and I disliked the evening discussions because of the now hardly imaginable attitude of disrespect which the very foremost of his followers adopted toward the person of Herzl.[40]

There then follows the paragraph about the various varieties of disrespect reproduced in the autobiography.

Clearly, in 1941 Zweig wanted at once to present himself as far more positively predisposed towards the Zionist movement than he had in 1929 and yet at the same time more aloof from its actual activities than he had in his earlier essay. In the autobiography we hear nothing about his attending Zionist meetings or about the differences between his attitude to Judaism and that of the Zionist students, and, very importantly, the name Martin Buber is never once mentioned. Gelber has found that these sentences were in fact included in the typescript of the autobiography preserved in the Zweig archive in Jerusalem, but crossed out in what appears to be Zweig's own hand![41] Moreover, in *The World of Yesterday*, Zweig added several paragraphs that wax quite lyrically about the great wisdom of Herzl's Zionism—words entirely missing from the earlier piece. Similarly, whereas the former piece ended with a brief description of Herzl's funeral in Vienna, culminating in the words "And only when he was being lowered into his grave did those who had been too close to him in Vienna recognize at last the universal scope of his work and his life," the same funeral is described at some length in the autobiography, with masses of Jews from the West, the East, Russia, and Turkey streaming into Vienna, which finally realized how important and beloved was the deceased.

Thus, quite in contrast to Arendt's characterization of the autobiography, its representation of Zweig's relationship to Herzl and to Zionism is far more positive than that written twelve years earlier, before the assumption to power of Nazism. But, in fact, neither the 1941 nor the 1929 version accurately depicted the admittedly complex story of Zweig's views on Zionism and Jewishness as they developed over the decades. First, several scholars have established that no piece by Zweig was published in the *Neue Freie Presse* before 1902—in other words, that Zweig's rendition of his first encounter with Herzl was, at the very least, factually imprecise.[42] Then, as Gelber and others have demonstrated, at the turn of the century, before he met Herzl, Zweig was rather close to Buber and the cultural Zionist "Jung-Jüdisch" movement: his novella "Im Schnee" was first published in the Zionist newspaper *Die Welt*, edited by Buber, on August 2, 1901, and his poems "Das Gedicht" and "Spinoza" appeared there later that autumn. "Im Schnee" was then reprinted in the *Jüdischer Almanach*, a publication of the Buberian cultural Zionists, in 1902 and 1904, in which Zweig was listed as one of the "literary contributors." Among the editors of this anthology was Zweig's close friend, the Zionist artist Ephraim

Moses Lilien, about whom Zweig recalled in *The World of Yesterday:* "[in Lilien] I encountered for the first time an Eastern Jew, and a Judaism which in its strength and stubborn fanaticism had hitherto been unknown to me."[43]

But one must be careful not to overstate Zweig's ideological affiliation with the new Jewish nationalist movement, even in its most humanistic Buberian guise. One of his first preserved letters, written on June 22, 1900, to the Austrian-Jewish writer Karl Emil Franzos (who, not incidentally, is credited with the quip "every country gets the Jews it deserves"), was a request to have "Im Schnee" published in the prestigious literary journal *Deutsche Dichtung* that Franzos edited. The nineteen-year-old aspiring writer wrote:

> I have written many novellas, which could comprise a separate volume. Several of these have already been published, others will soon appear in major newspapers such as the Berlin *Morgenpost.* But I have not sent off this novella, not because I think it bad—on the contrary, I think it rather better than the others, but because it is a Jewish novella [einer Judennovelle]. This makes it infinitely difficult—you personally, as a famous poet, no longer have to experience this—to have it published in a newspaper. . . . I do not want to give it to a Jewish paper, since it has *absolutely no nationalist take to it* [*absolut keine nationale Sendung enthalten ist*] unlike most other Jewish novellas.[44]

In the event, Franzos rejected the novella for his journal, and Zweig's decision to submit it to a Zionist publication was undoubtedly not so much ideological as expedient. Similarly, in 1903 Zweig wrote a long, virtually Buberian introduction to an album of Lilien's drawings, in which he gushed, inter alia, that his artist friend's work "was the first page in the history of nationally conscious Jewish art . . . the end and greatness of which are still incalculable."[45] At the very same time, however, he privately confessed to another friend in their circle that writing this introduction "marked me with the title Zionist which I personally am not very fond of."[46]

For almost the next decade, as his fame grew, Zweig left no extant documents about his inward feelings about these matters. Not surprisingly, the chapters of *The World of Yesterday* that chronicle these years never once mention his Jewishness, except, via negativa, for a telling marginal remark that in America he was pleasantly astonished that "no one had asked me about my nationality, my religion, my origin, and—fantastic as it might seem to the world of today with its fingerprinting, visas, and police certificates—I had traveled without a passport."[47] All we can know about this part of his inner world from his correspondence is that in 1912 Buber approached him to contribute to a book he was editing for the Prague Jewish Student Society; Zweig declined, on the grounds both that he was too busy and that it would tax him too much to spend weeks pondering this all-too-complex subject.

The next chapter of the autobiography, "The First Hours of the War of 1914"—whose misrepresentation of Zweig's position at this time has been well analyzed by Prater—only mentions the Jews en passant in describing his friendship with the pathetic Ernst Lissauer, "the most Prussian or Prussian-assimilated Jew" he had ever known, who penned the most patriotic German poem of the period, "Hymn of Hate," expressing sharp hatred of England and undying devotion to the Kaiser and his Reich; twenty years later, Zweig noted, Lissauer "was driven out by Hitler from the Germany to which he had been attached with every fiber of his heart, to die forgotten, the tragic victim of the one poem which had raised him so highly only to dash him to the lowest depths."[48] Most of the next chapter, entitled "Intellectual Brotherhood," describes his wartime experiences at the Austrian military's Kriegsarchiv, including his trips to Galicia, where he used Jewish agents to gather material for his work. He does not mention that, early in the war, he was once more approached by Buber for a written statement on his position on the "Jewish Question." At this point Zweig was more responsive, writing that in line with his overarching cosmopolitan stance, he disdained nationalism of any kind, including Jewish nationalism, but nevertheless believed that Judaism—or Jewishness (in German "Judentum" means both)—was central to his worldview and his artistic core:

As for my position on Judaism . . . I will only tell you that, in keeping with my nature, which is based entirely on integration, or synthesis, I would never like to choose Judaism as a prison of emotion, with bars shutting out comprehension of the other world. In fact, everything in Judaism that pits itself against the other world is antipathetic to me. But I know that I nevertheless dwell within that world and never want to be or will turn apostate. . . . In the professions of Jewishness that I so often read, everything that bespeaks pride seems to me to be an exposure of insecurity, a reversed anxiety, a twisted inferiority feeling. What we lack is *security, composure*—I have these feelings more and more strongly as a Jew as well. Being a Jew does not burden me, does not uplift me, does not torment me, and does not separate me. I feel it as part of my being, like my heartbeat, feel it when I think of it and do not feel it when I do not think of it.[49]

We know, of course, that the experience of the First World War, and particularly its breaching of the barriers between German and Eastern European Jews, led many German-Jewish intellectuals to reconsider their views on Judaism; Franz Rosenzweig's reaction is only the most famous in this regard. And Zweig seems to have gone through his own reconsideration of his Jewishness at the same time, as he soon wrote to Buber:

Never before have I felt so liberated by the Judaism within me as I do now in this period of national insanity—and what separates me from you and yours is only this, that I have never wanted the Jews to become a nation again and thus to lower itself to taking part with the others in the rivalry of realities. I love the Diaspora and affirm it as the meaning of Jewish idealism, as Jewry's cosmopolitan human mission. And the only union I would wish for would be in the spirit, in our sole real element, never in a language, in a nation, in mores or customs of any of those syntheses which are as dangerous as they are beautiful. To my mind, the present condition of the Jews is the most glorious in all of mankind: this oneness without language, without ties, without a homeland, solely out of the essence of our beings. As I see it, any narrower, any more real coalescence, would be a diminution of this incomparable condition. And the one point wherein we have to strengthen ourselves is to feel this condition not as a humiliation, but with love and awareness, as I do.[50]

This was closer to Rosenzweig's position than to Buber's, though to be sure, without either's philosophical and spiritual depth and consequent commitment to refashioning the religious basis of Judaism. Unfortunately, Buber's response to this letter has not been preserved, but we do have Zweig's response to it, dated May 25, 1917, in which he sets forth his most outspoken and passionate articulation of his views:

> My position on the Jewish question, which in the past may well have been unclear because I unconsciously fended off any preoccupation with this problem, has in the course of time become remarkably precise. What previously I had vaguely sensed, and have confirmed by ten years of a wandering life, is the value of absolute freedom to choose among nations, to feel oneself a guest everywhere, to be both participant and mediator. This supranational feeling of freedom from the madness of a fanatical world has saved me psychologically during these trying times, and I feel with gratitude that it is Judaism that has made this supranational feeling possible for me. I consider nationalistic ideas, and in fact the idea of any kind of restriction, as dangerous. The concept that Judaism should establish itself in the real world actually seems to me a debasement and a renunciation of its highest mission. Perhaps the purpose of Jewry is to show through the centuries that communion is possible even without soil, merely as the consequence of blood and spirit, merely by means of the Word and the faith. And for us to give up this uniqueness means to me voluntarily surrendering a high office which history has conferred on us, closing a book that was written on a thousand pages but still has room for thousands upon thousands of years of pilgrimage. . . .
>
> Just because I personally have no faith in the achievement of a national community, in the rebuilding of an ancient nation into a new one, does not mean that I lack respect for those who devote themselves to the creative effort of building one. Czech literature and Hungarian literature as well show how dead languages can be artificially revived by the exertion of a national will, and perhaps in hundreds and hundreds of years there will actually arise, in a real Jerusalem, the kind of cultural renewal you long for and are trying to create. But neither of us will live to see it. . . .

I am very happy that these matters do not cause a rift between us, and I can love you exactly as if you fully agreed with me.[51]

It was at precisely this time that Zweig wrote his most famous play, *Jeremiah,* which in many ways brought to the fore, and to the stage, this conception of Judaism. In the autobiography, he feigned unconsciousness about the ideological core of this play:

> [I]n choosing a Biblical theme I had unknowingly touched upon something that had remained unused in me up to that time: that community with Jewish destiny whether in my blood or darkly founded in tradition. Was it not my people that again and again had been conquered by all other peoples, again and again, and yet outlasted them because of some secret power—that power of transforming defeat through will, of withstanding it again and again? Had our prophets not presaged this perpetual hunt and persecution that today again scatters us upon the highways like chaff, and had they not affirmed this submission to power, and even blessed it as the way to God? Had trial not eternally been of profit to all and to the individual? Happily, I realized this while working on my drama, the first of all my works that means something to me.[52]

Once more, this was rather different than his contemporary position; in an undated letter probably written at the end of January 1918, he wrote to Buber:

> I would so have liked to talk with you sometime to find out what effect [*Jeremiah*] has had in nationalist circles, whether as a profession of faith or as a repudiation of the national idea. For I am quite clear in my mind: the more the dream threatens to become a reality, the dangerous dream of a Jewish state with cannons, flags, medals, the more than ever am I resolved to love the painful idea of the Diaspora, to cherish the Jewish destiny more than Jewish well-being. In well-being, in fulfillment, the Jews were never with anything—they found their strength only under pressure, and their unity only in dispersal. Once they are together they will disperse of their own accord. What is a nation if not a transformed destiny? And

what is left of it if it evades its destiny? Palestine would be a terminus, the circle returning on itself, the end of a movement that has thoroughly shaken Europe, in fact the whole world. And it would be a tragic disappointment, like every repetition.[53]

Buber of course vehemently rejected Zweig's analysis, responding characteristically that

> I know nothing about a "Jewish state with cannons, flags and medals," not even in the form of a dream. What will be depends on those who create it, and for that very reason those who have human and humanitarian aims like myself must help to direct its course of affairs. . . . At any rate, I prefer to join in the tremendous venture of something new, in which I see not much "well-being" but a series of great sacrifices; I prefer to join in this rather than endure any longer a Diaspora that for all its lovely and painful fruitfulness hands over piece by piece the fruits of that movement to inner corruption, and I would prefer even a tragic disappointment to continual and hopeless, though not tragic, degeneration.[54]

Zweig, in turn, was not convinced by Buber, and continued steadfastly to maintain his antinationalist and non-Zionist stance throughout the next decade and a half.[55] "Non-Zionist" is a precise term in Jewish ideological history, referring to those Jews who did not share the Zionist diagnosis of the essential pathology and inevitable demise of Diaspora Jewry, but at the same time supported Jewish colonization in Palestine and were willing to work with the Zionists in various collaborative projects, including most importantly the building of the Hebrew University in Jerusalem and the establishment of the Jewish Agency for Palestine, which in fact had a stipulated number of seats set aside precisely for "non-Zionists." This was in sharp contrast to the overt anti-Zionism of the vast majority of Orthodox rabbis who rejected Zionism as a heretical movement rebelling against the basic eschatological and messianic beliefs of Judaism; of the vast majority of Reform rabbis who rejected Zionism as a heretical movement that misrepresented Judaism as a nation, not a religion, and rejected the Jews' supernaturally revealed mission to spread ethical monotheism to the rest of humankind; and of the Jewish socialist parties, especially but not only the Bund, which condemned Zionism as a bourgeois nationalist heresy, misleading the Jewish working classes into rejecting the true solution to their woes, i.e., socialism, which had to be fought for in the Diaspora, not in some colonialist, and necessarily murderously anti-Arab, adventure in Palestine.

To be sure, Zweig's views on these matters have been described in countless places as that of an "assimilated Jew." As I have explained at length elsewhere,[56] I regard the term "assimilated Jew" as heuristically and conceptually meaningless, covering an enormously wide and self-obliterating spectrum of Jewish self-perceptions, prescriptive solutions, and descriptive realities. Most importantly, from the late nineteenth century on, "assimilation" and "assimilated Jews" became highly politicized terms of opprobrium in the internal wars of the Jews, especially used to describe non- or anti-Zionists who were otherwise committed to Judaism; this stance is now called "integrationist" by the most careful students of Jewish politics. But Zweig's Jewishness was hardly so central to his life as it was for most "integrationists," though neither was he an "assimilationist"—one who advocated the dissolution of the Jews as a religious or ethnic entity.

Rather, I suggest, Stefan Zweig was emblematic of a type of Jew—and Jewish writer—even more common in our day than his: one who acknowledges his or her Jewish origins, never considers conversion, steadfastly opposes anti-Semitism, may or may not be married to a non-Jew, is sympathetic to the Zionist movement (or later the State of Israel) without identifying as a Zionist or a Jewish nationalist, and may indeed use Jewish themes and subject matter in creative or artistic work—but for whom Jewishness is neither central to their conscious worldview nor entirely absent from it. To be sure, Zweig's attitude to Jewishness was far more cognitive, ideational, and articulated than, say, Osip Mandelstam's. For Austrian Jews of Zweig's generation this rather agnostic stance became increasingly impossible after 1933, as Zweig himself recognized.

The chapters of *The World of Yesterday* on the interwar period are among the most interesting in the autobiography, detailing Zweig's rise to unprecedented success throughout a good part of the world, his trip to Soviet Russia, and his move to Salzburg with Fridericke—still mentioned only by default through the occasional slip into the pronoun "we" instead of "I" in describing domestic arrangements. So insistent was Zweig's deliberate hiding of his private life from his readers, that at one point he all but teases us with the following: "In my personal life the most notable happening of these years was the presence of a guest who settled himself most benevolently, a guest whom I had never expected"—but this turns out to be "success" and this comment is importantly linked with the over-archingly retroactive cast of the autobiography as a whole:

> It is understandable that I do not feel at ease in mentioning the public success of my books, and in normal times I would have avoided even the most casual reference which might be interpreted as bragging. But I have a particular right and am even compelled not to pass over this fact in the story of my life, because this success, upon Hitler's advent nine years ago, passed into history. Of the hundreds of thousands and even millions of my books which had their secure place in the book shops and in innumerable homes in Germany, not a single one is obtainable today; whoever still has a copy keeps it carefully hidden and in the public libraries they remain locked away in the so-called "poison cabinet" for those few who with a special permit from the authorities want to use them "scientifically"—mostly for the purposes of defamation. . . . Nor is this all: in France also, in Italy, in all the countries now enslaved and in which my books in translation were among those most widely read, they have been similarly banned by Hitler's command. Today, as a writer I am, in [the famous nineteenth-century Austrian poet] Grillparzer's words, one "who living follows his own corpse."[57]

A few pages later, he admits, "if I could start all over again today, I should try . . . publishing my works under another, an invented name, a pseudonym"[58] and one wonders whether, in some profound though hardly conscious way, this was connected to his subsequent fate as a banned Jewish writer.

Thus finally we come to 1933, and his soon-to-be controversial reaction to the rise of Nazism. The chapter entitled "Incipit Hitler" focuses—understandably—on the effects of the assumption to power of the Nazis on Zweig himself: the fate of *The Silent Woman*, the opera he wrote with

Richard Strauss; his decision to abandon his home in Salzburg, at first temporarily, and then permanently after a police search; and his move to London. Barely a word is said about the implications of this move on Friderike and her two (non-Jewish) daughters from a previous marriage, and not much more on the inner psychic turmoil the entire turn of events must have caused him. Writing with hindsight now becomes extraordinarily more difficult than ever before, since the "handwriting on the wall" is as terrifyingly legible now as it was indecipherable beforehand. Although in theory he could have claimed clairvoyantly to have understood the incomprehensible, since he left Austria in time and intact, he did not replicate his deceptively self-serving retelling (or recollection) about his stance in World War I; all he can say is:

> One cannot easily dispose of thirty or forty years of deep faith in the world inside of a few brief weeks. In the clutch of our conception of justice we believed that there was a German, a European, a world conscience and were convinced that there existed a measure of barbarousness that would make its own quietus, once and for all, because of mankind.[59]

Immediately though, the omniscient "we" becomes a pathetically nescient "I" and for the first and only time in *The World of Yesterday* Zweig admits that telling the truth about the past is both painful and inherently problematic: "Since I am trying here to stick to the truth *as much as possible* [my italics], I have to admit that none of us in Germany and in Austria in 1933 and even in 1934 thought that a hundredth, a thousandth, part of what was to break upon us within a few weeks would be possible."[60] The fact that others shared in this inability to see—his publisher, Austrian Jews as a whole, other writers and intellectuals—does not assuage the pain, specifically since for the first time he also admits that for years he had attempted to keep aloof from all politics and had not even voted. Appropriately, perhaps, the next chapter is entitled "The Agony of Peace," in which he describes his early years of exile in England, in which he claims that "the sharper the political tension became the more I withdrew from discussions and from any public participation"—hence eliciting Arendt's later ire, as well as contemporary, if largely privately conveyed, indigna-

tion from friends and colleagues such as Joseph Roth and Klaus Mann
who urged him to join public protests against the Nazis and fumed
against him when he didn't.

What is most complex about this matter is that we know that Zweig was
not nearly so detached from politics as a whole and from anti-Nazi public
statements in particular as both he and others would later claim, though
his position in general, and especially on appropriate responses to the persecution of the Jews, was characteristically, and perhaps characterologi-
cally, idiosyncratic. As soon as Zweig arrived in London in 1933 one of the
first things he asked his English friend Joseph Leftwich to do was to circu-
late a press release denying the rumors that he was refusing to join the
protests against the Nazi regime:

> There is nothing further from my mind than the thought of shutting my-
> self out from the common fate of my comrades and brethren-in-blood;
> and I would despise any attempt on my part to surrender my moral inde-
> pendence in return for any advantages whatsoever. I declare openly and
> unambiguously that the fate of my brethren-in-blood is obviously a thou-
> sand times more important to me than all literature.[61]

Even more interestingly, on November 30, 1933, Zweig gave a fascinating speech—not mentioned in the autobiography, and not analyzed, to
my knowledge, anywhere in the vast literature on him—at the house of
Mrs. Anthony de Rothschild, to the "Committee for the Luncheon in Aid
of German Jewish Women and Children." This speech, published as a
pamphlet several months later by the German Relief Fund of the Joint
Distribution Committee, began with a citation of Dmitri Karamazov's
plea about the sufferings of children, and drew the following analogy:

> I, too, wish to speak now not of the entire tragedy of the Jews in Germany,
> which staggers imagination, but only and solely of the terrible plight of the
> children.
>
> Certainly, the catastrophe that has come upon the Jews of Germany has
> affected all alike, people of all ages, men and women. It has torn away in-
> numerable people from their homes, from their work, from all that life

meant to them, from a community of which they formed part for centuries, and the record of this devastation has already filled many volumes.

But grown-up men and women, no matter how deeply hurt they are, must not acknowledge defeat. They already have the strength, or think they have, to master their fate, and to build a new home on the ruins of the old. The adult may find consolation in the history of his ancestors, in similar events in the past, and he has the comfort of knowing that by far the greater part of the world condemns what is now being done in Germany. A strong man may actually be strengthened by this experience, and suffering may lead to creative expression. Real men and women are spiritually able to defend themselves.

It is the defenseless, the children, the young people, the growing generation, who must have all their care, for they are in danger, almost in mortal danger, faced with a double peril.[62]

Citing Freud, Zweig elaborated the first danger, the sense of inferiority and the daily humiliation that German Jewish children face. The psychological effects of their persecution, he explained, is the "terrible epidemic that is menacing the Jewish children of Germany today." He continued in a vein that resonated with many Zionist diagnoses of the "ghetto mentality":

We Jews know better than anyone else the sinister nature of this malady, for it has affected our whole people for centuries. It has been the endemic disease of our race, the terrible infection to which we succumbed for centuries in the Ghetto. For a century we hoped we had once and for all finally conquered this innermost malady. We had thought that in Germany, as everywhere else in the world, we had brought our release from the reproach of inferiority by taking part in all fields of cultural life, in poetry, painting, music, science, philosophy, by rendering equal service in citizenship with the best of all other nations. We saw a new generation that no longer walked furtively, with cast-down eyes, but looked up with the calm, confident gaze that a sound and undisturbed childhood and a sense of spiritual straightness bestows upon every human being.

And now, is this old malady to begin its ravages again in a new generation? Are Jewish children once more, in Germany of all places, in the heart of Europe, to become cowering and crippled souls, an anxious, terrified, broken generation? It must not be![63]

But equally dangerous, he continued, was the second danger facing German Jewish children, "that their souls may be poisoned by the hatred implanted in them" towards other peoples, and especially the Germans. Conscious that he was here expressing a belief that was "contrary to that of many of my brethren in blood," he repeated his oft-expressed antagonism to nationalist hatred or calls for revenge:

> We are an ancient people, and our experience goes back to ancient times. We have for 3000 years encountered the enmity of numerous nations who have long since vanished, Egyptians and Chaldeans, Rome and Spain, France and Germany and Russia. There is scarcely a town in Europe in which ancestors of ours have not been burnt at the stake, nor a street through which our forefathers have not fled into exile. Yet—and this is the pride of the Jewish people—we have not become a people of hate. We have always tried faithfully to serve the general cause of humanity. We have loved the land in which we dwelt, and its language which we speak. There is nothing that I find, as a Jew, nobler in our people than the fact that we have always been the masters and not the slaves of our sufferings, that we did not convert the misery inflicted upon us into lasting enmity against the nations that wronged us. . . . We grown-up people must force ourselves to reply to this humiliation proudly: without vulgar abuse, without humiliating words of hatred, we must look our enemies straight in the face without fear.[64]

But this the children cannot do, he concluded, and thus they must be removed as soon as possible from Germany:

> They should either be planted in the native soil of Palestine, or for a time find a home among nations, such as your own, that respect themselves and elevate themselves by the liberty that they grant in matters of religion of every form to every race upon this earth.[65]

Calling on English Jewish women and men to serve as foster mothers and fathers of these children, he concluded:

> From the books of our forefathers we have learnt that no good deed is ever lost in obscurity, and free and happy Jewish men and women will one day, with bright and shining eyes, thank you for having saved their youths for them and thus retained in them the capacity of loving with unbroken souls this world that is common to us all.[66]

After the Nuremberg Laws, Zweig came to advocate the emigration of Jewish grown-ups, to Palestine as well as anywhere else that would take them. In a foreword to Leftwich's book, *What Will Happen to the Jews?* published in 1936, he wrote:

> The Jewish problem is to-day much greater than Palestine, and calls for a more accelerated subsistence. I agree with [Leftwich's] train of thought, that national and international emigration should proceed side-by-side, and this dual form of action seems to me entirely in the tradition of Jewish history.[67]

At the same time, he donated a good chunk of his archives to the Jewish National Library at the Hebrew University of Jerusalem. This was hardly a conversion to Zionism, as evidenced by an article he wrote for the first issue of a new Yiddish periodical published in 1939 in Paris by the Russian-Jewish émigré scholar Elias Tcherikover, in which he argued that Jews should stay out of leadership positions in the political life of countries other than Palestine, since "nothing has so promoted the anti-Semitic movement as the fact that Jews have been too much in evidence in political life." Almost anticipating Arendt's later fury, he asked:

> Should a Jew then take no part in political life? Is he to resign his citizenship rights? Not at all. There is nothing that proves a man's loyalty to a party or an idea more than to have the ability to hold the first, the most prominent position, and to serve voluntarily in the ranks. It is not by pushing forward, but by deliberately holding back that a man reveals his moral strength. The example of Disraeli no longer applies to our time.[68]

Although his former friend Max Brod—among many other things, Kafka's publisher—advocated a similar conclusion from a decidedly Zionist perspective, Zweig's basic ideological position on the Jewish question was still unchanged, as Europe descended into war.

All this he of course did not—and could not—detail in his autobiography, which is silent about all these pamphlets, speeches, and articles, and reveals only that in 1938, when he heard about the death of his mother in Vienna, "I am not ashamed to say that I was not shocked and did not mourn. . . . on the contrary, I even felt something like composure in the knowledge that she was now safe from suffering and despair."[69] Far more emotional was his response to the plight of Sigmund Freud and his consequent delight when Freud arrived in London and greeted him in his new Hampstead home, and his reaction to the multitudes of Jewish refugees he encountered in London:

What was most tragic in this Jewish tragedy of the twentieth century was that those who suffered it knew that it was pointless and that they were guiltless. Their forefathers and ancestors of mediaeval times had at least known what they suffered for; for their belief, for their law. . . . They lived and suffered in the proud delusion that they were selected by the Creator as a people chosen for a special destiny and a special mission and the promise of the Bible was to them commandment and law. . . . As long as their religion bound them together they were still a community and therefore a power. . . . But the Jews of the twentieth century had for long not been a community. They had no common faith, they were conscious of their Judaism rather as a burden than as something to be proud of and were not aware of any mission. They lived apart from the commandments of their once holy books and they were done with the common language of old. To integrate themselves and become articulated with the people with whom they lived, to dissolve themselves in the common life, was the purpose for which they strove impatiently, for the sake of peace from persecution, rest on the eternal flight. Thus the one group no longer understood the other, melted down into other peoples as they were, more Frenchmen, Germans, Englishmen, Russians than they were Jews. Only now, since they were swept up like dirt in the streets and heaped together, the bankers from their Berlin

palaces and sextons from the synagogues of orthodox congregations, the
philosophy professors from Paris and Rumanian cabbies, the undertaker's
helpers and Nobel Prize winners, the concert singers, and hired mourners,
the authors and the distillers, the haves and the have-nots, the great and the
small, the devout and the liberals, the usurers and the sages, the Zionists
and the assimilated, the Ashkenazim and the Sephardim, the just and the
unjust besides which the confused horde who thought that they had long
since eluded the curse, the baptized and the semi-Jews—only now, for the
first time in hundreds of years the Jews were forced into a community of
interest to which they had long ceased to be sensitive, the ever-recurring—
since Egypt—community of expulsion.[70]

No longer the prophet singing hallelujahs to the Diasporic genius of the
Jews, Stefan Zweig still did not align himself to any ideological solution to
what he confessed was one of the greatest mysteries of all time:

But why this fate for them and always for them alone? What was the reason, the sense, the aim of this senseless persecution? They were driven out
of lands without a land to go to. They were repulsed but not told where
they might be accepted. They were held blameful but denied expiation.
And thus, with smarting eyes, they stared at each other on their flight: Why
I? Why you? How do you and I who do not know each other, who speak
different languages, whose thinking takes different forms and who have
nothing in common happen to be here together? Why any of us? And none
could answer. Even Freud, the clearest seeing mind of this time, with whom
I often talked in those days, was baffled and could make no sense out of the
nonsense. Who knows but that Judaism because of its mysterious survival
may not, in its ultimate significance, constitute a reiteration of Job's eternal
cry to God, so that it may not be forgotten on earth.[71]

At last Zweig was speaking here, I think, directly from his heart, lifting
ever so slightly the veil of self-insouciance that obscured so much of the
autobiography. Not incidentally, only a few pages later we are finally told
that "it was my intention to contract a second marriage [and] I did not
want to lose a minute, in order not to be separated for long from my fu-

ture life-partner."[72] But as quickly as possible, the self-obliterating conceit of autobiographical full disclosure reasserts itself, and the mask is quickly donned again, as the long autobiography comes to a halt with the news of the German invasion of Poland, and England's declaration of war on September 3, 1939. His life, he wrote two years later, had been transformed into a paradox—he still wrote and thought in the German language, but was committed with his whole being to the enemies of Germany who "stood in arms for the freedom of the world." That which he had feared more than his own death—the war of all against all—had been unleashed again, and he was left to wander, not only as a refugee but as a "war alien" through the streets of Bath, "to have a last look at peace." His world, he knew, was gone, never to be retrieved; "something new, a new world began, but how many hells, how many purgatories, had to be crossed before it could be reached?"[73]

The World of Yesterday ends with a paragraph meant, one supposes, to have been poignant, but which reads in retrospect merely as maudlin:

> The sun shone full and strong. Homeward bound I suddenly noticed before me my own shadow as I had seen the shadow of the other war behind the actual one. During all this time it has never budged from me, that irremovable shadow, it hovers over every thought of mine by day and by night; perhaps its dark outline lies on some pages of this book, too. But, after all, shadows themselves are born of light. And only he who has experienced dawn and dusk, war and peace, ascent and decline, only he has truly lived.[74]

The Viking edition ends with a "publisher's postscript," an anonymous addendum that repeats the certitude of the author of the introduction to the volume, Harry Zohn, that Zweig "did not write this book as a farewell message" on the strange grounds that it was "an old project to which he sometimes adverted in his happier days," and that he "undertook it with gusto during his last visit to the United States."[75] But whatever Zweig's intentions, *The World of Yesterday* does, perforce, serve as his extended, if deliberately obfuscated, farewell message to his readers and the world which defined his existence.

On February 23, 1942, in Petropolis, Brazil, as a good Austrian bour-

geois clad in a suit and tie, and with Lotte by his side and sharing in his
fate, Stefan Zweig took his own life, leaving behind a suicide note that
ended: "I think it better to conclude in good time and in erect bearing a
life in which intellectual labor meant the purest joy and personal freedom
the highest good on earth. I salute all my friends! May it be granted them
yet to see the dawn after the long night! I, too impatient, go on before."[76]
No instructions were left regarding the burial, and an unseemly dispute
arose between the Orthodox chief rabbi of Brazil and the mayor of Petropolis over whether the Zweigs would be buried in the Christian cemetery of that town or be transported to Rio to be buried in Jewishly conse-
crated ground. In the end, a compromise was reached: a Reform rabbi and
cantor officiated at the town cemetery, and Stefan and Lotte Zweig's
graves stand to this day, bedecked with Stars of David, in a Christian
graveyard in an obscure Brazilian town.[77]

5 / Autobiography as Farewell II

SARAH KOFMAN

Less than five months after the Zweigs' suicide—on July 16, 1942—12,884 Jews were rounded up in their beloved Paris by 9,000 Vichy French policemen, from lists carefully prepared in advance. Most of the deportees were first brought to the Velodrome d'Hiver, the large indoor sports arena in the fifteenth arrondissement, and then transported to Drancy, the notorious detention camp northeast of Paris from which approximately 70,000 Jews were ultimately sent to Auschwitz. Among those arrested on July 16 was Berek Kofman, a forty-two-year-old Polish Jew who was the rabbi of a small synagogue in the eighteenth arrondissement. Thirteen days later, on July 29, 1942, he was sent to Auschwitz in convoy number twelve, comprising 1,000 deportees, 270 men and 730 women, aged 36 to 54. He died in Auschwitz one year later.[1]

We know this from the "memorial" list of those deported, and from *Rue Ordener, Rue Labat*, the remarkable autobiography published by his daughter Sarah Kofman in Paris in 1994.[2] Sarah Kofman was an extraordinarily prolific philosopher at the Sorbonne who penned over twenty books on philosophers and philosophical problems from Socrates to Nietzsche and Freud. A fervent adherent of the post-structuralist and deconstructionist movements in post–World War II French thought, she became one of the most important and revered feminist and postmodern thinkers in France; the editor, along with Jacques Derrida, of a widely influential series of French philosophical and literary texts; and the subject of much acclaim in the English-speaking world as well.

I have chosen *Rue Ordener, Rue Labat* as the last text to study here not primarily because of its somewhat macabre juxtapositional possibilities with Zweig's autobiography, but because it stands out, in my mind, among the dozens of memoirs and autobiographies I have read, in English, Hebrew, Yiddish, German, and French, written by men and women who were children at the time of the Holocaust but who were themselves not subjected to the murderous brutality of the Nazis. This is so primarily because of its starkly beautiful prose, but also because it provides serious, but not insurmountable, theoretical challenges to the student of the genre today. For years before writing her autobiography, Kofman denied that such a feat was possible. In her first book, *L'enfance de l'art: Une interprétation de l'esthétique freudienne*, Kofman was highly critical of Freud's psychoanalytic reading of art and literature, but accepted as fact that Freud has proven that

> both the individual and the collective past are constituted phantasmally by an individual or a people, rather than recovered. . . . Analytic examination reveals that there is no guarantee of the accuracy of [all childhood memories]. Most are falsified, incomplete, or have undergone spatial or temporal displacement, but not because of faulty memory. The distortions are due to the intervention of a bias—powerful psychic forces shape and orient our way of evoking the past, just as they render our childhood years incomprehensible. One can only conclude therefore that "in the so-called earliest childhood memories we possess not a genuine memory-trace but a later revision of it . . . which acquires the significance of 'screen memory.'"[3]

Several years later, in speaking about her own psychoanalysis in an essay entitled "'*Ma vie*' et la psychanalyse,"—with "my life" tellingly italicized—she confessed that she wanted to write her autobiography but could not, since her life was literally indescribable.[4] And a few years after that, in an interview in *Le Monde,* she repeated the claim that she wanted to write her autobiography, but now added that she feared that she did not know who she was or whether she was nothing at all (*Je ne sais qui je suis, peut-être, ne suis-je rien*)[5], from which stemmed her need to identify with the authors she studied. Was there, she wondered, a "self" called "Sarah Kofman" whose story could be told, separable from her philosophical work?

I'm like [Hoffman's] cat, Murr, whose autobiography is no more than an assemblage of citations of diverse authors. . . . This "myself," isn't that an illusion? Isn't it an illusion to believe that I have any autobiography other than that which emerges from my bibliography?[6]

This was, of course, totally in line with much postmodern thought, but to me—and I hope by now, to readers of this book as well—Kofman's denial of the existence of her "self" and the possibility of its retelling in autobiographical form can also be read as merely the latest variation on the canonical demurral of interest in the self proclaimed by most autobiographers before they engage in their work.

At the very least, we must attend to the grammar of her denial of self, which was posed as a question, not a statement of fact—something not recognized in the scholarship on Kofman which takes such comments, as well as the facticity of every detail of her subsequent autobiography, as true—a paradoxical lack of critical reading on the part of adherents of the culture of deconstruction and its highly suspicious hermeneutic. And this same hagiographic approach marks the literature on several early autobiographical essays and on her book *Paroles suffoquées* (translated into English as *Smothered Words*), published in 1987,[7] in which she first spoke publicly about her father's death and the overarching problem of writing about the Holocaust. Before we come to *Rue Ordener, Rue Labat*, then, it is necessary to spend a bit of time on the earlier autobiographical pieces and on *Smothered Words*, which give us, bit by bit, a foretaste of the complex narrative that will ensue.

The first fragment, entitled "Sacrée nourriture" (translated into English as "Damned Food," thus losing the crucial playfulness of the French *sacré* which can, like the Hebrew *qadosh*, mean both "sacred" and "damned"), begins with a rather embittered version of the classic portrayal of the *yidishe mama* encouraging her child to eat:

Damned [or sacred] food! And twice damned [or sacred].

"You must eat," said my mother. And she stuffed and stuffed and stuffed us. Not a chance of being deprived of dessert with her.

"You must not eat everything," said my father. Not mix milk with meat, not eat just any meat; not eat off just any dish; not mix plates and silver-ware, *milchig* and *fleishig*; purify once a year at Passover; in case of an inadvertent mistake, etc.

My mother, the high priestess, officiated in the kitchen, where it was not rare to see a piece of salted beef dripping blood for hours, or a carp wriggling in a basin while my father, a rabbi and ritual slaughterer, killed chickens in the bathroom according to the law.

Was it fear of transgressing some taboo, or the consequence of being stuffed, that I had hardly any appetite, and resisted with all my might the maternal categorical imperative? To accomplish her goal, my mother would follow me to school with a bowl of cafe au lait, making the teacher the witness of my crime: "She didn't eat anything this morning!"

During the war things became complicated. How to find anything to eat? How to continue eating kosher?

During the exodus, in the train that took us to Brittany, the Red Cross distributed cocoa and ham and butter sandwiches. "Don't eat that," said my mother. "Let the children eat," my father intervened, "it's wartime." The ham and butter, once decreed impure, I found delicious, now purified by circumstances and paternal authority.

A few years later my father was deported.

We could no longer find anything to eat.[8]

This episode will not be included in *Rue Ordener, Rue Labat*, though its immensely complicated themes will resonate throughout that work: for now we see that her father's sacred authority, based on law, is paradoxically far more malleable than her mother's enforcement of that law, her "categorical imperative" based on coercion masquerading (as in Sarah Kofman's reading of Kant) as solicitude and love. To Kofman, desecrating that maternally interpreted paternal law was "delicious," though always tinged with disaster, and linked with possible, though always ultimately unbearable, surrogate mothering by Christian women. Thus, this fragment continues:

After countless turns of fortune I was "saved" just in time by a woman who kept me in her home in the middle of Paris until the end of the war.

At the same time that she taught me what it was "to have a Jewish nose," she put me on a totally different diet: the food of my childhood was decreed bad for my health, held responsible for my "lymphatic state." Very rare red meat (raw horsemeat in bouillon) was supposed to "restore my health." From then on it was my daily ration (until the day when we really no longer had anything to eat and had to go begging at the soup kitchen for a mess tin of macaroni or beans).

Put in a real double bind, I could no longer swallow anything and vomited after each meal.[9]

As we shall see, the motif of the young Sarah vomiting the food necessary for her sustenance but which she cannot bear to digest, will also be central to her autobiography, as will be her love for her deported father and hatred of her surviving but all so threatening mother. It is crucial even at this point to understand, without overstating its biographical basis, that this latter theme came to dominate Kofman's philosophical writings, especially her work on Freud. In her *L'énigme de la femme: La femme dans les textes du Freud*, first published in 1980, she claimed, inter alia, that his theory of women's penis envy was but a screen solution to men's—and Freud's own—incestuous desire for the mother leading to a deeply repressed matricidal fantasy. As the Kofman scholar Kelly Oliver well put it:

Kofman interprets Freud's interpretation of his dream of the Three Fates as his attempt to master the mother and thereby master death. By translating or sublimating the mother/death into his scientific discourse, Freud tries to claim as his own the lessons learned from his maternal pedagogy and thereby assume the position of master. The mother remains a silent image associated with natural bodily needs that are later sublimated through the intervention of paternal agency into socially accepted forms of communication and love. The relation with the maternal body is forbidden and dangerous. It is associated with a return to nature that threatens murder and death. To deny the maternal pedagogy, however, is to try to insist that one is born without a mother; it is to try to insist that one gives birth to oneself. To deny that the mother knows or teaches the lessons of science is to commit matricide. But, as Kofman asks, can the mother/death be sublimated?[10]

This question is posed again, if in a rather gruesome way, in Kofman's next autobiographical fragment, "Nightmare: At the Margins of Medieval Studies," published in 1983 as a review of/homage to the French medievalist Bernard Cerquiglini and his neo-Nietzschian anti-etymological study of Old French, *La parole médiévale: Discours, syntaxe, texte*.[11] Focusing on Cerquiglini's study of the lexeme *mar*, signifying misfortune, in its many permutations and combinations, including "margins," "marginality," and the "typically female *'mar fui'*—Woe is me!" leads Kofman to recounting and analyzing one of her dreams, or rather night-<u>mar</u>es/*cauche<u>mar</u>s*:

> Neither a linguist nor a medievalist, I would just like to underline the "profound" interest that "I" took in reading this book (which at first I read rather superficially) by reporting a dream here—an epic dream?—a dreadful night-*mar*. The particle *mar*, that segment of a vanished language, induced the return of an entire buried past, belonging to an entirely other age, to my dark ages: it reappeared in a text ruled by a singular code, an entirely personal syntax and grammar.
>
> *I am in a room from my childhood, with my mother, my brothers and sisters, at night. A bird enters, a kind of bat with a human head, pronouncing in a loud voice: "Woe unto you! Woe unto you."*
>
> *My mother and I, terrorized, run away. We are in tears in the rue Marcadet; we know we are in great danger and fear death.*
>
> *I awake very anxious.*[12]

Under the rubric "Context" Kofman then writes:

> I must take a plane on Tuesday [*mardi*]. An airplane strike forces me to delay my departure, to reserve a seat on a night flight. I am worried.
>
> Night flight—night bird—bird of misfortune. . . .
>
> I associate this with a sinister event from my childhood. In February 1943—almost 40 years ago—a Tuesday [*mardi*] perhaps, at 8 o'clock in the evening (the evil hour, *la mala hora*), a man from the *Kommandatur*—the bird of misfortune—comes to warn us, me and my mother (we are eating a vegetable soup in the kitchen) "to go hide as quickly as possible because we were on the list for that night"; my mother and her 6 children (my fa-

ther already having been "picked up" on the 16th of July 1942). My mother and I fled in all haste (my brothers and sisters were hidden in the country). We lived in the rue Ordener, and in order to get to the rue Labat, where there was a woman who generously took us in on the nights of round-ups, we took the long rue Marcadet. During this forced nocturnal walk, clenched in anxiety, I vomited my dinner onto the rue Marcadet.

For the rest of the war, we lived hidden in the rue Labat, marginally, "Woe is me!"[*Com mar fui*].[13]

Kofman then proceeds to an orthodox Freudian interpretation of this dream as wish fulfillment, reassurance before the new anxiety, her unconscious promising herself "You won't die this time any more than the last when you feared the worst." But her "personal dark ages" return in a postscript to this analysis, in which she claims that three months after having this nightmare, she learned that one of the privileged representations of Lilith in Jewish folklore is a bat, which leads her to discuss Mardewitch, another avatar of Lilith, which haunted her entire childhood:

When I was bad my mother locked me in a dark closet where "Mardewitchale" was supposed to come, if not to eat me, at least to take me far away from home: that was the threat. I imagined her to myself not as a bat, but as a very old woman. My unconscious possessed an "unofficial knowledge" that knew much more than the "official knowledge." The dreamwork was able to condense in one image the two terrifying figures of my childhood: the man from the *Kommandatur*, the bird of misfortune, and the old sorceress *Mardewitch*.[14]

We are therefore not entirely surprised to read, three years later, her interview in *Le Monde*, which begins with the statement:

I am not a mother. Nature bores me very quickly. I am an unconditional fan of culture. I love big cities, the cinema, painting, museums, and have a horror of the country. I do not feel close to nature. I have no desire for maternity. I am not a woman, if by that one means a being subjected to sentiment, in love with her body, allied with nature or *épannoui* in maternity.[15]

As if to conform with the Freudian script, Kofman then summoned "the intervention of paternal agency"—in her case, the story of her father, which was first broached, as already noted, in *Paroles suffoquées*, published in 1987, a year after the *Le Monde* interview. This highly impacted text was originally written for a volume planned in honor of Maurice Blanchot, the French philosopher and literary critic, and was dedicated to him; to Robert Antelme, the author of *The Human Race*, one of the earliest and most searing memoirs of imprisonment in a German camp in World War II, admired by Blanchot and analyzed at length by Kofman in this book; and in memory of her father. Kofman begins with four quotations from Blanchot which frame and define the central problem of the work as a whole: first, that the "fact of the concentration camps, the extermination of the Jews and the death camps . . . are for history an absolute which interrupted history; this one *must* say, without, however, being able to say anything else. Discourse cannot be developed from this point . . . "; second, the corollary that since we cannot truly "know" what happened at Auschwitz, we have to accept "not to know" in the face of the necessity to attempt to know and not to forget; third, that we must attend to the "immeasurable absence" that words cannot convey, but that defines everything that happened in the wake of the Holocaust, "Israel, all of us;" and finally, given the insufficiency of words, "how can thought be made the keeper of the holocaust where all was lost, including guardian thought?"[16]

Kofman then takes on seriatim each of these questions. She begins with a bold gesture:

> If, since Auschwitz, the categorical imperative has become the one which Adorno has formulated in the style of Kant, though ridding it of its abstract and ideal generality, "to arrange one's thoughts and actions so that Auschwitz will not repeat itself, so that nothing similar will happen," if, with Auschwitz, an absolute has been reached before which other rights and duties must be judged; if Auschwitz is neither a concept nor a pure name, but a name beyond naming (or in Lyotard's terms, a name which designates that which has no name in speculative thought, the name of the anonymous, the name of that which remains without result and without

profit for the speculative), it behooves me, as a Jewish woman intellectual who has survived the holocaust, to pay homage to Blanchot for the fragments on Auschwitz scattered throughout his texts; writing of the ashes, writing of the disaster which avoids the trap of complicity with speculative knowledge, and therefore complicit with the torturers of Auschwitz.[17]

While others have characteristically read this as a simple declarative paragraph expressing Kofman's innermost thoughts, I would like—to some degree emulating Kofman's own mode of subversive close reading—to stress the conditional nature of this opening: *if* Adorno, Lyotard, and Blanchot were correct about Auschwitz signaling a new post-Kantian categorical imperative, an "end to discourse," and the inevitable complicity of any speculative thinker with the Nazi torturers, then Kofman must pay homage to Blanchot. This, I suggest, is a fruitful way to read this text, since it brings out into the open two of the abiding, if here silent, paradoxes of Kofman's tribute to Blanchot. First, Kofman must have been responding in some way to the very public "affaire Blanchot" of the previous decade, in which Blanchot's own collaboration with right-wing French nationalists and to some extent with their anti-Semitism before, and even more dramatically, during the war, was exposed and debated[18]— a controversy, not unlike that surrounding Paul de Man, that may in some highly complex way be connected to Blanchot's claim of the unknowability of Auschwitz and the impossibility of either narrative or speculative writing thereafter: if anyone engaged in philosophical work after Auschwitz is in some way complicit with the Nazi torturers, does this not lessen, or at the least flatten out, the guilt of those who actually did collaborate? Which leads to the second paradox, that Kofman will continue to insist on the possibility, and indeed the necessity, of speculative writing after the Holocaust, if in a supposedly "non-complicit" manner.

What is not conditional in this opening paragraph, not preceded by an "if" clause, is Kofman's self-identification as a "Jewish woman intellectual who has survived the Holocaust"—a four-point definition that reminds us of Zweig's five-point "Austrian, Jew, author, humanist, pacifist." But then, citing Blanchot, Kofman rhetorically calls into question the very possibility of such designators, and especially that of Jew/non-Jew:

[Blanchot's texts] teach us (without making this the object of a lesson) to remember that which must henceforth constitute the ground of our memory; which teach us all, young or old, Jews or non-Jews, if this senseless breaking of the human race can, after Auschwitz, still make sense—a break desired by the anti-Semites and the Nazis so that the Jew would signify repulsion, the Other in all his horror, the abject man who must be kept at a distance, expelled, exiled, exterminated.[19]

Without quite saying so, Kofman seems to understand that to answer "no" to her (and Blanchot's) questions would be in some sense to accomplish that which the Nazis strove for: the extinction of the Jews. If, after the Holocaust, there can be no sense in preserving the "senseless" distinction between Jew and non-Jew, then there are two, and only two, options left: either the Jew melds into the non-Jew, or the non-Jew melds into the Jew. Kofman seems to advocate the second option, and, indeed, her second-to-last published work before her autobiography, and her last of a long series of books on Nietzsche, was *Le mépris des Juifs: Nietzsche, les Juifs, l'antisémitisme*, in which she argued not only that Nietzsche was not an anti-Semite, but that "Nietzsche must be read as a Jew"—positing (extremely problematically) that for him "the Jew who had become a great man—even more than the Renaissance man—could serve as a model for the 'Übermensch,'" that the true Sabbath, in whose advent Nietzsche takes delight, "will be a celebration not so much of the birth of a new Adam as a return of the Jew of the biblical age, of the Jew who, at the peak of his power, was able to create in his own image and in the likeness of his prophets and of Moses a majestic, omnipotent, choleric, and jealous God."[20]

Here, in *Smothered Words*, she takes a rather different tone:

What the Nazis could not tolerate, what they tried to commit to the invincible power of death, is that which no form of power can overcome, because it does not encounter it, that which is not measured in terms of power: the infinite distance which never ceases to reaffirm the relation with the infinite of which the Jew, for Blanchot (even if he is not only that), is the emblematic figure, he who has been able to preserve throughout his history the vocation of foreignness, of exile, of the outside.[21]

Here, again, the parenthetical is critical: "even if he is not only that" challenges head-on Blanchot's oft-stated and oft-cited identification of the Jew with the Other and Jewish monotheism with "the revelation of the word as the place in which men maintain a relation to that which excludes all relation: the infinitely Distant, the absolutely Foreign."[22] Not, once more, that Kofman rejects these definitions, but—consistent with her style of heterodox fidelity to Nietzsche and Freud—she restates them while stressing often insoluble questions in Blanchot's thought. She knows, but does not tell us, that the Jew is more than the consummate foreigner or outsider, the *autrui*; that there is specific content in Judaism and Jewish monotheism that challenges, if not refutes, Blanchot's highly problematic representation of them. But all this is left hanging in *Paroles suffoquées*, to be foregrounded in *Rue Ordener, Rue Labat*. For now, she continues to ponder Blanchot—first, his claim that humanity itself died in Auschwitz. She responds affirmatively: "Since Auschwitz all men, Jews [and] non-Jews die differently: they do not really die; they survive death, because what took place, death in Auschwitz, was worse than death."[23] Though the second part of this statement is entirely comprehensible, what can the first part possibly mean? How can death post-Auschwitz be survival of death? Again, Kofman does not answer this question, but instead summons head-on, for the first time in her oeuvre, the story of her father:

Because he was a Jew, my father died in Auschwitz: How can it not be said? And how can it be said? How can one speak of that before which all possibility of speech ceases? Of this event, my absolute, which communicates the absolute of history, and which is of interest only for this reason. . . . And how can one not speak of it, when the wish of all those who returned—and he did not return—has been to tell, to tell endlessly, as if only an "infinite conversation" could match the infinite privation?[24]

Here then, is her answer to Blanchot's first challenge: in order to continue to write speculatively after 1945 one must "speak without power." "To speak: it is necessary—*without power*: without allowing the language, too powerful, sovereign, to master the most aporetic situation, absolute powerlessness and very distress."[25] And indeed her disciples claim that after writing this, Kofman did change the style of her published philosophical work, to one which was less assertive, less authoritative/authoritarian. To Blanchot's call for attentiveness to the "immeasurable absence" that words cannot convey, she responds with the facts about her father's deportation, not only citing the evidence from Serge Klarsfeld's "Memorial" to the deported, but literally reproducing the page that includes her father's name, date, and place of birth, chilling columns of name after name, Jews from all parts of Europe and even from Palestine, who were swept up in the deportation of July 16. Kofman then notes how this list's "neutral voice . . . takes your breath away . . . leaves you without a voice, makes you doubt your common sense and all sense, makes you suffocate in silence."[26]

This leads to the next chapter, which begins with the Blanchot-like claim: "About Auschwitz and after Auschwitz no story is possible, if by a story one means: to tell a story of events which makes sense."[27] But again, as if to challenge, if not to subvert, that claim, she continues with a long analysis of Blanchot's pre-1939 story "The Idyll," which describes the persecution and murder of a stranger within a closed community, which leads back once more to her father:

> My father, a rabbi, was killed because he tried to observe the Sabbath in the death camps; buried alive with a shovel for having—or so the witnesses reported—refused to work on that day, in order to pray to God for them all, victims and executioners, reestablishing, in this situation of extreme powerlessness and violence, a relation beyond all power. And they could not bear that a Jew, that vermin, even in the camps, did not lose faith in God. As he did not lose faith in God on that afternoon of July 16, 1942, when a French policeman came to round him up with a pained smile on his lips, almost as if he, too, were excusing himself. Having gone to warn the Jews of the synagogue to go and hide because he knew there would be a raid, he had returned to the house to pray to God that he be taken, so long as his wife and his children were spared. And instead of hiding, he left with the policeman; so that we would not be taken in his place, as hostages, he suffered, like millions of others, the infinite of violence: death in Auschwitz.[28]

What Kofman does *not* say here, however, and which she only reveals in her later autobiography, is that her father was in fact not killed by the Nazis but by a Jewish *kapo*, a butcher in Paris before the war who returned to his butcher-shop after the war. "They" who could not tolerate that a Jew not lose faith in God in the death camps thus included a Jew. Again, one might say, the Jew and the non-Jew merge in highly unsettling ways. Why Kofman hid, or at the least did not include, this information here we cannot really know, but it seems safe to speculate that her autobiographical will was not yet sufficiently strong to disclose the terribly disruptive details of her father's death. And once more, her rhetorical point was otherwise:

> In this unnamable "place" he continued to observe Jewish monotheism, if by this, with Blanchot, we understand the revelation of the word as the place in which men maintain a relation to that which excludes all relation: the infinitely Distant, the absolutely Foreign. A relation with the infinite, which no form of power including that of the executioners of the camps, has been able to master, other than by denying it, burying it in a pit with a shovel, without ever having encountered it.[29]

Yet once more, the conditional "if": *if* we understand Jewish monotheism with Blanchot. But ought we not rather assume that Rabbi Kofman believed precisely the opposite, that his God was both immanent and intimate? Once more, these questions are not posed, much less answered, in *Paroles suffoquées*, whose second half turns to a discussion of Antelme's memoir, without returning overtly to Berel Kofman and the problem of the Jews, their faith, or their murder. More covertly, however, the rest of the book does present a response to the death of Rabbi Kofman and the other victims of the Nazis, and hence to Blanchot's last challenge, by proposing, through an analysis of one of his favorite texts, Antelme's *The Human Race*, a "new humanism" that supplants the old humanism of Western culture "dead and buried" at Auschwitz:

> The fierce affirmation of the unity of the species does not amount to the denial of differences, or indeed, oppositions. On the contrary, it is because no community is possible with the SS that there is also the strongest com-

munity, the community (of those) without community. It is not founded on any specific difference or on a shared essence—reason—but on a shared power to choose, to make incompatible through correlative choices, the power to kill *and* the power to respect and safeguard the incommensurable distance, the relation without relation. This community does not imply universal reconciliation: everyone laughing or crying together at the same things, in the illusory spirit of Christmas Day. . . .

"Man is the yet undetermined animal," says Nietzsche. Yes and no would say Antelme. No, if we must take this to mean that a transformation of the species is possible; yes, if this aphorism signifies that in man there is multiplicity of powers, none of which is ever sure to triumph. Among these powers is that of killing, of "forgetting" the Other. . . . And since these powers are not independent of specific historical or economic contexts, even if they cannot be reduced to them; since, even after Auschwitz, Auschwitz could still return—eternally—which is to say that power to kill could again take the upper hand, it is necessary, it is our duty, after Auschwitz, to continue, "to go on."[30]

Which Kofman does, to be sure, in the immensely productive years between *Paroles suffoquées* and *Rue Ordener, Rue Labat*. But the questions left unresolved in the former work apparently still tortured her, and around New Year's Day 1993, she began to write the autobiography she earlier claimed she could, literally, not write, and that would be her next-to-last work.

Rue Ordener, Rue Labat is a relatively short work—ninety-nine pages in the French original, divided into twenty-three sections ranging from two paragraphs to seven pages long. In the text of the autobiography proper, the individual chapters are signified only with numbers, but in the table of contents placed, in French custom, at the end of the book, they are given interesting and, at times, highly significant names (unfortunately omitted in the English translation.) As we shall see, it is not at all by chance that the longest section, number seven, called "Metamorphosis," comes precisely at the middle of the book—the pivot of the narrative. Since the canonical demurral of self, in its postmodern form, has already been given by Kofman in her earlier interview, the text here begins rather abruptly:

Of him, all I have left is the fountain pen. I took it one day from my mother's purse, where she kept it along with some other souvenirs of my father. It is a kind of pen no longer made, the kind you have to fill with ink. I used it all through school. It "failed" me before I could bring myself to give it up. I still have it, patched up with Scotch tape; it is right in front of me on my desk and makes me write, write.

Maybe all my books have been the detours required to bring me to write about "that."[31]

No one, to my knowledge, has read this opening in a Kofmanian manner, which undoubtedly would include pondering not only the veracity of the story itself, but what she would call its disruptive "sexual economy": the daughter surreptitiously steals the phallic, and grammatically masculine, "stylo" of her dead father from her mother, who has kept it among other tokens of her murdered husband's memory. We already know, from the autobiographical fragments, how tortuous and complex Sarah's relationship with her mother was (or, rather, has been represented to readers), and how crucial the more benign paternal authority. This pen, so obviously a totem of that authority, cannot be replaced by another, since it is (counterfactually?) of a kind that is made no more: it is this pen, and only this pen, that enabled her to study, but then failed her before she could abandon it—just like her father, we might propose, who failed her, in some ineffable way, by volunteering for deportation when she was but a child, before she could abandon him in the "normal" way, as a teenager or young adult. The maimed pen (circumcised phallus?) is preserved, "patched up" with Scotch tape, urging and indeed enabling her to write, but not, until now, to write about "that." Most commentators on this text have read that "that"—*ça*—as referring to the story of her father's deportation and death. But she had already broken that barrier in *Paroles suffoquées*, and I would propose—and will later demonstrate textually—that this *ça* refers rather to the even more difficult story that takes up by far the bulk of this autobiography: the push and pull over her and within her, between her real, Jewish mother, and the non-Jewish woman who saved them both.[32]

But we are not yet told this tale. Rather, the next section returns to the story of Rabbi Kofman's arrest and deportation, though this time without the mute documentary evidence provided seven years earlier, but with far more detail. Now we learn:

> On 16 July 1942, my father knew he was going to be picked up. It had been rumored that a big roundup was planned for that day. He was rabbi of a small synagogue on the Rue Duc in the 18th arrondissement. He had left home very early that day to warn as many Jews as he could to go into hiding immediately.
>
> Then he came home and waited: he was afraid that if he were to hide his wife and six young children would be taken in his place. He had three girls and three boys between two and twelve years old.
>
> He waited and prayed to God that they would come for him, as long as his wife and children could be saved.[33]

After rereading this opening several times, the reader is able to bracket the horror and realize that there is a gaping question left unposed, much less unanswered here: since her mother was subsequently able to hide herself and all her children, why couldn't Rabbi Kofman do the same? (The Vel d'Hiv roundup was not only of men or heads of households, or only of foreign-born Jews; it tragically included thousands of women and children.) Why was the only alternative his hiding alone? Could he have been more concerned about the members of his congregation than, it seems, his own life?

To begin to understand, we are led by his daughter into his study:

> In a corner of the room (my father's room, the biggest and nicest of the apartment, the best furnished, paneled, and papered, mysterious and invested with a sacred quality—for my father carried out all kinds of religious ceremonies there, marriages, divorces, circumcisions), I watched his every gesture, fascinated. The memory of the sacrifice of Isaac (whose depiction in an illustrated Bible, in which I learned Hebrew in early childhood, had often worried me) fluttered through my mind.[34]

This is, of course, a jarring and hardly random or benign biblical evocation, especially for a quasi-Freudian like Sarah Kofman. First, there are the unspoken Oedipal resonances of choosing a story about Abraham, Sarah's husband (sometimes, crucially, masked as her brother), and not only any story about Abraham but specifically the most Oedipally charged story of them all, the binding of Isaac. Here, though, it is the father who leads himself to the slaughter, and no angel of the Lord appears to spare him. To complicate matters even further, although we never learn the name of Mrs. Kofman, we soon learn that the Kofman's youngest child was indeed named Isaac. Then we learn that when the French policeman came to pick up Rabbi Kofman, Mrs. Kofman first lied that he wasn't home, at which point the cop was ready to leave, until the rabbi appeared, voluntarily, to his wife and children's mounting horror. Then his wife lies again, claiming that she was pregnant:

> My mother is lying! My brother had just turned two on 14 July. And she wasn't pregnant, as far as I knew! I couldn't be as certain on this point as on the first, but I felt very ill at ease. I didn't know yet what a "white lie" was (at that time they weren't taking fathers of children under two years old, so if the cop had believed my mother my father would have been saved), and I didn't understand very well what was happening: the idea that my mother could lie filled me with shame, and I said to myself, anxiously, that perhaps after all I was going to have another little brother.[35]

One wonders about the coincidence of this Isaac being born on Bastille Day and just two days older than the age that would have spared his father, and why the young Sarah is presented as worried that she would have another brother, rather than a sister. Moreover, the intertextual inversion of Abraham's lying, presenting Sarah as his sister rather than his wife, is hard to ignore. But to the older Sarah Kofman, her younger self is far more "shamed" by her mother's lies than by her father's curious passivity and self-destructive commitment to "truth." Is it too simplistic to link her subsequent skepticism about the objective neutrality of truth-claims to this episode—or rather, vice versa: that her subsequent skepticism about the objective neutrality of truth-claims shades, if not determines, the telling of this tale? In the event, her parents go off to the police station to establish the "truth," and their six children stand in the street, sobbing, wailing, like a Greek chorus, "knowing"—we are told retrospectively—that their father would never return.

In the next chapter we read that he never did return home, and that his only communication with them thereafter was a postcard from Drancy announcing his deportation eastward, written by someone else in French, rather than the Yiddish or Polish he used with his family, asking for cigarettes, and that his wife take good care of the baby. Here, once more, the inverted evocation of the Isaac story is striking: this Abraham, on his road to Moriah, a.k.a. Auschwitz, asks his wife only to take care of his Isaac, forgetting about his other children. But then this wife—the non-Sarah, we might say—loses, or deliberately fails to preserve, this single note, to the real Sarah's lasting chagrin:

> When my mother died, it wasn't possible to find that card, which I had reread so often and wanted to save. It was as if I had lost my father a second time. From then on nothing was left, not even that lone card that he hadn't even written.[36]

This is the only reference in the entire autobiography to her mother's death, related only to underscore Mrs. Kofman's cruelty in stealing her husband away from her daughter yet a second time. It is now that we are told the "whole story" of Berek Kofman's death:

> After the war the death certificate arrived from Auschwitz. Other deportees returned. One Yom Kippur, at the synagogue, one of them claims to have known my father at Auschwitz. According to him my father survived for a year. One day when he refused to work, a Jewish butcher-turned-kapo (on returning from the death camp, he reopened his shop on Rue des Rosiers) supposedly beat him to the ground with a pickax and buried him alive. It happened on Shabbat: my father, according to the story, said that he had been doing no harm, only beseeching God for all of them, victims and murderers alike.
>
> For that, my father along with so many others suffered this infinite violence: death at Auschwitz, the place where no eternal rest would or could ever be granted.[37]

Beyond the issue of whether or not it is credible that a rabbi at Auschwitz would pray to God on behalf of the Nazis, perhaps it is fortunate that, given the subsequent errors in this text recalling simple Jewish ceremonies (in the next chapter she refers to the Havdalah prayer on Saturday night as "kiddush," refers to Sukkot as "Shoukott,"[38] and, even more curiously, recalls only "seven plagues" at the Passover seder), it is unlikely that Sarah Kofman knew enough about Judaism and Jewish law to raise the issue of *pikuah nefesh*—the halachic requirement of violating a commandment in order to save one's life. Thus, if the earlier story about the ham-and-butter sandwich on the train was truthful, Rabbi Kofman's actions would have conformed to this requirement. According to Jewish law he was legally obligated to work on the Sabbath rather than be killed for not doing so. His self-sacrifice was, therefore, in a profound sense transgressive of his faith rather than demanded by it. This, once more, Sarah Kofman does not seem to have known, but in the next chapter she intertextually reveals acquaintance with a different central motif of Jewish lore:

> On Rosh Hashanah, which was also my birthday, we would listen to my father blow the shofar. My mother was very proud of him, insisting that he did it better than anyone else. He practiced at home, and I would see him take out the shofar and put it away again in the drawer of a wardrobe where he kept it next to his tallith, his tefilin, and the razor with which he slaughtered chickens according to the ritual.[39]

We then read what we already learned in "Damned Food," that in addition to his rabbinic duties, her father was also a *shohet*, a ritual slaughterer, who every Friday afternoon killed chickens in their bathroom for women waiting in the entryway to the Kofman home. Here, though, we are told that to the young Sarah this "mysterious" scene was alarming as a young child, not only because of the gore but more so because she "associated the shohet's razor with Abraham's knife, and the guttural sounds of the shofar with cries from the chickens' severed throats."[40] The unstated but enormously powerful symbolism is dizzying: the shofar, the ram's horn that replaces Isaac on the sacrificial altar, is here transposed with her father's slaughtering knife; the shofar's notes, meant to hearken redemption or at the very least to summon the most intimate connection between God and the Jews on the Days of Awe, in which life and death are inscribed in the heavenly accounts, resound instead with the cries of innocent chickens' severed throats, killed like her father, by a Jewish slaughterer, out of obeisance to Jewish law!

At this point, roughly a fifth of the way through the work, Berek Kofman all but drops out of his daughter's autobiography; we only hear a bit more about his background later in the narrative. By far the bulk of *Rue Ordener, Rue Labat*, then, is not concerned with Sarah Kofman's father or the Holocaust per se, but with the extraordinarily painful story of her and her mother's joint survival through the war years. But before we come to this central issue, we are stalled just a bit by an important intervening chapter, which describes the progressive worsening of the Kofman family's situation in Paris after the July roundups, though the chronology here is confused and confusing, since at one and the same time we are told that the children no longer dared to go to school, for fear of being picked up, and that at school young Sarah was called a dirty Jew by a schoolmate, and heard of the death of two of her former classmates—one who was deported in the Vel d'Hiv roundup, and one who was killed when her mother, unable to bear her husband's deportation, turned up the gas in the apartment during the night.

But the point of this short chapter is not these horrifying details but the heroism of Madame Fagnard, the head of the second year of the elementary program in which young Sarah was enrolled, who became her first surrogate mother: she took charge of the children during air raids, gave Sarah free piano lessons, brought toys to her home, gave her books for her birthday, took her and her sisters to the zoo, brought food to the elderly when rationing started, and served Sarah as much milk and cookies as she wanted, beyond her ration. But as always in this book (and, as already noted, in Kofman's oeuvre as a whole), mother figures are never quite so benign as they first appear:

> One day during my last year, I drank so much milk at recess that I vomited in the middle of class. I was put in a corner, on my knees. This incident was

all the more upsetting to me because my family had always forbidden me Christian genuflections, too Christian [*Je fus d'autant plus accablée de cet incident que dans ma famille on m'avait toujours interdit les génuflexions chrétiennes, trop chrétiennes*].[41]

The problematic syntax here alerts us to the fact that is the first indication of what we already read about earlier and will become an increasingly central motif in this text: the young Sarah vomits in response to acts of kindness towards her on the part of Christian surrogate mothers. What can be more maternal an image than feeding a child milk? As a Freud expert, however, Kofman well knew the relevant proof text:

> No one who has seen a baby sinking back satiated from the breast and falling asleep with flushed cheeks and a blissful smile can escape the reflection that this picture persists as a prototype of the expression of sexual satisfaction in later life. The need for repeating the sexual satisfaction now becomes detached from the need for taking nourishment—a separation which becomes inevitable when the teeth appear and food is no longer taken in only by sucking, but is also chewed up. The child does not make use of an extraneous body for his sucking, but prefers a part of his own skin because it is more convenient . . . because in this way he provides himself, as it were, with a second erotogenic zone . . . It may be assumed that those children do so in whom there is constitutional intensification of the erotogenic significance of the labial region. If that significance persists, these same children when they are grown up will become epicures in kissing, will be inclined to perverse kissing, or, if males, will have a powerful motive for drinking and smoking. If, however, repression ensues, they will feel disgust at food and will produce hysterical vomiting.[42]

Only later in the autobiography will Kofman reveal to us, if in a highly muted way, that her own hysterical vomiting was indeed coupled first with thumb-sucking and then with homosexual attraction to her surrogate Christian mothers. Never, though, will she overtly make the obvious Freudian next move, considering her vomiting "defensive regression" against positive Oedipal wishes. As one psychoanalyst recently put it, to the child and the unconscious, food is the paternal phallus, ingestion of which undoes castration and conceives the oedipal baby. . . . The expulsive act of vomiting desexualises the receptive wish, symbolically rejects and re-stores the ingested phallus-baby, sadistically punishes the thwarting object, and masochistically relieves the guilt evoked by the desire to castrate and possess the father[43]

—or, as Kofman's would argue, to kill the mother.

Whether any of this is "true" in the sense of scientifically explaining the etiology of anorexia or other eating disorders is, of course, not the point here. What is relevant is that Kofman was convinced of this mode of analysis. The narrative then continues with rather symbolically overde-termined intermediaries appearing to save the day—Jewish Communist women (thus neither Christians nor law-abiding Jews) who hide the Kof-man children in the countryside and give them, or at least, everyone but Sarah, fake Christian names; Sarah only takes on Madame Fagnard's sur-name as her alias. But for Sarah alone, both the hiding and the name-change are unsuccessful: she cannot stand being separated from her mother, and refuses to eat nonkosher food, especially pork:

> This refusal, whose pretext was obedience to my father's law, must also have
> served, without my being completely aware of it, as a means of returning to
> my mother. Indeed, my sister Rachel wrote to her that she would have to
> take me back, for my behavior threatened to make it obvious to everyone
> that we were Jews.[44]

She is then returned to Paris, first to Madame Fagnard's, but this is only a temporary haven for one night, and hence there is no vomiting.

At this point, chapter eight, Kofman finally begins to grapple with the "real danger: separation from my mother"[45]—which leads to remem-brances of two painful separations, at the ages of two-and-a-half and three-and-a-half. Curiously enough, the second story ends with the young Sarah's delight in seeing her father, rather than her mother: "The Gare du Nord: glued to the train window, I watch for my parents and at last catch sight of my father's smile. I am saved." And then, once more as if to conform to a predetermined Freudian script, "After this episode my character changed. I became irritable and whiny and sucked my thumb incessantly."[46]

Now, crucially, Kofman can move on to the central drama of the story, her being hidden by the woman she will come to call "mémé" (Granny),[47] though their relationship was hardly typical of grandmother and grandchild. Mémé is the last resort: Sarah is first sent to Picardy, where she cried and refused to eat, and came back to her mother after two days; to a family in the rue du Département, where she lasts one week; at the Claude-Bernard Hospital, for three days; in a home in the rue des Petits-Ménages, where once again, she refused to eat pork and begged for her mother to rescue her; in a shelter for Jewish children in the rue Lamarck, where she could have kosher food, but nonetheless vomited when she got there and was immediately removed by her mother—a "miracle," they both agreed, since the following night the Gestapo raided the shelter and deported all the children. At this point her mother "resolved to keep me with her from then on, no matter what happened. 'It' was not long in happening."[48]

In other words, the "it," the *ça* that all of Kofman's previous books have been detours required to bring her to write about, is clearly the story of her relationship with mémé, not that of her father's death. At this point, we read a far shortened, almost rushed, version of the warning to her and mother on that February night of 1943: it is only "a man" who arrives to give them the news, not a German from the *Kommandatur*. Finally, we meet mémé:

> Our most frequent haven was "the lady on the rue Labat." She had been my parents' neighbor when they lived on the Rue des Poissonniers. She had noticed my mother pushing the baby carriage in the street with "such beautiful little blond children," and always asked after our health. "Now there is a woman who loves children," my mother had said. "She wouldn't let us go without a roof over our heads." Leaving our vegetable broth unfinished, and not even quite realizing what the stranger had said, we set out for her house. One Métro stop separates Rue Ordener from rue Labat; between them, rue Marcadet. It seemed endless to me, and I vomited the whole way.[49]

The cause of the hysterical vomiting is retrospectively all too clear: "the lady" is home, caring for a sister with—what else—"stomach cancer"; she agrees to take them in, serves them Floating Island and "looks lovely in her peignoir—so gentle and affectionate that I almost forgot what had brought us to her house that evening."[50]

This safe house is then horrifically contrasted to the Kofman's flat. The next chapter abruptly begins: "There were seals on the door. They had indeed come. At midnight. Six men from the Gestapo: one for each child."[51] The Germans in their anger smash the furniture, destroy everything. "Never again, except in dreams, have I ever gone back."[52] Mother and daughter return to the rue Labat; "the lady" agrees to keep them, until a solution is found. She proposes that Sarah be hidden in a nearby monastery, which would require that she be baptized, a conversion that could (ostensibly) be annulled after the war. Somehow, "the lady" convinces Rebbetzin Kofman to agree to this, and the three of them appear one fine morning at the Institut Notre Dame de Sion: "The 'lady' had just lost her sister and was in deep mourning. She was dressed in black and I was struck by her blond hair and the soft melancholy in her blue eyes."[53] The two older women go off to confer with the priest, and Sarah is overcome with a strange malaise, vaguely sensing that something more was at stake than separation from her mother. The door is open. She flees, tells the métro ticket-taker "I've lost my mother," and runs back to the rue Labat: "The lady decided to keep me."[54]

Now we come to the crucial chapter twelve, the "Metamorphosis." We learn that the apartment is tiny, only three rooms: Mrs. Kofman is given the nicest room, Sarah sleeps on a sofa in the dining room, adjoining the bedroom of the woman who now "asked me to call her mémé, while she christened me Suzanne because that was the saint's name closest to hers (Claire) on the calendar."[55] But, in fact, whether Kofman knew it or not, St. Claire and St. Suzanne share the *same* date on the Roman Catholic saints' calendar: August 11; did Kofman, with her delight in Nietzschian paronomasia, ever ponder that *mémé* is ever so close to *même*?

The question of Sarah's selfhood and her relationship to her two mothers soon pivots, of course, on food. At first, Mrs. Kofman goes out to find kosher food for her and her daughter, risking her life at every turn, but:

Very soon, mémé declared that the food of my childhood was unhealthy; I was pale, "lymphatic," I must change my diet. From then on it was she who would take care of me. Besides, my mother could scarcely ever go out, and I could not do without fresh air. Children were rarely asked for their papers; I could pass for her daughter.[56]

This increasingly intimate relationship was only interrupted for mémé's weekly sexual trysts with a male friend who came over to have dinner and spend the night. Sarah was conscripted into setting the scene for the dinner, setting the table with the best tablecloth and the nicest flatware, and was then sent off to her mother's room for the evening. As can well be imagined, her mother

> found this state of affairs harder and harder to tolerate; she considered it to be unhealthy but of course could say nothing. It was especially hard for her to endure mémé's tenderness toward me; she thought it excessive. She knew very well that woman adored children (she was indeed keeping another little girl during the daytime—Jeanine, of whom I quickly grew jealous) and that she also took in stray cats to feet and pet, but still! Why did she kiss me so often? In the morning, at bedtime, on the slightest pretext! And to be sure, at home we had never gone in for ritual morning or bedtime kisses or such a lot of hugging and commotion.[57]

The sexualization of their relationship is intense, if gingerly depicted: until this time Sarah's hair was cut short, "like a boy's," by her mother; mémé let her grow her hair out long, made two little coils on the top of her head and brought her a pretty black velvet ribbon. She then revamped Sarah's wardrobe, making her clothes to order and teaching her how to sew. And then, of course, the food issue reasserts itself, now focused on the issue—not surprisingly—of the feminine symbol of blood:

> Rare meat had always been forbidden. On the Rue Ordener my mother let pieces of salted beef drip in the kitchen for hours and then boiled them; on the Rue Labat, I had to "restore my health" by eating raw horsemeat in broth. I had to eat pork and "acquire a taste" for food cooked in lard.[58]

The reader can now predict the result—"I vomited frequently"—if not the consequence—"mémé would get angry." Even though mémé was an excellent cook, Sarah's body rejected "this foreign diet that was so unfamiliar to me and so unwelcome." For her part, mémé was fixated on food and on digestive problems—"she could detect the tiniest quiver of discontent from her 'tube' or mine." She kept a medical dictionary on the dining-room table, and Sarah was "especially impressed by the pictures of Siamese twins."[59] In the next paragraph, we hear that unlike the all-too-Jewish Mrs. Kofman, mémé never showed any sign of panic when Sarah was sick. When Sarah has her tonsils removed in a clinic, both women are there: when she cries out in pain her mother "proceeds to talk very loudly, sympathizing with me in Yiddish"; we can all but hear the malediction "vey iz mir." But mémé remains calm, assuring Sarah that she'll get ice to suck on: "Immediately I stop crying. On that day I feel vaguely that I am detaching myself from my mother and become more and more attached to the other woman."[60]

One is tempted to believe that Kofman is here challenging the reader to extend the Kofmanian "sexual economy" analysis further, in a way that begins to feel parodic: the indigestability of the (homosexually charged) nonkosher food is now frozen by the ice she sucks on; she becomes attached to mémé, and the vomiting ceases; the hysteria is cured by the successful ingestion of the prohibited.

This is the "metamorphosis" of which the chapter title speaks ("erased," as Kofman and her disciples would say, in the English translation), and the chiasmatic descent into the second half of the autobiography begins. Presently we learn only, not surprisingly, that on Mother's Day she buys mémé a nicer present than her real mother; that as a schoolgirl she won a prize on that day given by Marshal Pétain, who was restoring "work, family, and fatherland" to their place of honor; and, in a paragraph much cited in the literature on Kofman,

Knowingly or not, mémé had brought off a tour de force: right under my mother's nose, she had managed to detach me from her. And also from Judaism. She had saved us, but was not without anti-Semitic prejudices.

She taught me that I had a Jewish nose and made me feel the little bump that was the sign of it. She also said, "Jewish food is bad for the health; the Jews crucified our savior, Jesus Christ; they are all stingy and love only money; they are very intelligent, no other people has as many geniuses in music and philosophy." Then she'd cite Spinoza, Bergson, Einstein, Marx. It is from her lips and in that context that I first heard those names, which are so familiar to me today.[61]

Tellingly not Freud, whose abiding, yet so disruptive, influence is yet once more intertextually hinted at: mémé punishes her not by locking her in a closet with threats of Mardewitch, as her mother did, but by withdrawing her affection, directing it to Jeanine, and inducing all-but-expressed homosexual jealousy, here deliberately conflated with sibling rivalry over maternal love. Sarah's response is yet again entirely predictable: sucking her thumb, refusing to eat. She entirely conforms to mémé's wishes, and is even allowed to join her and her male lover at dinner, thus ceasing the final connection with her abandoned mother in the next room.

Soon, Sarah even adopts mémé's family as her own—at their gatherings, she claims, she first discovers what "a family and family spirit" meant. This chilling renunciation of her own large biological family evokes the only recollection of her father in the second half of the book: his whole family died in the Warsaw ghetto, including nine brothers and sisters. One brother had moved to Yugoslavia before the war, where he married a non-Jewish woman and was thus rejected by all his relatives, save Rabbi Kofman, who lived with him for two years, it seems, before immigrating to France. But the uncle is nonetheless shot by the Nazis, and in response, yet again, the non-Jew merges with the Jewish in Kofman's vision: her non-Jewish aunt converts to Judaism in response to her husband's murder, and moves to Israel, where she and her children found a collective settlement.

But this recollection of her father leads immediately to the most overtly sexual scene in the book: after a visit to mémé's family they get back to Paris late, miss the last métro, and mémé decides to spend the night in a hotel:

I was relieved and at the same time, without knowing why, extremely worried.

Mémé got undressed behind a big mahogany screen, and I, curious, watched from the bed to catch sight of her when she emerged. Back on the Rue Labat, to the amazement and irritation of my mother, she routinely walked around the apartment in pajamas, her chest uncovered, and I was fascinated by her bare breasts.

I have no memory of that night in the hotel, save of that undressing scene behind the mahogany screen.

The next day we took the first métro. My mother was waiting, sick with worry, certain we'd been arrested and obviously unable to inquire at the police station.

I had completely forgotten her. I was simply happy.[62]

This scene dictates the title of the chapter in French—"Paravent" (Screen)—and once more it is as if Kofman is here playing with her readers, daring us to contest this "screen memory," both literally and metaphorically, with the obvious Freudian proof text, which Kofman cited in her first book and in which Freud came closest to the notion held by neuroscientists in our day about the nature of episodic memory as a whole:

It may indeed be questioned whether we have any memories at all *from* our childhood: memories *relating to* our childhood may be all that we possess. Our childhood memories show us our earliest years not as they were but as they appeared at the later periods when the memories were aroused. In these periods of arousal, the childhood memories did not, as people are accustomed to say, *emerge;* they were *formed* at that time. And a number of motives, with no concern for historical accuracy, had a part in forming them, as well as in the selection of the memories themselves.[63]

Kofman's claim of forgetting everything that happened after mémé emerged from that screen is, therefore, incredible, in both senses of that term; and no one to my knowledge has pointed out that the quasi-orgasmic ending engages in a sort of Schadenfreude in regard to her mother that we have not yet encountered in this autobiography. Not surprisingly, then, the next chapter links Sarah's happiness with mémé, her mother's suffering in silence with no word from Rabbi Kofman, and no means of visiting her brothers and sisters in the countryside (which, we recall, the mature Kofman told us in the *Le Monde* interview, she detests—hating, we might deduce, the safety of the countryside as opposed to the dangers of the city!). It is precisely at this point, Kofman now tells us, that she buried her "entire past"—not, as in the nightmare analyzed years before, when she and her mother fled their home, not when her father was picked up, but when she found happiness, sexual and digestive, with mémé:

> My mother . . . had no power to prevent mémé from transforming me, detaching me from herself and from Judaism. I had, it seemed, buried the entire past: I started loving rare steaks, cooked in butter and parsley. I didn't think at all any more about my father, and I couldn't pronounce a single word in Yiddish despite the fact that I could still understand the language of my childhood perfectly.[64]

Perhaps this is why, in this autobiography, virtually every Hebrew/Yiddish word is mistranscribed? But this paragraph ends with the most shocking confession in the book as a whole: "Now I even dreaded the end of the war."[65] And indeed, when liberation comes, and her mother quite naturally sought to restore her family, reclaiming her children from their various hiding places, a battle begins between her and mémé over Sarah. Mémé used the "pretext," as Kofman calls it, that Mrs. Kofman had more than enough to handle with five other children and wasn't looking after Sarah's best interests. Her mother retorted that mémé simply wanted to steal her daughter, and felt nothing other than contempt and hatred for the "woman who'd saved our lives." "It tore me in two. Overnight I had to take leave of the woman I now loved more than my own mother."[66]

Incredibly, she now has to share a bed with her mother, and she uses the oldest trick in her repertoire to return to mémé: she refuses to eat! Of course, her mother relents, allowing her one hour a day with her beloved, but beating her with a strap if she was even one minute late. The Schadenfreude now turns to hatred: "Strangely enough, she had thought to bring that strap with her the day we escaped" from their family home in the rue

Labat. "I was soon covered with bruises and began[!] to detest my mother."[67] She escapes to mémé, but the law requires that she return to her mother, who therefore brings a lawsuit against mémé:

> The hearing took place before an improvised Free French tribunal in the playground of a school. Mémé was accused of having tried to "take advantage" of me and of having mistreated my mother. I didn't understand the expression "take advantage" but I was convinced that my mother was lying.[68]

We, of course, know that this time—unlike the last time, when her lies could have saved her husband's life!—she was telling the truth. But, Kofman continues,

> I was outraged to see her falsely accuse the woman to whom we owed our lives and whom I loved so much! I in turn accused my mother, showing the court my thighs covered with bruises, and I succeeded in making everyone feel sorry for me. The Jewish friend who had taken us in and who had heard the worst imaginable stories about what had happened on the Rue Labat was herself scandalized and promptly switched sides. She confirmed that my mother beat me with a strap.
> The Free French tribunal decided to entrust me to mémé.[69]

But Sarah is not free, not liberated by this victory. As she left with mémé her stomach was in a knot; she was afraid, peering around the street as if she had committed a crime, "as if once again I were 'wanted.'"[70] Her mother wanting her back is thus equated with the Nazis "wanting" her: Returning to her mother, to Judaism, (to heterosexuality?) is thus not very subtly equated with death, to being killed because she was Jewish, to "the senseless breaking of the human race" into Jewish and non-Jewish queried in *Paroles suffoquées*. But her mother would not heed the verdict of a law foreign to her very being, however "free" the tribunal; on the fifth floor of the building in the rue Labat, she waits with two men, who violently tear Sarah from her Gentile protectress and carry her out the door. Her mother screams at her in Yiddish "I am your mother! I am your mother!" and Sarah writes, decades later, "I struggled, cried, sobbed. Deep down, I was relieved."[71]

At precisely this point, the narrative is interrupted with two chapters that appear to have nothing to do with Kofman's story per se: The first is an analysis of Leonardo da Vinci's painting of the Virgin Mary, St. Anne, and child; the second, of Alfred Hitchcock's film *The Lady Vanishes*. In fact, however, both these chapters are highly convoluted citations (or, as we shall see, under-citations) from previous Kofman books, and we are thus forced to return to these texts in order to ponder the precise relationship between her bibliography and her autobiography.

Unlike the page marking her father's deportation in *Paroles suffoquées*, the Leonardo image is not here reproduced: Kofman merely informs us that she chose it, or rather the extant London cartoon version of it, for the cover of her first book, *The Childhood of Art*: "Two women, the Virgin and Sainte Anne, each with the same 'blissful smile,' bend side by side over the infant Jesus, who is playing with St. John the Baptist."[72] She then cites Freud's interpretation of the painting: The maternal figure that is further away from the boy, the grandmother, corresponds to Leonardo's "true mother" from whom he was taken away at an early age, and the mother represents his younger stepmother, who raised him as well. Freud believed that Leonardo used the blissful smile on St. Anne's face "to disavow and to cloak the envy which the unfortunate woman felt when she was forced to give up her son to her better-born rival, as she had once given up his father as well."[73] The implication seems to be that the St. Anne figure corresponds to Mrs. Kofman, who was forced to give up her husband to the Gentiles, and then her daughter to the better-born, and Gentile, mémé/Virgin Mary, and that the smile on the former's face is a disavowal of the envy which Mrs. Kofman felt at losing her daughter to her rival.

Had this chapter come earlier in the narrative, this may have been a convincing interpretation. But it does not in the least relate to, much less explain, Sarah's feeling "relief" at being returned to her real mother. To decode this further, then, we must return to Sarah Kofman's first book, *L'enfance de l'art*, in which she carefully examined the rest of Freud's interpretation of the Leonardo painting. Freud had speculated that the London cartoon, which had St. Anne and the Virgin Mary fusing together to the extent that it is difficult to discern the contours of each, predated the Louvre version of this painting, in which they are separated. The latter was therefore a "counterinvestment" of the former's meaning: Leonardo's anxiety about his homoerotic fantasy of St. Anne and the Virgin Mary "fusing together" had made him want to conceal it. Thus, Freud argued, Leonardo went from a painful childhood memory, essentially "phantasmal" in character, to adult memory constituted through his art. This process eventually allowed him to triumph over his own unrealized homosexual desires, but only in his art; there, his repression was lifted, but it remained potent in his persistent disguising of his homosexuality in real life.[74]

It is virtually impossible to believe that by summoning this analysis at precisely this point (again, where she expresses relief at being returned to her mother) Kofman was not challenging us to read her "life" through this citation, especially since, only a few pages earlier in *L'enfance de l'art*, she had cited Freud's view of screen memories, which I have cited above in part, but which continued:

> The displacement affected by screen memory can be carried out in two different temporal directions. The screen memory may belong to the earliest years of childhood, while the repressed memory it represents is part of a later period, which is instance of retrogressive displacement (*ruckgreifende oder rucklangige*). Or, as is more frequently the case, the displacement works in the other direction, so that an indifferent repression belonging to a later period functions as a screen memory for the repressed memory. The latter is an anticipatory screen memory, one that has been *displaced forward* (*vorgreifende oder vorgeschoben*). The key memory is behind the screen memory. . . . Generally speaking, screen memories function as counterinvestments intended to maintain repression.[75]

The textual linking of "counterinvestment" rather clinches the point: Kofman seems to be intimating that there is a "key memory" behind the screen memory just recounted; that the recollection of feeling relief over being returned to her mother is but a "counterinvestment intended to maintain repression"; that like Leonardo, she can partially overcome that repression—of homosexuality—through art, that is, through autobiographical narrative, but not in real life. Or, more subversively, is she suggesting that the entire story we have just been told, the fight between the two women, the childhood memory of the screen incident—that all of these are simply fantasies formed in the present state of arousal caused by writing her autobiography, "and a number of motives, with no concern for historical accuracy, had a part in forming them, as well as in the selection of the memories themselves?" In other words, that in fact she had no life separable from her bibliography?

A clue to resolving this tension lies in the next chapter of *Rue Ordener, Rue Labat*, which is a reprint of the beginning of the last chapter of her last book before the autobiography, *L'imposture de la beauté*.[76] Thus we go from the first item in her bibliography to her last. In the part actually cited here, Kofman repeats the claim that Hitchcock's *The Lady Vanishes* is one of her favorite films, and each time she sees it she is "seized with the same visceral anguish" when the nice little old lady, Miss Froy, vanishes; the most "intolerable" part for her is to perceive, all of a sudden, instead of the good maternal face of the old lady, the face of her replacement, a horribly hard, shifty face, and instead of the good lady's sweet smile, the menacing and false smile of her replacement: "the bad breast in place of the good, the one utterly separate from the other, the one changing into the other."[77] It is very difficult to discern which of these figures is meant to represent Mrs. Kofman, and which mémé, since the one changes into the other too dizzyingly. Here the citation stops in the autobiography. In *L'imposture de la beauté*, on the other hand, the analysis just begins: Miss Froy, Kofman elaborates, is not really as "good" and as maternal as we first thought. It turns out she is a spy, if for a good cause—which Kofman interprets, along with others, as anti-Nazism—and has lied about her identity. Her beautiful image is to some extent contaminated, and her position as protector of her daughter is lost, taken over by the latter (whom Kofman calls a "young girl" though in the film she is clearly an adult), who saves her from the evil ones. Thus, to Kofman this film is not a mere spy story but an "initiation ritual" into maternal ambivalence —i.e., ambivalence about one's mother. From Truffaut's study of the film she has learned that the source of the story is a legend set in Paris in 1889: a woman and her daughter arrive in Paris, check into a

hotel, and the mother falls sick in the hotel bed. The doctor arrives, ex-
amines the woman, confers with the owner of the hotel, and then sends
the daughter off to another part of Paris to get needed medications.
When she returns, four hours later, and asks the owner how her mother
is, he responds, "which mother?" and when she is taken to their former
room, she discovers that it has different furniture and different wallpaper.
For Kofman, who of course has just told the story of her relief at being
removed from the clutches of the woman who presumably seduced her
in a hotel room in Paris, and back into the arms of her despised mother,
the agony of the spectator is a repetition of "profound archaic agony," the
paranoid anguish of the infant who, in Melanie Klein's famous scheme,
unconsciously "splits" his or her mother into the good mother and the
bad mother in order to repress hatred of the real, beloved mother. Thus,
Kofman suggests, Iris, the young heroine of the film, is not so innocent as
it first appears: the spectator begins to suspect that Iris feels guilty about
the disappearance of the old woman, and therefore out of guilt represents
her as totally pure and good, as opposed to her replacement (and the
other travelers on the train) who are seen by her as sinister. But earlier in
the film we have been led to view Iris negatively, as a spoiled rich brat,
who bribes the previous hotel manager to get rid of the male clarinetist,
who soon becomes her accomplice in finding the old woman on the
train. To Kofman, the clarinetist represents the brother in the mother-
daughter-son triangle that soon emerges; Iris is thus both duplicitous
and ultimately incestuous. In this way, Kofman argues, the film as a whole
can be read as the incarnation of the heroine's fantasies, caused by her
paranoid anguish and her unconscious guilt. Or, on the contrary, as pure
illusion: The old woman is hidden in the trunk of an illusionist, and
thereby Hitchcock may be revealing himself as the ultimate illusionist.
He disproves any reductionist, psychoanalytic reading that takes the film
too seriously; the true force of the illusion, and the psychic pain that it
evokes, lies in the reaction of the spectator, on whose unconscious the
film has such a powerful effect. Indeed, Kofman says, watching it several
times evoked in her an identification with the heroine and hence her own
most archaic agonies, "apparently surmounted a long time earlier." But,
in the end, she concedes, the tale has cathartic power: it permits the

agony to be relieved through recognition that this is but a film, and through the laughter that ensues.[78]

What results from these long and admittedly rather obscure digressions is that Kofman seems to be signaling to the reader that her own memories of her childhood are, in fact, unstable, and highly influenced by the context of their retroactive summoning: writing an autobiography. By definition, we cannot trust the veracity of these memories, for like all childhood memories, they are but screen memories, "counterinvestments" of the key memories that she cannot summon—not even, we suppose, through her own psychoanalysis. Her own recorded memories, then, must have been displaced in her writings, which, like Leonardo's art, or for that matter, Hitchcock's, succeed only in hiding the truth: her matricidal fantasies and consequent homosexual desires. Thus, to what extent the story of her mother and mémé is factually "true" we cannot ever know. All we can know for certain about her life is her bibliography, which she claims constitutes her true self, but which now necessarily and only seemingly paradoxically includes this autobiography! Thus, the "paranoid anguish" at the core of her being, her own doubly complex matricidal fantasies, are partially resolved through her art.

The rest of *Rue Ordener, Rue Labat* is therefore a rather thin denouement: While living with her mother (and again sleeping in one bed.) she continues surreptitiously to visit mémé; then, her mother has to leave Paris to rescue her other children, and (hard to believe.) entrusts Sarah back to mémé. Now, the (still unstated) lesbian relationship flourishes, and Sarah is happy, until her mother demands her return once more. Now Sarah visits mémé only with the protection of one of her sisters. To protect her further, her mother places Sarah in a Jewish scouting home outside of Paris where she returns to Judaism and seems to forget about mémé, and forges close ties with yet another older women. In the face of her mother's disapproval, she becomes a scholar, entering the Ecole Normale Supérieure, where, for the first time, she has a room of her own. By this point, mémé has moved to the seashore, and Sarah visits her, but soon cuts off all contact with her, since she can't stand to hear her talk about the past, or to hear her calling her "little bunny."[79] When she does visit her, she always brings a friend.

The book ends:

> She died recently, in a hospice in Les Sables. Seriously disabled, half blind, she couldn't do anything anymore except listen to "great music." On the telephone she'd hum to me various Beethoven melodies she'd heard. I was unable to attend her funeral. But I know that at her grave the priest recalled how she had saved a little Jewish girl during the war.[80]

Or, we might add, how she both saved and condemned to misery a little Jewish girl during the war.

On October 15, 1994, just a few months after the appearance of her autobiography, Sarah Kofman committed suicide.[81] She was sixty years old. Her bibliography was complete.

Conclusion

In *Rue Ordener, Rue Labat* Sarah Kofman demonstrated, perhaps to her own profound dismay, that she had a singular gift to do two things she held to be philosophically impossible: first, to articulate a highly idiosyncratic "selfhood"; and secondly, to do so in a narrative form she believed to be untenable after Auschwitz. Both these claims were, as I hope this study documents and demonstrates, incorrect. However fashionable and oft repeated, the notion that autobiographical narrative, philosophical analysis, or poetry were impossible "after Auschwitz" was never philosophically serious, and—although this argument may not seem directly relevant to the bulk of this book—I firmly believe that the counter-Enlightenment analysis upon which it is based has served to mute, rather than advance, our ability to understand the horrors of the Holocaust, just as the overarching Heideggerrian thesis behind it has served vastly to distort our collective understanding of, and indebtedness to, the values whose destruction, rather than reification, led to Auschwitz.[1]

Be that far larger argument as it may, I do not think it credible to maintain that Sarah Kofman, as well as Josephus Flavius, Asher of Reichshofen, Glikl of Hameln, Moshe Leib Lilienblum, Osip Mandelstam, or Stefan Zweig failed to present to us, through their autobiographies, a keen sense of their selfhoods, even as those can and must be distinguished from the facts of their life-stories. As I hope I have demonstrated, although we can no longer read these autobiographies, or any others, as veridical depictions of their authors' lives and times, these texts can still yield great profit to the historian, illuminating not only the search for selfhood in discrete historical contexts, but the culturally specific and thus highly historically informative and repercussive articulations of the quest for self-fashioning in changing temporal, geographical, and ideational contexts.[2] Indeed, I hope that my argument demonstrates, contrary to many postmodernist claims, that a conceptually and contextually rigorous analysis of autobiographical texts can yield insights into historical processes that lie "outside the text," clearly demarcating the boundaries between the fictive and the historical domains and the ongoing validity of the historian's quest for truth.

For reasons which I laid bare in the introduction to this book, I do not for a moment believe that the problems we encountered in reading and analyzing the particular texts we have studied here are in any sense unique to the Jews, or to something called "Jewish autobiography." Whether written in Greek, Hebrew, Yiddish, Russian, German, or French, or any other language, the dynamics of writing about one's self are, I believe, essentially the same, even as the cultural contours and rhetorical contexts of doing so are infinitely variable. In a profound sense, I hope not so much to have "reclaimed" Mandelstam, Zweig, and Kofman for "Jewish history" but to have demonstrated, as I have tried to do in all my other books, that the all but canonical boundary between Jewish and a presumptive "general" history is a fictive artifact that obscures sound historical analysis.

In the end, I hope that this small volume adds an important dimension to the ongoing debate about the boundaries between history and memory that have so concerned historians and theorists for the last several decades, and that was so productively initiated in regard to Jewish history by Yosef Yerushalmi in 1982, in his famous book in this series.[3] As Andreas Huyssen has recently put it, after so much "intense public and academic discussions of the uses and abuses of memory, many feel that the topic has been exhausted. Memory fatigue has set in."[4] I hope that shifting the analysis from collective memory to individual memories—and hence from one presumed Jewish history and collective memory to many Jewish histories and memories—serves to sharpen our understanding of this so complex and fascinating issue. The basic lesson of this volume is that from all that we have collectively learned from literary theory and the neuroscience of memory about human beings' all too fragile recollection of their pasts and its transmission through language and narrative, we—

as historians or quite simply as readers—can no longer read autobiographies as factual first-person accounts. And yet, at the same time, we can continue to read with great profit, as well as much pleasure, such fascinating and engaging autobiographies as Josephus's *Vita,* Asher of Reichshofen's *Sefer zikhronot,* Glikl's *Zikhroynes,* Lilienblum's *Hatot neurim,* Mandelstam's *Shum vremeni,* Zweig's *Die Welt von Gestern,* and Kofman's *Rue Ordener, Rue Labat,* so long as we do so with the recognition, or perhaps the painful self-confession, that if we ourselves were to sit down to tell the stories of our own lives, we would necessarily not tell the truth, the whole truth, and nothing but the truth, but a highly selective account that historians of later generations would be well advised to treat skeptically.

NOTES

ABBREVIATIONS

SZ   *Sefer zikhronot* (Levy)

KO   *Ketavim otobiografiim* (Lilienblum)

NT   *The Noise of Time* (Mandelstam)

RORL   *Rue Ordener, Rue Labat* (Kofman)

SS   *Sobranie sochinenii* (Mandelstam)

SW   *Smothered Words* (Kofman)

WY   *The World of Yesterday* (Zweig)

INTRODUCTION

1. Roy Pascal, *Design and Truth in Autobiography* (Cambridge, Mass.: Harvard University Press, 1960), 69.

2. Ibid., 63–64.

3. James Olney, *Memory and Narrative: The Weave of Life-Writing* (Chicago: University of Chicago Press, 1998), xv.

4. Edward Said, "Presidential Address 1999: Humanism and Heroism," *Publications of the Modern Language Association of America* 115, no. 3 (May 2000): 285–91.

5. Shmuel Werses, "Darkhei ha-otobiografiah be-tequfat ha-haskalah," *Gilyonot* 4 (1945): 175–83.

6. Alan Mintz, *Banished from Their Father's Table: Loss of Faith and Hebrew Autobiography* (Bloomington: Indiana University Press, 1989).

7. Marcus Moseley, "Jewish Autobiography in Eastern Europe: The Pre-history of a Literary Genre" (Ph.D. diss., Oxford University, 1990).

8. Mark R. Cohen, ed., *The Autobiography of a Seventeenth-Century Venetian Rabbi: Leon Modena's Life of Judah* (Princeton, N.J.: Princeton University Press,

1988); Jacob J. Schacter, "History and Memory of Self: The Autobiography of Rabbi Jacob Emden," *Jewish History and Jewish Memory: Essays in Honor of Yosef Hayim Yerushalmi* (Hanover, N.H.: University Press of New England, 1998), 428–52; Elisheva Carlebach, *Divided Souls: Converts from Judaism in Germany, 1500–1750* (New Haven, Conn.: Yale University Press, 2001); David Ruderman, *A Valley of Vision: The Heavenly Journey of Abraham ben Hananiah Yagel* (Philadelphia: University of Pennsylvania Press, 1990).

9. Natalie Zemon Davis, *Women on the Margins: Three Seventeenth-Century Lives* (Cambridge, Mass.: Harvard University Press, 1995).

10. Mintz, *Loss of Faith*, 7, 206.

11. Jacob J. Schacter, *Jewish Memory*, 428–29.

12. Israel Yuval, "A German-Jewish Autobiography of the Fourteenth Century," *Binah* 3 (1994): 79–99; originally published as "Otobiografiah ashkenazit me-hameah ha-arbah-esreh," *Tarbiz* 55 (1986): 541–66. I am grateful to David Assaf for bringing this article to my attention.

13. Georges Gusdorf, cited in Moseley, "Jewish Autobiography," 51–52.

14. Salman Rushdie, *Step Across this Line* (New York: Random House, 2002), 178; see also the new edition of the *Baburnama*, trans. Wheeler Thackston (New York: Modern Library, 2002).

15. Stephen Greenblatt, *Renaissance Self-fashioning: From More to Shakespeare* (Chicago: University of Chicago Press, 1980), 9, 256.

16. David Gross, *Lost Time: On Remembering and Forgetting in Late Modern Culture* (Amherst: University of Massachusetts, 2000), 31–33.

17. Isaac Rosenfeld, *The Invention of Memory: A New View of the Brain* (New York: Basic Books, 1988), 158.

18. See Larry R. Squire and Eric R. Kandel, *Memory: From Mind to Molecules* (New York: Scientific American Library, 1998), 77.

19. Fredric Bartlett, *Remembering: A Study in Experimental and Social Psychology* (Cambridge: Cambridge University Press, 1964), 213.

20. See Squire and Kandel, *Memory*; Eric Kandel et al., *Principles of Neural Science*, 4th ed. (New York: McGraw-Hill, Health Professions Division, 2000), 1227–46; Michael Gazzaniga, *The New Cognitive Neurosciences*, 2nd ed. (Cambridge, Mass.: MIT Press, 2000), 727–842.

21. Daniel L. Schacter, *The Cognitive Neuropsychology of False Memories* (Hove, U.K.: Philadelphia Psychology Press Ltd., 1999); Daniel L. Schacter and Elaine

Scarry, eds., *Memory, Brain, and Belief* (Cambridge, Mass.: Harvard University Press, 2000); and, most recently, Daniel L. Schacter, *The Seven Sins of Memory: How the Mind Forgets and Remembers* (Boston: Houghton Mifflin, 2001).

22. See, most importantly, the U.S. Department of Justice's *Eyewitness Evidence: A Guide for Law Enforcement* (October 1999) that fundamentally rethinks the use of eyewitness evidence in criminal proceedings.

23. A. S. Byatt, *The Biographer's Tale* (New York: Vintage International, 2000), 248.

1 / JOSEPHUS'S LIFE

1. Louis Feldman, "Hail Caesar! How the Romans Saved Jewish Civilization," *Forward*, April 12, 2002.

2. Shaye J. D. Cohen, *Josephus in Galilee and Rome: His Vita and Development as a Historian* (Leiden: Brill, 1979), 101.

3. Uriel Rappaport, "Where was Josephus Lying—in his Life or in the War?" in Fausto Parente and Joseph Sievers, eds., *Josephus and the History of the Greco-Roman Period: Essays in Memory of Morton Smith* (Leiden: Brill, 1994), 279–89.

4. Josephus, *The Life*, trans. Joseph Thackeray (Cambridge, Mass.: Harvard University Press, 1926), 3.

5. Cohen, *Josephus in Galilee and Rome*, 107–8, n. 33.

6. Josephus, *Life*, 5–7.

7. Cohen, *Josephus in Galilee and Rome*, 107.

8. Seth Schwartz, *Josephus and Judaean Politics* (Leiden and New York: Brill, 1990), 23, 209.

9. Ibid.

10. Gohei Hata, "Imagining Some Dark Periods in Josephus' Life," in Parente and Sievers, *Essays*, 309–28.

11. Per Bilde, *Flavius Josephus, between Jerusalem and Rome: His Life, His Works and Their Importance* (Sheffield, England: JSOT Press, 1988), 108–9.

12. Schwartz, *Josephus and Judaean Politics*, 6.

13. Steve Mason, "An Essay in Character: The Aim and Audience of Josephus's Life" (unpublished paper); I am grateful to Professor Mason for sending me an early copy of this study, and to Shaye Cohen for making this connection.

14. Cicero, *Tusculan Disputations*, trans. J. E. King (Cambridge, Mass.: Harvard University Press, 1927), vol. 2, xviii, 43.

15. Josephus, *Life*, 7–9.

16. Ibid., 37–39.

17. Ibid., 53–55.

18. Ibid., 55–57.

19. Ibid., 63–67.

20. Ibid., 153–55.

2 / IN THE CULTURE OF THE RABBIS

1. See John Van Engen, "The Christian Middle Ages as an Historiographical Problem," *The American Historical Review* 91 (June 1986): 519–52.

2. Peter Brown, *The Cult of the Saints: Its Rise and Function in Latin Christianity* (Chicago: University of Chicago Press, 1981), 21–22.

3. Stephen Greenblatt, *Renaissance Self-fashioning: From More to Shakespeare* (Chicago: University of Chicago Press, 1980), 1-2.

4. See Daniel Carpi's edition of *Sefer Haye Yehudah* (Tel Aviv: Tel-Aviv University, 1985).

5. See Dorothy Bilik, "The Memoirs of Glikl of Hameln: The Archeology of the Text," *Yiddish* 8 (1991): 5–22. Bilik repeats an earlier suggestion that it was Alfred Feichenfeld, the translator of the memoirs into German, who first used the "pompous" term "Denkwurdigkeiten" rather than the more appropriate "Memoiren" used by David Kaufmann in his original publication of Glikl's text. But, in fact, Kaufmann himself used "Denkwurdigkeiten" throughout his introduction to refer to this text. And as we shall see, Bilik's repetition of the claim that Glikl was a "simple woman" is highly debatable.

6. See Samuel Landauer, *Katalog der hebräischen, arabischen, persischen und türkischen Handschriften der Kaiserlichen Universitäts- und Landesbibliothek zu Strassburg* (Strassburg: Truebner, 1881), 65–66.

7. *Die Memoiren des Ascher Levy aus Reichshofen im Elsass, 1598-1635*, ed. and trans. M. Ginsburger (Berlin: Lamm, 1913); hereafter cited as *SZ*, for the original Hebrew *Sefer zikhronot*.

8. I have been able to find only one scholarly analysis of Ha-levi's text, a short

and rather dismissive discussion in Marcus Moseley's brilliant, if idiosyncratic and still unpublished, doctoral dissertation.

9. *SZ,* "Vorwort," 5 (German). Henceforth, all page numbers will refer to the original Hebrew text.

10. Desiderus Erasmus, *Colloquia,* ed. Craig Thompson, (Toronto: University of Toronto Press, 1997), vol. 39, 143.

11. *SZ,* 3.

12. Ibid., 37.

13. Ibid., 32.

14. Ibid., 32–33.

15. Ibid., 40. There is, of course, an ongoing tradition of reciting a special prayer, the *tefillah zaqah,* to avoid sins, including nocturnal emissions, on Yom Kippur.

16. Ibid., 41.

17. Ibid., 44.

18. David Kaufmann, ed., *Die Memoiren der Glückel von Hameln, 1645–1719* (Frankfurt a/M: Kaufmann, 1896).

19. See the excellent new article by Chava Turniansky, "Glikls Werke und die zeitgenössige jiddische Literatur," in Monika Richarz, ed., *Die Hamburger Kauffrau Glikl: Jüdische Existenz in der Frühen Neuzeit.* (Hamburg: Christians Verlag, 2001) 68–90. This volume contains interesting material on various aspects of Glikl's context, but never addresses the assumption of the veracity of Glikl's account.

20. Marvin Lowenthal, ed. and trans., *The Memoirs of Gluckel of Hameln* (1932; reprint, New York: Schocken Books, 1977).

21. Beth-Zion Abrahams, trans., *The Life of Gluckel of Hameln, 1646–1724, Written by Herself* (New York: Yoseloff, 1963).

22. This matter would require a long and detailed review essay not possible here. Suffice it to say that the *only* source Natalie Zemon Davis (1995) cites for the claim that Glikl "argued with God" (the title of the study itself!) is the passage describing the last moments of her first husband's life, when she asked him if she could hold him despite the fact that she was ritually unclean—that is, she had had her period and had not yet gone to the mikveh. He responds, "God forbid, my child. It will not be long until you go to the bath," to which she replies, according to Davis, "But, alas, he did not live till then." From which Davis concludes that "we should not underestimate the range" of her arguments with God, and "the cost to

her of the constraints of ritual purity." In fact, however, there is no "alas" here. Glikl writes: "velkhes er bav'r nit erlebt." The acronym here stands for the Yiddish/Hebrew *be-avonoseynu ha-rabim*—"because of our many sins"—and is standard usage for Glikl, and any other traditional Jew, prefacing any description of a tragic event. There is absolutely no cause to read into this formulaic phrase any dissent whatsoever from God's will, or the laws of menstrual purity.

23. Chava Turniansky, "Vegn di literatur-mekoyrim in Glikl Hamels zikhroynes," in Ezra Mendelsohn et al., eds., *Ke-minhag Ashkenaz u-Folin: Sefer yovel le-Hone Shmeruk: Kovets mehkarim be-tarbut yehudit* (Jerusalem: Merkaz Zalman Shazar le-Toldot Yisra'el, 1993), 153–77.

24. Shmuel Rozhanski, ed., *Zikhroynes,* trans. Yosef Bernfeld (Buenos Aires: Yivo, 1967).

25. Israela Klayman-Cohen, *Die hebräische Komponente im Westjiddischen am Beispiel der Memoiren der Glückel von Hameln* (Hamburg: Buske, 1994).

26. See Günther Marwedel, "Glückel von Hameln und ihre Familie in der Steuerkontenbüchern der aschkenasischen Gemeinde Altona," in Peter Freimark et al., eds., *Judentore, Kuggel, Steuerkonten: Untersuchungen zur Geschichte der deutschen Juden, vornehmlich in Hamburger Raum* (Hamburg: Hans Christians Verlag, 1983), 73–74.

27. Kaufmann, *Memoiren,* 1.

28. Ibid., 4.

29. *Zikhronot Glikl* (Tel Aviv: Devir, 1929).

30. Kaufmann, *Memoiren,* 1.

31. Ibid., 2–3.

32. On this, see M. Ginsburger (the same as the M. Ginsburger who published the Asher Ha-levi manuscript!), "Samuel Lévy, rabbin et financier," *Revue des études juives* 65 (1913): 274–300; 66 (1913): 111–33, 263–84; 67 (1914): 82–117, 262–87; and 68 (1914): 84–109.

33. Kaufmann, *Memoiren,* 298–99.

34. Ibid., 300.

35. See Gunter Marwedel, "Probleme der Chronologie in Glikls Memoiren," in Richarz, *Hamburger Kauffrau Glikl,* 123–33.

36. See, for example, D. Simonson, "Eine confrontation zwischen Glückel Hameln's Memoiren und den alten Hamburger Grabbüchern," *Monatsschrift für Geschichte und Wissenschaft des Judentums* 49 (1905): 96–106.

37. Marwedel, cited in note 26 above.

38. Ibid.

39. Kaufmann, *Memoiren*, 76–77.

40. See note 2 above.

3 / TWO RUSSIAN JEWS

1. *Hatot neurim* was first published in Vienna in 1876, and reprinted in *Kol kitvei Moshe Leib Lilienblum* (Cracow/Odessa: n.p., 1910–13), vol. 2, 201–410. *Derekh teshuvah* was first published in Warsaw in 1899, and was not included in the collected works just cited. Here I will cite the latest edition of these texts, edited by Shlomo Breiman and published as *Ketavim otobiografiim* (Jerusalem: Mosad Bialik, 1970); hereafter cited as *KO*, followed by volume and page number.

2. The first edition was published as Osip Mandelstam, *Shum vremeni* (Leningrad: Vremia, 1925); a fuller version of the text was then published in *Egipet-skaia marka* (Leningrad: Priboi, 1928). My citations (hereafter cited under the abbreviation *SS*), will be from the authoritative Russian edition, O. E. Mandel'shtam, *Sobranie sochinenii*, ed. G. P. Struve and B. A. Filippov (Moscow: Terra, 1991).

3. *KO*, 1: 81; 2: 126–41.

4. I owe this observation to Marcus Moseley.

5. See introduction, note 8.

6. Moseley, "Jewish Autobiography," 75–79.

7. M. A. Gunzburg, *Aviezer* (Vilna: Fuenn, 1863).

8. See Moseley, "Jewish Autobiography," 447–62.

9. *Oxford English Dictionary* (Oxford: Oxford University Press, 1989), item 00188918.

10. Julius Carlebach, "Family Structure and the Position of Jewish Women," in Werner Mosse et al., eds., *Revolution and Evolution: 1848 in German-Jewish History* (Tubingen: Mohr, 1981), 157–88.

11. David Biale, "Eros and Enlightenment: Love against Marriage in the East European Jewish Enlightenment," *Polin* 1 (1986): 49–67.

12. Yosef Klausner, *Historiah shel ha-sifrut ha-ivrit ha-hadashah* (Jerusalem: Ahiasaf, 1953), vol. 4, 237–38.

13. Alan Mintz, *Banished from Their Father's Table: Loss of Faith and Hebrew Autobiography* (Bloomington: Indiana University Press, 1989), 29–54; Ben-Ami

Feingold, "Ha-otobiografiah ke-sifrut: Iyun be-'Hatot neurim' le-M. L. Lilien-blum," *Mehkarei yerushalayim be-sifrut ivrit* 4 (1984): 86–111.

14. A. Druyanov, "Mi-'sefer-ha-zikhronot' shel M. L. Lilienblum," *Reshumot* 2 (1927): 390–405.

15. *KO,* 2: 153.

16. Ibid.

17. Druyanov, "M. L. Lilienblum," 403.

18. Ibid., 391.

19. M. Vinchevsky, "Lilienblum ve-yahaso le-sozialiyut," *Luah aviever* 2 (1921): 292–300.

20. *KO,* 1: 131–32.

21. *KO,* 1: 134.

22. *KO,* 2: 61.

23. Druyanov, "M. L. Lilienblum," 397–98.

24. *KO,* 2: 180.

25. *KO,* 2: 188.

26. *KO,* 2: 188–89.

27. Roy Pascal, *Design and Truth in Autobiography* (Cambridge, Mass.: Harvard University Press, 1960), 11.

28. Osip Mandelstam, *The Noise of Time,* ed. and trans. Clarence Brown (New York: Penguin, 1965); hereafter cited as *NT.* In my translations I will generally follow Brown's, with occasional changes of my own.

29. Ibid., 33.

30. Cited in ibid.

31. *NT,* 109; *SS,* 99.

32. Charles Isenberg, *Substantial Proofs of Being: Osip Mandelstam's Literary Prose* (Columbus: Slavica, 1987), 54.

33. Jane Gary Harris, *Osip Mandelstam* (Boston: Twayne, 1988), 51.

34. *NT,* 113; *SS,* 103.

35. Cited in Omry Ronen, "Osip Mandelshtam, 1891–1938," in *European Writers,* ed. George Stade (New York: Scribners, 1983–91), vol. 10, 1623.

36. Nadezhda Mandelstam, *Hope against Hope* (New York: Penguin, 1980), 289–91.

37. See the advertisements on the back cover of the first edition of *Shum vremeni.*

38. See Ronen, "Osip Mandelshtam," 1624.

39. Clare Cavanagh, *Osip Mandelstam and the Modernist Creation of Tradition* (Princeton, N.J.: Princeton University Press, 1995), 295.

40. Ronen, "Osip Mandelshtam," 1632.

41. *NT*, 69; *SS*, 45.

42. Clarence Brown in *NT*, 232 n. 1.

43. *NT*, 69; *SS*, 45.

44. *NT*, 70–71; *SS*, 47–48.

45. Nadezhda Mandelstam, *Hope Abandoned* (New York: Atheneum, 1974), 513.

46. Ibid.

47. Ronen, "Osip Mandelshtam," 1620.

48. Evgeny Mandelstam, "Excerpts from Memoirs," *Glas: New Russian Writing* 5 (1993): 149–50. For the Zagare/Zhagory tax lists, see the "All Lithuania Revision List Database" at www.jewishgen.org.

49. *Evreiskaia entsiklopediia* (St. Petersburg: Brockhaus-Efron, n.d.), vol. 7, 535.

50. See my article "The Tsarist Mishneh Torah: A Study in the Cultural Politics of the Russian Haskalah," *Proceedings of the American Academy for Jewish Research* 50 (1983): 165–83.

51. See *Evreiskaia entsiklopediia*, vol. 10, 591.

52. *NT*, 85–86; *SS*, 67–68.

53. Ibid.

54. For the best version of this thesis, see Cavanagh, *Osip Mandelstam*, 295.

55. *NT*, 85; *SS*, 67.

56. Clarence Brown, *Mandelstam* (Cambridge: Cambridge University Press, 1973), 13–14.

57. *NT*, 85; *SS*, 67.

58. Evgeny Mandelstam, "Excerpts from Memoirs," 150.

59. *NT*, 81; *SS*, 61.

60. *NT*, 84–85; *SS*, 66–67.

61. Nadezhda Mandelstam, *Hope Against Hope*, 210.

62. See my *Zionism and the Fin-de-Siècle* (Berkeley: University of California Press, 2001), 123–25.

63. The invitation is reproduced in O. Mandel'shtam, *Sobranie sochinenii v chetyrekh tomakh* (Moscow: Art-Biznes-Tsentr, 1997), vol. 4, 472.

64. Evgeny Mandelstam, "Excerpts from Memoirs," 151.

65. Ibid., 156.

66. Ibid., 170.

67. Ibid., 152–53.

68. Nadezhda Mandelstam, *Hope Abandoned*, 210.

69. Clarence Brown, *NT,* 16.

70. See the conversion certificate reproduced in O. Mandel'shtam, *Sobranie,* vol. 4, 478.

71. Evgeny Mandelstam, "Excerpts from Memoirs," 172.

72. I follow here the translation in Clarence Brown, *NT,* 35; the original letter is reproduced in O. Mandel'shtam, *Sobranie,* vol. 4, 11–12.

73. See Nadezhda Mandelstam, *Hope Abandoned,* 27.

74. Among the studies of this subject see Patrick Kegel, "Ethnicity and Culture in the Poetry and Prose of Osip Mandelstam," (Ph.D. diss., Indiana University, 1994); Holt Meyer, "Das Übersetzen des 'chaos iudejskij' in Osip Mandel'stam's 'Rauschen der Zeit,'" *Juden und Judentum in Literatur und Film des slavischen Sprachraums* (Wiesbaden: Harrassowitz, 1999), 193–226.

75. See Cavanagh, *Osip Mandelstam,* passim.

76. *Encyclopedia Judaica* (Keter), vol. 11, 867.

77. Nikita Struve, "Khristianskoe mirovozzrenie Mandel'shtama," in Robin Aizlewood and Diana Myers, eds., *Stoletie Mandel'shtama* (Tenafly, N.J.: Ermitazh, 1994), 244.

78. Ibid.

79. Robert Alter, "Mandelstam's Witness," *Commentary* 57 (1964): 76.

80. *NT,* 73–74; *SS,* 50–52.

81. *NT,* 74; *SS,* 52.

82. *NT,* 74–75; *SS,* 52–53.

83. *NT,* 76–77; *SS,* 55.

84. Nadezhda Mandelstam, *Hope Abandoned,* 232.

85. *NT,* 77; *SS,* 56.

86. Ibid.

87. *NT,* 78; *SS,* 57.

88. Ibid.

89. Heinrich Graetz, *Istoriia evreev ot drevnieishikh vremen do nastoiashchago,* 2 vols. (Odessa: Sherman, 1900–1905).

90. *Sobranie,* vol. 3, 151.

91. "Fourth Prose," in *NT,* 186.

92. "Ia nastaivaiu na tom, chto pisatel'stvo v tom vide, kak ono slozhilos' v Evrope, i v osobennosti v Rossii, nesovmestimo s pochetnym zvaniem iudeia, kotorym ia gorzhus'," *Sobranie,* vol. 3, 175.

93. Kiril Taranovsky, "The Black-Yellow Light," in Kiril Taranovsky, *Essays on Mandel'stam* (Cambridge, Mass.: Harvard University Press, 1976), 48–67.

94. *Sobranie,* vol. 1, 123–34.

95. *NT,* 78; *SS,* 57–58.

96. *NT,* 82; *SS,* 62.

97. *NT,* 82–83; *SS,* 63.

98. *NT,* 83; *SS,* 65.

99. *NT,* 83–84; *SS,* 65.

100. *NT,* 84; *SS,* 65. Why Brown uses the highly obscure "philo-progeneity" for "chadoliubivye" is not clear to me, despite its being the first entry in the Russian-English dictionary issued by the *Great Soviet Encyclopedia.*

101. Ibid.

102. Franz Kafka, *Letter to His Father* (New York: Schocken, 1953), 77.

103. *NT,* 84; *SS,* 65.

104. *NT,* 106–7; *SS,* 95.

105. *NT,* 99; *SS,* 86.

106. *NT,* 101; *SS,* 89.

107. Peter Maggs, *The Mandelstam and "Der Nister" Files: An Introduction to Stalin-era Prison and Labor Camp Records* (Armonk, N.Y.: M. E. Sharpe, 1996), M/2 and M/3.

4 / AUTOBIOGRAPHY AS FAREWELL I

1. Stefan Zweig, *Die Welt von Gestern: Erinnerungen eines Europäers* (Stockholm: Bermann-Fischer, 1942).

2. Stefan Zweig, *The World of Yesterday* (New York: Viking, 1943; republished by University of Nebraska Press, 1964); hereafter cited as *WY.*

3. Irwin Erdman, "World Not Without End," *New Republic* 109 (May 3, 1943): 600–601.

4. Hannah Arendt, "Portait of a Period," in *The Jew as Pariah* (New York: Random House, 1986), 112.

5. Ibid., 113.

6. Ibid., 121.

7. Ibid., 114.

8. Ibid., 115–16.

9. See Ulrich Weinzierl, ed., *Stefan Zweig: Triumph und Tragic* (Frankfurt a/M: Fischer, 1991).

10. Donald Prater, *European of Yesterday: A Biography of Stefan Zweig* (Oxford: Oxford University Press, 1972).

11. Leon Botstein, "Stefan Zweig and the Illusion of the Jewish European," in Marion Sonnenfeld, ed., *Stefan Zweig: The World of Yesterday's Humanist Today* (Albany: SUNY Press, 1983), 82–110.

12. Mark Gelber, "Sholem Asch, Joseph Leftwich, and Stefan Zweig's *Der begrabene Leuchter*," in Mark Gelber, ed., *Identity and Ethos: A Festschrift for Sol Liptzin* (New York: Peter Lang, 1986), 101.

13. *WY*, xvii.

14. *WY*, xxii.

15. See his *Begegnungen mit Menschen, Buchern, Stadten* (Vienna: Reichner, 1937).

16. Prater, *European of Yesterday*, 301–2.

17. Friderike Zweig, *Stefan Zweig* (New York: Thomas Crowell, 1946), 253–54.

18. *WY*, xxii–xxiii.

19. Prater, *European of Yesterday*, 71.

20. Ibid., 79.

21. *WY*, 5.

22. *WY*, 6.

23. Leo Spitzer, "Into the Bourgeoisie: A Study of the Family of Stefan Zweig and Jewish Social Mobility," in Sonnenfeld, *Stefan Zweig*, 70–74.

24. *WY*, 8.

25. *WY*, 9.

26. Friderike Zweig, *Stefan Zweig*, 2–3.

27. *WY*, 9.

28. *WY*, 9–10.

29. See Spitzer, "Into the Bourgeoisie."

30. Friderike Zweig, *Stefan Zweig*, 4–7.

31. *WY*, 11.

32. *WY*, 22.

33. *WY*, 24, 63.

34. *WY*, 98.

35. Stefan Zweig, "'Konig der Juden': The Man of Letters and the Man of Action," in Meyer Weisgal, ed., *Theodor Herzl: A Memorial* (New York: Zionist Organization of America, 1929), 55–57.

36. Theodor Herzl, *Briefe, 1903–Juli 1904* (Frankfurt a/M: Propylaen, 1996), 440.

37. *WY*, 101.

38. *WY*, 106.

39. *WY*, 106–7.

40. Stefan Zweig, "Konig der Juden," 56–57.

41. Mark Gelber, "Stefan Zweig und die Judenfrage von Heute," in Mark Gelber, ed., *Stefan Zweig Heute* (New York: Lang, 1987), 165.

42. Gelber, "Stefan Zweig und die Judenfrage," 166.

43. *WY*, 117. Apart from the studies already cited, see Gelber's "Stefan Zweig auf Hebräisch," in Sigrid Schmid-Bortenschlager et al., eds., *Stefan Zweig Lebt: Akten des 2. Internationalen Stefan Zweig Kongresses in Salzburg 1998* (Stuttgart: Hans-Dieter Heinz, 1999), 121–30; "Stefan Zweig und E. M. Lilien: Aspekte der Begegnung von jüdischen Ost und West um die Jahrhundertwende," *Austriaca* 34 (1992): 17–31; "Stefan Zweigs verspätete Bekehrung zum Judentum?" *Bulletin des Leo Baecks Instituts* 63 (1982): 3–11; "Karl Emil Franzos, Achad Ha-am und Stefan Zweig," in ibid., 37–49; and two studies by Jeffrey B. Berlin: "Unveröffentliche Briefe über Stefan Zweigs USA-Reise im Jahre 1935 und sein Projekt einer jüdischen Zeitschrift," in *Stefan Zweig Lebt*, 59–82; and "The Unpublished Correspondence between Albert Einstein and Stefan Zweig," in Amy Colin et al., eds., *Brücken über dem Abgrund* (Munich: Fink, 1994), 337–63.

44. Knut Beck et al., eds., *Stefan Zweig Briefe, 1914–1919* (Frankfurt a/M: Fischer, 1995), 19. The phrase "absolut keine nationale Sendung enthalten ist" is underscored in the original.

45. Stefan Zweig, *E. M. Lilien* (Berlin: n.p., 1903), 21. On this matter, see my

Zionism and the Fin-de-Siècle (Berkeley: University of California Press, 2001), 98–115.

46. Letter to Georg Busse-Palma, Beck et al., *Briefe*, 68.

47. *WY*, 109.

48. *WY*, 231–33.

49. Beck et al., *Briefe*, 106–8; I follow here the translation in Nahum Glatzer et al., eds., *The Letters of Martin Buber: A Life of Dialogue* (New York: Schocken Books, 1991), 187–88.

50. Letter of January 24, 1917, Beck et al., *Briefe*, 130–32; Glatzer et al., *Letters of Martin Buber*, 202–4.

51. Letter of May 25, 1917, Beck et al., *Briefe*, 142–244; Glatzer et al., *Letters of Martin Buber*, 217–18.

52. *WY*, 253.

53. Beck et al., *Briefe*, 202–3; Glatzer et al., *Letters of Martin Buber*, 228.

54. Glatzer et al., *Letters of Martin Buber*, 229–30.

55. Gelber insistently portrays Zweig as a cultural Zionist throughout this period, confusing support of the projects of the cultural Zionists, such as the Hebrew University, with their ideology itself. Thus, the speech Zweig wrote in support of the University, cited by Gelber in *Stefan Zweig Heute*, was entirely typical of other non-Zionists' words and positions at this time.

56. Stanislawski, *Zionism and the Fin-de-Siècle*, 6–9.

57. *WY*, 316–17.

58. *WY*, 325.

59. *WY*, 364.

60. *WY*, 364–65.

61. Joseph Leftwich, "Stefan Zweig and the World of Yesterday," *Yearbook of the Leo Baeck Institute* 3 (1958): 92–93.

62. Stefan Zweig, "Their Souls a Mass of Wounds: An Address on the Jewish Children in Germany" (Reprint, New York: German Relief Fund of the Joint Distribution Committee, 1934), 2–3.

63. Ibid., 5.

64. Ibid., 5–7.

65. Ibid., 7.

66. Ibid., 8.

67. Leftwich, "Stefan Zweig," 95.

68. Ibid., 96–97.

69. *WY,* 406–7.

70. *WY,* 427–28.

71. *WY,* 428–29.

72. *WY,* 433.

73. *WY,* 425.

74. *WY,* 436.

75. *WY,* 439.

76. *WY,* 437.

77. Alberto Dines, "Death in Paradise: Some Revelations about Stefan Zweig's Presence in Brazil," in Sonnenfeld, *World of Yesterday's Humanist Today,* 299.

5 / AUTOBIOGRAPHY AS FAREWELL II

1. Serge Klarsfeld, *Le memorial de la deportation des juifs de France* (Paris: Klarsfeld, 1978).

2. Sarah Kofman, *Rue Ordener, Rue Labat,* trans. Ann Smock (Lincoln: University of Nebraska Press, 1996); originally published as *Rue Ordener, Rue Labat* (Paris: Galilée, 1994); Hereafter cited as *RORL,* following Smock's translation except when noted.

3. Sarah Kofman, *The Childhood of Art: An Interpretation of Freud's Aesthetics* (New York: Columbia University Press, 1988), 58–59; originally published as *L'Enfance de l'art: Une interpretation de l'esthetique freudienne* (Paris: Payot, 1970).

4. Sarah Kofman, "'*Ma vie*' et la psychanalyse," *La Part de l'Oeil* 9 (1993): 83.

5. Sarah Kofman, "Apprendre aux hommes à tenir parole: Portrait de Sarah Kofman par Roland Jaccard," *Le Monde,* 27–28 April 1986, 7.

6. Ibid.

7. Sarah Kofman, *Smothered Words,* trans. Madelaine Dobie (Evanston, Wyo.: Northwestern University Press, 1998); originally published as *Paroles suffoquées* (Paris: Galilée, 1987; Cited hereafter as *SW.*

8. Sarah Kofman, "Damned Food," *Substance* 49 (1986): 8–9, trans. Frances Bartkowski. Originally published as "Sacrée negritude," *La Part de l'Oeil* 9 (1993): 85.

9. Ibid.

10. Kelly Oliver, "Sarah Kofman's Queasy Stomach and the Riddle of the Paternal Law," in Penelope Deutscher and Kelly Oliver, eds., *Enigmas: Essays on Sarah Kofman* (Ithaca, N.Y.: Cornell University Press, 1999), 176.

11. Sarah Kofman, "Cauchemar: En marge des études médiévales," in *Comment s'en sortir?* (Paris: Galilée, 1983), 103–12; Kofman, "Damned Food," 10–13.

12. Ibid., 12.

13. Ibid.

14. Ibid., 13.

15. Sarah Kofman, *Le Monde*, 7.

16. *SW,* 5–6.

17. *SW,* 7–8.

18. See Michael Holland, ed., *The Blanchot Reader* (Oxford: Blackwell, 1995), 1–15.

19. *SW,* 8.

20. Cited in Deutscher and Oliver, *Enigmas,* 209.

21. *SW,* 8.

22. See his "Being Jewish," in Holland, *Blanchot Reader,* 228–35.

23. *SW,* 9.

24. *SW,* 9.

25. *SW,* 10.

26. *SW,* 10–11.

27. *SW,* 14.

28. *SW,* 34.

29. *SW,* 34–35.

30. *SW,* 72–73.

31. *RORL,* 3.

32. See below. My colleague Gil Anidjar has interestingly suggested that this *ça,* meaning "it," can also be read as "id."

33. *RORL,* 5.

34. *RORL,* 5–6.

35. *RORL,* 6–7.

36. *RORL,* 9.

37. *RORL,* 9–10.

38. These "errors" are "corrected" by the translator in the English version. See following note.

39. *RORL*, 15; again, virtually every Hebrew/Yiddish term is distorted in the original.

40. *RORL*, 14.

41. *RORL*, 21; 27–28 in the original.

42. Sigmund Freud, *Three Essays on the Theory of Sexuality* (New York: Basic Books, 1962), 48.

43. Em Farrell, *Lost for Words: The Psychoanalysis of Anorexia and Bulimia* (London: Process Press, n.d.), chap. 2.

44. *RORL*, 24.

45. *RORL*, 27.

46. *RORL*, 27.

47. As opposed to the translator of this text into English, I prefer to leave mémé in lower case, to preserve the intimate feeling of the original.

48. *RORL*, 30.

49. *RORL*, 31.

50. *RORL*, 32.

51. *RORL*, 33.

52. *RORL*, 33.

53. *RORL*, 36.

54. *RORL*, 37.

55. *RORL*, 39.

56. *RORL*, 40.

57. *RORL*, 40–41.

58. *RORL*, 42. I translate the opening "rare" rather than "red" meat.

59. *RORL*, 43.

60. *RORL*, 43–44.

61. *RORL*, 47.

62. *RORL*, 55–56.

63. Sigmund Freud, "Screen Memories," *The Standard Edition of the Complete Psychological Works of Sigmund Freud* (London: The Hogarth Press, 1953–74), vol. 3, 322.

64. *RORL*, 57.

65. *RORL*, 57.

66. *RORL*, 58.

67. *RORL*, 59.

68. *RORL*, 59–60.

69. *RORL*, 60.

70. *RORL*, 61.

71. *RORL*, 61

72. *RORL*, 63.

73. *RORL*, 63–64.

74. See Kofman, *Childhood of Art*, 78–85.

75. Ibid., 59.

76. Sarah Kofman, *L'imposture de la beauté* (Paris: Galilée, 1995).

77. *RORL*, 65–66.

78. Kofman, *L'imposture*, 141–45.

79. *RORL*, 84.

80. *RORL*, 85.

81. Astonishingly, the introduction to *Smothered Words* gets this date wrong.

CONCLUSION

1. On this crucial matter, I am most impressed by the work of Christopher Norris; see, among others, his recent book *Against Relativism: Philosophy of Science, Deconstruction, and Critical Theory* (Oxford: Blackwell, 1997).

2. To some extent, this argument parallels that of the psychoanalyst Donald Spence, who (as Yosef Yerushalmi has pointed out to me) advanced a distinction between "narrative truth" and "historical truth" in Freudian theory, rejecting Freud's reconstructive archeological model for a constructivist and aestheticist approach to the truth claims of the analytic process. See his *Narrative Truth and Historical Truth: Meaning and Interpretation in Psychoanalysis* (New York: Norton, 1982). But Spence's distinction partakes too much of a Foucault-based relativism which I wholeheartedly reject.

3. Yosef Hayim Yerushalmi, *Zakhor: Jewish History and Jewish Memory* (Seattle: University of Washington Press, 1982).

4. Andreas Huyssen, *Present Pasts: Urban Palimpsests and the Politics of Memory* (Stanford: Stanford University Press, 2003), 3.

BIBLIOGRAPHY

PRIMARY SOURCES

Abrahams, Beth-Zion. *The Life of Gluckel of Hameln, 1646–1724, Written by Herself.* New York: Yoseloff, 1963.

Berlin, Jeffrey B. "The Unpublished Correspondence between Albert Einstein and Stefan Zweig." In Amy Colin et al., eds., *Brücken über dem Abgrund.* Munich: Fink, 1994.

———. "Unveröffentliche Briefe über Stefan Zweigs USA-Reise im Jahre 1935 und sein Projekt einer jüdischen Zeitschrift." In Sigrid Schmid-Bortenschlager et al., eds., *Stefan Zweig Lebt: Akten des 2. Internationalen Stefan Zweig Kongresses in Salzburg 1998,* 59–82. Stuttgart: Hans-Dieter Heinz, 1999.

Buber, Martin. *The Letters of Martin Buber: A Life of Dialogue.* Edited by Nahum Glatzer et al. New York: Schocken Books, 1991.

Cicero. *Tusculan Disputations.* Translated by J. E. King. Cambridge, Mass.: Harvard University Press, 1927.

Druyanov, A. "Mi-'sefer-ha-zikhronot' shel M. L. Lilienblum." *Reshumot* 2 (1927): 390–405.

Glikl of Hameln. *Die Memoiren der Glückel von Hameln, 1645–1719.* Edited by David Kaufmann. Frankfurt a/M: Kaufmann, 1896.

Gunzburg, M. A. *Aviezer.* Vilna: Fuenn, 1863.

Herzl, Theodor. *Briefe, 1903–Juli 1904.* Frankfurt a/M: Propylaen, 1996.

Holland, Michael, ed. *The Blanchot Reader.* Oxford: Blackwell, 1995.

Josephus. *The Life.* Translated by Joseph Thackeray. Cambridge, Mass.: Harvard University Press, 1926.

Kafka, Franz. *Letter to His Father.* New York: Schocken, 1953.

Kofman, Sarah. "Apprendre aux hommes à tenir parole: Portrait de Sarah Kofman par Roland Jaccard," *Le Monde,* April 27–28, 1986, 7.

———. "Cauchemar: En marge des études médiévales." In *Comment s'en sortir?* Paris: Galilée, 1983, 103–12.

———. *The Childhood of Art: An Interpretation of Freud's Aesthetics.* Translated by Winifred Woodhull. New York: Columbia University Press, 1988. Originally published as *L'Enfance de l'art: Une interpretation de l'esthetique freudienne* (Paris: Payot, 1970).

———. "Damned Food." Translated by Frances Bartkowski. *Substance* 49 (1986): 8–9. Originally published as "Sacrée negritude" (*La Part de l'Oeil* 9 [1993]: 85).

———. *L'imposture de la beauté.* Paris: Galilée, 1995.

———. "'Ma vie' et la psychanalyse." *La Part de l'Oeil* 9 (1993): 83.

———. *Rue Ordener, Rue Labat.* Translated by Ann Smock. Lincoln: University of Nebraska Press, 1996. Originally published as *Rue Ordener, Rue Labat* (Paris: Galilée, 1994).

———. *Smothered Words.* Translated by Madelaine Dobie. Evanston, Wyo.: Northwestern University Press, 1998. Originally published as *Paroles suffoquées* (Paris: Galilée, 1987).

Levi, Asher. *Die Memoiren des Ascher Levy aus Reichshofen im Elsass, 1598–1635.* Edited and and translated by M. Ginsburger. Berlin: Lamm, 1913.

Lilienblum, Moshe Leib. *Ketavim otobiografiim*, Shlomo Breiman, ed. Jerusalem: Mosad Bialik, 1970. Originally published as *Hatot neurim* (Vienna: G. Breg, 1876); reprinted in *Kol kitvei Moshe Leib Lilienblum.* (Cracow/Odessa: n.p., 1910–13).

Lowenthal, Marvin, ed. and trans. *The Memoirs of Gluckel of Hameln.* 1932. Reprint, New York: Schocken Books, 1977.

Mandelstam, Evgeny. "Excerpts from Memoirs." *Glas: New Russian Writing* 5 (1993): 148–91.

Mandelstam, Nadezhda. *Hope Abandoned.* New York: Atheneum, 1974.

———. *Hope against Hope.* New York: Penguin, 1980.

Mandelstam, Osip. *Complete Poetry.* Translated by Burton Raffel et al. Albany: State University of New York Press, 1973.

———. *The Noise of Time.* Edited and translated by Clarence Brown. New York: Penguin, 1965. Originally published as *Shum vremeni* (Leningrad: Vremia, 1925); second edition published as *Egipetskaia marka* (Leningrad: Priboi, 1928).

Mandel'shtam, O. E. *Sobranie sochinenii.* Edited by G. P. Struve and B. A. Filipov. Washington: Mezhdunarodnoe literature sodruzhestvo, 1991.

Mandel'shtam, O. *Sobranie sochinenii v chetyrekh tomakh*. Moscow: Art-Biznes-Tsentr, 1997.

Modena, Leon. *The Autobiography of a Seventeenth-Century Venetian Rabbi: Leon Modena's Life of Judah*. Edited and translated by Mark R. Cohen. Princeton, N.J.: Princeton University Press, 1988. Originally published as *Sefer Haye Yehudah*, edited by Daniel Carpi (Tel Aviv: Tel-Aviv University, 1985).

Rozhanski, Shmuel, and Yosef Bernfeld. *Zikhroynes*. Buenos Aires: Yivo, 1967.

Zweig, Frederike. *Stefan Zweig*. New York: Thomas Crowell, 1946.

Zweig, Stefan. *Begegnungen mit Menschen, Buchern, Stadten*. Vienna: Reichner, 1937.

———. *Briefe*. 1914–1919. Edited by Knut Beck et al. Frankfurt a/M: Fischer, 1995.

———. *The World of Yesterday*. 1943. Reprint, Lincoln: University of Nebraska Press, 1964. Originally published as *Die Welt von Gestern: Erinnerungen eines Europäers* (Stockholm: Bermann-Fischer, 1942).

———. *E. M. Lilien*. Berlin: n.p., 1903.

———. "'Konig der Juden': The Man of Letters and the Man of Action." In Meyer Weisgal, ed., *Theodor Herzl: A Memorial*. New York: Zionist Organization of America, 1929, 55–57.

———. "Their Souls a Mass of Wounds: An Address on the Jewish Children in Germany." Reprint, New York: German Relief Fund of the Joint Distribution Committee, 1934.

SECONDARY SOURCES

Alter, Robert. "Mandelstam's Witness." *Commentary* 57 (1964): 69–77.

Arendt, Hannah. "Portait of a Period." In *The Jew as Pariah*. New York: Random House, 1986, 112–21.

Bartlett, Frederic. *Remembering: A Study in Experimental and Social Psychology*. Cambridge: Cambridge University Press, 1964.

Biale, David. "Eros and Enlightenment: Love against Marriage in the East European Jewish Enlightenment." *Polin* 1 (1986): 49–67.

Bilde, Per. *Flavius Josephus, between Jerusalem and Rome: His Life, His Works and Their Importance*. Sheffield, England: JSOT Press, 1988.

Bilik, Dorothy. "The Memoirs of Glikl of Hameln: The Archeology of the Text." *Yiddish* 8 (1991): 5–22.

Botstein, Leon. "Stefan Zweig and the Illusion of the Jewish European." In Marion

Sonnenfeld, ed., *Stefan Zweig: The World of Yesterday's Humanist Today*. Albany: SUNY Press, 1983, 82–110.

Brown, Clarence. *Mandelstam*. Cambridge: Cambridge University Press, 1973.

Brown, Peter. *The Cult of the Saints: Its Rise and Function in Latin Christianity*. Chicago: University of Chicago Press, 1981.

Byatt, A. S. *The Biographer's Tale*. New York: Vintage International, 2000.

Carlebach, Elisheva. *Divided Souls: Converts from Judaism in Germany, 1500–1750*. New Haven, Conn.: Yale University Press, 2001.

Carlebach, Julius. "Family Structure and the Position of Jewish Women." In Werner Mosse et al., ed., *Revolution and Evolution: 1848 in German-Jewish History*. Tubingen: Mohr, 1981, 157–88.

Cavanagh, Clare. *Osip Mandelstam and the Modernist Creation of Tradition*. Princeton, N.J.: Princeton University Press, 1995.

Cohen, Shaye J. D. *Josephus in Galilee and Rome: His Vita and Development as a Historian*. Leiden: Brill, 1979.

Davis, Natalie Zemon. *Women on the Margins: Three Seventeenth-Century Lives*. Cambridge, Mass.: Harvard University Press, 1995.

Dines, Alberto. "Death in Paradise: Some Revelations about Stefan Zweig's Presence in Brazil." In Marion Sonnenfeld, ed., *Stefan Zweig: The World of Yesterday's Humanist Today*. Albany: SUNY Press, 1983.

Erdman, Irwin. "World Not Without End." *New Republic* 109 (May 3, 1943): 600–601.

Evreiskaia entsiklopediia. St. Petersburg: Brockhaus-Efron, n.d.

Farrell, Em. *Lost for Words: The Psychoanalysis of Anorexia and Bulimia*. London: Process Press, n.d.

Feingold, Ben-Ami. "Ha-otobiografiah ke-sifrut: Iyun be-'Hatot neurim' le-M. L. Lilienblum." *Mehkarei yerushalayim be-sifrut ivrit* 4 (1984): 86–111.

Feldman, Louis. "Hail Caesar! How the Romans Saved Jewish Civilization." *Forward*, 12 April 2002.

Freud, Sigmund. "Screen Memories." In *The Standard Edition of the Complete Psychological Works of Sigmund Freud*. Vol. 3. London: The Hogarth Press, 1953–74, 3.

———. *Three Essays on the Theory of Sexuality*. New York: Basic Books, 1962.

Gazzaniga, Michael. *The New Cognitive Neurosciences*. 2d ed. Cambridge, Mass.: MIT Press, 2000.

Gelber, Mark. "Karl Emil Franzos, Achad Ha-am und Stefan Zweig."

———. "Sholem Asch, Joseph Leftwich, and Stefan Zweig's *Der begrabene Leuchter*." In Mark Gelber, ed., *Identity and Ethos: A Festschrift for Sol Liptzin*. New York: Peter Lang, 1986.

———. "Stefan Zweig auf Hebräisch." In Sigrid Schmid-Bortenschlager et al., ed., *Stefan Zweig Lebt: Akten des 2. Internationalen Stefan Zweig Kongresses in Salzburg 1998*. Stuttgart: Hans-Dieter Heinz, 1999, 121–30.

———. "Stefan Zweig und die Judenfrage von heute." In Mark Gelber, ed., *Stefan Zweig Heute*. New York: Lang, 1987.

———. "Stefan Zweig und E. M. Lilien: Aspekte der Begegnung von jüdischen Ost und West um die Jahrhundertwende." *Austriaca* 34 (1992): 17–31.

———. "Stefan Zweigs verspätete Bekehrung zum Judentum?" *Bulletin des Leo Baecks Instituts* 63 (1982): 3–11.

Ginsburger, M. "Samuel Lévy, rabbin et financier." *Revue des études juives* 65 (1913): 274–300; 66 (1913): 111–33, 263–84; 67 (1914): 82–117, 262–87; 68 (1914): 84–109.

Graetz, Heinrich. *Istoriia evreev ot drevnieishikh vremen do nastoiashchago*. 2 vols. Odessa: Sherman, 1900–1905.

Greenblatt, Stephen. *Renaissance Self-fashioning: From More to Shakespeare*. Chicago: University of Chicago Press, 1980.

Gross, David. *Lost Time: On Remembering and Forgetting in Late Modern Culture*. Amherst: University of Massachusetts, 2000.

Harris, Jane Gary. *Osip Mandelstam*. Boston: Twayne, 1988.

Hata, Gohei. "Imagining Some Dark Periods in Josephus' Life." In Fausto Parente and Joseph Sievers, ed., *Josephus and the History of the Greco-Roman Period: Essays in Memory of Morton Smith*. Leiden: Brill, 1994, 309–28.

Huyssen, Andreas. *Present Pasts: Urban Palimpsests and the Politics of Memory*. Stanford: Stanford University Press, 2003.

Isenberg, Charles. *Substantial Proofs of Being: Osip Mandelstam's Literary Prose*. Columbus: Slavica, 1987.

Kandel, Eric, et al. *Principles of Neural Science*. 4th ed. New York: McGraw-Hill, Health Professions Division, 2000.

Kegel, Patrick. "Ethnicity and Culture in the Poetry and Prose of Osip Mandelstam." Ph.D. diss., Indiana University, 1994.

Klarsfeld, Serge. *Le memorial de la deportation des juifs de France.* Paris: Klarsfeld, 1978.

Klausner, Yosef. *Historiah shel ha-sifrut ha-ivrit ha-hadashah.* Vol. 4. Jerusalem: Ahiasaf, 1953.

Klayman-Cohen, Israela. *Die hebräische Komponente im Westjiddischen am Beispiel der Memoiren der Glückel von Hameln.* Hamburg: Buske, 1994.

Leftwich, Joseph. "Stefan Zweig and the World of Yesterday." *Yearbook of the Leo Baeck Institute* 3 (1958): 81–100.

Maggs, Peter. *The Mandelstam and "Der Nister" Files: An Introduction to Stalin-era Prison and Labor Camp Records.* Armonk, N.Y.: M. E. Sharpe, 1996.

Marwedel, Günther. "Glückel von Hameln und ihre Familie in der Steuerkontenbüchern der aschkenasischen Gemeinde Altona." In Peter Freimark et al., ed., *Judentore, Kuggel, Steuerkonten: Untersuchungen zur Geschichte der deutschen Juden, vornehmlich in Hamburger Raum.* Hamburg: Hans Christians Verlag, 1983, 70–79.

———. "Probleme der Chronologie in Glikls Memoiren." In Monika Richarz, ed., *Die Hamburger Kauffrau Glikl: Jüdische Existenz in der Frühen Neuzeit.* Hamburg: Christians Verlag, 2001, 123–33.

Mason, Steve. "An Essay in Character: The Aim and Audience of Josephus's Life." Unpublished paper.

Meyer, Holt. "Das Übersetzen des 'chaos iudejskij' in Osip Mandel'stams 'Rauschen der Zeit.'" *Juden und Judentum in Literatur und Film des slavischen Sprachraums* (Wiesbaden: Harrassowitz, 1999): 193–226.

Mintz, Alan. *Banished from their Father's Table: Loss of Faith and Hebrew Autobiography.* Bloomington: Indiana University Press, 1989.

Moseley, Marcus. "Jewish Autobiography in Eastern Europe: The Pre-history of a Literary Genre." Ph.D. diss., Oxford University, 1990.

Norris, Christopher. *Against Relativism: Philosophy of Science, Deconstruction, and Critical Theory.* Oxford: Blackwell, 1997.

Oliver, Kelly. "Sarah Kofman's Queasy Stomach and the Riddle of the Paternal Law." In Penelope Deutscher and Kelly Oliver, ed., *Enigmas: Essays on Sarah Kofman.* Ithaca, N.Y.: Cornell University Press, 1999.

Olney, James. *Memory and Narrative: The Weave of Life-Writing.* Chicago: University of Chicago Press, 1998.

Pascal, Roy. *Design and Truth in Autobiography*. Cambridge, Mass.: Harvard University Press, 1960.

Prater, Donald. *European of Yesterday: A Biography of Stefan Zweig*. Oxford: Oxford University Press, 1972.

Rappaport, Uriel. "Where was Josephus Lying—in his Life or in the War?" In Fausto Parente and Joseph Sievers, ed., *Josephus and the History of the Greco-Roman Period: Essays in Memory of Morton Smith*. Leiden: Brill, 1994, 279–89.

Ronen, Omry. "Osip Mandelshtam, 1891–1938." In George Stade, ed., *European Writers*, vol. 10. New York: Scribners, 1983–91.

Rosenfeld, Isaac. *The Invention of Memory: A New View of the Brain*. New York: Basic Books, 1988.

Ruderman, David. *A Valley of Vision: The Heavenly Journey of Abraham ben Hananiah Yagel*. Philadelphia: University of Pennsylvania Press, 1990.

Rushdie, Salman. *Step Across this Line*. New York: Random House, 2002.

Said, Edward. "Presidential Address 1999: Humanism and Heroism." *Publications of the Modern Language Association of America* 115, no. 3 (May 2000): 285–91.

Schacter, Daniel L. *The Cognitive Neuropsychology of False Memories*. Hove, U.K.: Philadelphia Psychology Press, 1999.

———. *The Seven Sins of Memory: How the Mind Forgets and Remembers*. Boston: Houghton Mifflin, 2001.

Schacter, Daniel L., and Elaine Scarry, eds., *Memory, Brain, and Belief*. Cambridge, Mass.: Harvard University Press, 2000.

Schacter, Jacob J. "History and Memory of Self: The Autobiography of Rabbi Jacob Emden." *Jewish History and Jewish Memory: Essays in Honor of Yosef Hayim Yerushalmi*. Hanover, N.H.: University Press of New England, 1998, 428–52.

Schwartz, Seth. *Josephus and Judaean Politics*. Leiden and New York: Brill, 1990.

Simonson, D. "Eine confrontation zwischen Glückel Hameln's Memoiren und den alten Hamburger Grabbüchern." *Monatsschrift für Geschichte und Wissenschaft des Judentums* 49 (1905): 96–106.

Spence, Donald. *Narrative Truth and Historical Truth: Meaning and Interpretation in Psychoanalysis*. New York: Norton, 1982.

Spitzer, Leo. "Into the Bourgeoisie: A Study of the Family of Stefan Zweig and Jewish Social Mobility." In Marion Sonnenfeld, ed., *Stefan Zweig: The World of Yesterday's Humanist Today*. Albany: SUNY Press, 1983, 64–81.

Squire, Larry R., and Eric R. Kandel. *Memory: From Mind to Molecules*. New York: Scientific American Library, 1998.

Stanislawski, Michael. "The Tsarist Mishneh Torah: A Study in the Cultural Politics of the Russian Haskalah." *Proceedings of the American Academy for Jewish Research* 50 (1983): 165–83.

————. *Zionism and the Fin-de-Siècle*. Berkeley: University of California Press, 2001.

Struve, Nikita. "Khristianskoe mirovozzrenie Mandel'shtama." In Robin Aizlewood and Diana Myers, ed., *Stoletie Mandel'shtama*. Tenafly, N.J.: Ermitazh, 1994, 244–48.

Taranovsky, Kiril. *Essays on Mandel'stam*. Cambridge, Mass.: Harvard University Press, 1976.

Turniansky, Chava. "Glikls Werke und die zeitgenössige jiddische Literatur." In Monika Richarz, ed., *Die Hamburger Kauffrau Glikl: Jüdische Existenz in der Frühen Neuzeit*. Hamburg: Christians Verlag, 2001, 68–69.

————. "Vegn di literatur-mekoyrim in Glikl Hamels zikhroynes." In Ezra Mendelsohn et al., ed., *Ke-minhag Ashkenaz u-Folin: Sefer yovel le-Hone Shmeruk: Kovets mehkarim be-tarbut yehudit*. Jerusalem: Merkaz Zalman Shazar le-Toldot Yisra'el, 1993, 153–77.

U.S. Department of Justice. *Eyewitness Evidence: A Guide for Law Enforcement*. October 1999.

Van Engen, John. "The Christian Middle Ages as an Historiographical Problem." *American Historical Review* 91 (June 1986): 519–52.

Vinchevsky, M. "Lilienblum ve-yahaso le-sozialiyut." *Luah aviever* 2 (1921): 292–300.

Weinzierl, Ulrich. ed., *Stefan Zweig: Triumph und Tragic*. Frankfurt a/M: Fischer, 1991.

Werses, Shmuel. "Darkhei ha-otobiografiah be-tequfat ha-haskalah." *Gilyonot* 4 (1945): 175–83.

Yerushalmi, Yosef Hayim. *Zakhor: Jewish History and Jewish Memory*. Seattle: University of Washington Press, 1982.

Yuval, Israel. "Otobiografiah ashkenazit me-hameah ha-arbah-esreh." *Tarbiz* 55 (1986): 541–66. Translated as "A German-Jewish Autobiography of the Fourteenth Century." *Binah* 3 (1994): 79–99.

INDEX